How to
Be a
Working Actor

How to Be a Working Actor:

An Insider's Guide to Finding Jobs in Theater, Film, and Television

MARI LYN HENRY
AND
LYNNE ROGERS

M. EVANS AND COMPANY, INC.
NEW YORK

Library of Congress Cataloging-in-Publication Data

Henry, Mari Lyn.
  How to be a working actor.

  Bibliography: p.301
  1. Acting—Vocational guidance. I. Rogers, Lynne.
II. Title.
PN2055.H39   1986   792'.028'023   86-2464

ISBN 0-87131-473-8
ISBN 0-87131-482-7 (pbk.)

M. Evans and Company, Inc.
216 East 49 Street
New York, New York 10017

Design by Lauren Dong

Manufactured in the United States of America

9 8 7 6 5 4

This book is dedicated
to
our husbands

Contents

Acknowledgments

This book could not have been written without the generous assistance of our many friends, among them—

Bret Adams
Nancy Addison
Jane Alderman
Maxine Alters
Sharon Ambrose
Arthur Anderson
Gerry Anthony
Hy Anzell
Jean Arley
Jacqueline Babbin
Chris Barrett
Patricia Barry
Tex Beha
Phyllis Black
Gene Blythe
Ralph Braun
Bonnie Brewster
Danielle Brisebois
Mary Brisebois
Anthony Call
Lara Cody
Jack Coffey
Wendy Curiel
Diana Deane
Lezlie Deane
Ro Diamond
Barry Douglas
Richard Dunn
Ira Eaker
Sherry Eaker

Joyce Eliason
Patricia Elliott
Carol Emshoff
Neil Felshman
Douglas Fisher
Charles Frederickson
Ginger Friedman
Catherine Gaffigan
Flo Salant Greenberg
Sam Grey
Albert Hague
Peggy Hadley
Joseph Hardy
Cricket Haskell
William Hathaway
Doug Johanson
Bob Kaliban
Robbie Kass
Larry Keith
Pete Kelley
Leslie Kruhly
Mark La Mura
Carmen LaVia
Juliet Lewis
Lester Lewis
Judith Light
Bill Lipton
Rita Litton
Molly Lopata
Barbara Lowenstein

Carol Luiken
Kristina Malandro
Guy Manna
Maxine Marx
Marin Mazzie
Lee Melville
Mervyn Nelson
Kathleen Noone
Fifi Oscard
Renee Orin
Peggy O'Shea
Marvin Paige
Jay Perry
Elizabeth Popiel
Natalie Priest
Betty Rea
Mark Redanty
Shirley Rich
David Rosen
Catherine Rusoff
Chuck Saucier
Richard Schmenner
Yvette Schumer
Dorothy Scott
Nancy Niles Sexton
Meg Simon

Christian Slater
Mary Jo Slater-Wilson
Edgar Small
Gillian Spencer
Dorothy Spears
John Speicher
Alice Spivak
Sydne Squire
Maureen Stapleton
Monica Stewart
Robin Strasser
Stephen Sutherland
Maura Tighe
Michael Thomas
Arthur Toretzky
Tasia Valenza
David Varnay
Greg Villone
Fred Vogel
Walden Theatre
Wisner Washam
Bob West
Josleen Wilson
Sanford I. Wolff
Ann Wright
Jacklyn Zeman

and our special thanks to the American Broadcasting Companies, Inc., and to Lydia Howard

How to
Be a
Working Actor

Introduction

Acting is half shame, half glory; shame at exhibiting yourself, glory when you can forget yourself.
—Sir John Gielgud

You are about to enter a strange and wondrous land.

You are approaching that singular community of theater-TV-films which lies somewhere between the Twilight Zone and the Land of Oz and is known as The Business. It is a world of bright lights and frenzy, where the inhabitants love what they do with a passion that sustains them, often for years, and that enables them to exist under primitive conditions, working frequently for no compensation other than the thrill of participating in the endeavor and the prospect of future greatness.

The Business happens to be a very accepting community. There is always room, at least on the outskirts, for a newcomer—someone who responds to the brightness and the energy and the lure of personal satisfaction. The primary requisite is dedication. It is the devoted ones who establish permanent residence in this community and who, eventually, make their way toward the centers of recognition, money, and power.

It is this journey that concerns us now.

We are going to chart the territory for you, provide you with a map, show you how to proceed from where you are now to where you want to be—enjoying a career as a working performer, part of the delicious excitement that characterizes life in the two magical cities, New York and Los Angeles. Along the way we may open your eyes to opportunities in new production centers blossoming across the country—in places like Dallas, Chicago, and Miami.

We've been living in this community for a long time; we know the way. And we have asked our friends—performers whose names or faces you know very well and casting directors and talent agents whose names you will want to know—to share with us the benefit of their experiences in The Business. Their wisdom is here too.

Some sobering facts before we begin: as we write this guidebook, there are some 140,000 professional performers, by which we mean members of AEA (Actors Equity Association), SAG (Screen Actors Guild), and AFTRA (American Federation of Television and Radio Artists), in New York and Los Angeles. You should know that only 20 percent of these people earn more than $2,000 per year. Performers who earn more than $25,000 per year constitute about 8 percent of the membership. The number of actors who earn more than $100,000 per year is approximately 1,500 people. They are the ones you recognize working in commercials, and in major roles on soap operas; they're bankable names in feature films and starring on the Broadway stage.

Do these numbers mean that you should abandon the idea of trying to make your journey? Only if you are not serious about your commitment. If there are other things that you see yourself doing that will bring you just as much happiness, offer a higher ratio of success, and demand less application, then by all means involve yourself in those activities.

The gifted actor Jim Dale, speaking to a seminar of young AFTRA and SAG members, put it this way. "If you are looking for security, go into some other business. I don't want that. We create magic. That's what I want to do. It's what I've wanted ever since I was nine years old and my father first took me to see a live performance."

If that is how you feel, if acting is what you know you absolutely must do, welcome to our world.

We believe that despite the numbers there is always room for talent. Every day another new face "makes it." Each season—on Broadway, on television, or in films—brings new shows with new people, and some of them are marvelous and they will last.

One of the most important things to keep in mind is that the casting director (or the producer or the network) and the actor share aspects of the same problem: one is constantly hoping to find new, interesting, arresting talent; the other is talent hoping to be found.

Whenever these two forces get together, the result is always jobs. And careers and recognition and, sometimes, fame and fortune.

Fame and fortune, however, are accidental, and they are not the immediate goal of this journey. Too often they are the result of being in the right show in the right season, on the right day of the week, on the right channel, in the right time slot, or in the right commercial or some other outrageous, unpredictable bit of luck. Many people believe that appearing in a deodorant commercial was the spark that ignited Diane Keaton's illustrious career. Her sweetly daffy portrayal of an exhausted, but fastidious, jogger was viewed coast to coast, several times a day, for many months.

Before you can have a chance at fame and fortune, you need to have a job. And to do that you must be a talented, determined performer who knows how to get *seen* by the people who can give you a job. That is what we call knowledgeable job seeking, and that is what this book—this journey—is all about: getting to the centers of activity, knowing exactly how to function under the wackiest circumstances.

Jobs, careers, and recognition are what we hope you are after. Then you can try for fame and fortune.

Are you ready?

Part 1
Nuts and Bolts

Chapter 1
What You Will Need to Get Started

The best thing to have is wealthy (or powerful or famous) parents who are willing to support you in your chosen career.

No joke intended.

We are simply trying to be realistic—and inject a little humor into the reality.

If you were hoping for a career in dentistry, archaeology, or accounting instead of performing, you would not be at all surprised to learn that establishing yourself requires the mastery of specific skills and the investment of time and dollars. Yet The Business, more than any other field of endeavor, is so loaded with legends of success achieved by accident, of plucky, untrained amateurs winning out over seasoned professionals, that it is frequently perceived as a fantasy playground even by those who would make their living in it.

Every dramatic form has glorified the waif who gets off the bus in Los Angeles or New York with little more than a knapsack, a pair of tap shoes, and a load of moxie. The waif then collides with a producer, celebrity, or agent who, struck by her artless quality, declares, "You're what this tired old town needs," makes a few phone calls, and in minutes, transforms her into a superstar. Doesn't that sound like the plot of a movie you've seen a couple of times? It's a wonderful story. Let's hope you can audition for the part when they cast the next remake. In the meantime, let's not confuse that myth with reality.

The recipe for success in The Business, as in any other community, calls for a mixture of talent and study, plus hefty amounts of discipline and determination.

This book is all about how to be a *working* actor. We are not here to tell you how to enjoy being a struggling, out-of-work actor. While we have been going on about magic and passion and the enormous satisfactions of performing, we have been careful to point out that there are a great many people at the bottom of the ladder who earn very little money.

Landing an acting job is a difficult accomplishment. Doing the job once you get it, while not on a par with brain surgery, nevertheless demands total concentration. Having to contend with those pressures while at the same time worrying about whether you'll have enough money to pay the rent or the telephone bill is, to our way of thinking, worse than foolish. It's suicidal and should not be attempted.

Veteran soap opera actress Janice Lynde says:

> *I could never have succeeded without the help and understanding I received from my parents. Thanks to them I have been able to study with the best teachers and not worry about the time it takes for me to develop as an artist. And I have been able to develop projects for myself.*

Jackie Zeman, *General Hospital*'s Bobbi Spencer, says:

> *Don't put a time limit on yourself. Don't give yourself the added pressure of a time limit.*

Helen Wagner, who arrived in New York a generation earlier, says almost the same thing:

> *There were many other girls—friends of mine—who came here at the same time I did, and who knows if I was more or less gifted than they? But I saw their careers get postponed or sidetracked because of the need to do other things to earn money. I am so glad that I was able to hang in there until the work started to come.*

Among the jobs that started to come was a role in the audition telecast of a show that was, in 1956, considered a very daring project—a thirty-minute, live, soap opera! (At that time, TV soaps, like the radio serials they sprang from, were fifteen-minute programs, performed live each day.) The show was *As the World Turns*, and Helen appeared as Nancy Hughes on the first episode. In the thirty years that have elapsed since its premiere, *As the World Turns* has expanded into the standard sixty-minute taped format—and Helen Wagner still appears as Nancy Hughes. (And we say there's no security in this business!)

Let us imagine for a moment that you are not a talented performer but a computer programmer looking for a job. Would you pack your duffle bag, head for Silicon Valley, and merely hope for the best? Of course not. You'd make certain that you had sufficient resources to enable you to lead a relatively normal life until you found the position you were seeking. Aware that you'd be interviewed by a slew of personnel directors, you'd want nothing to interfere with your ability to impress them as the ideal candidate for their needs: the best person they could consider adding to the corporate team.

The aspiring performer requires and deserves no less.

Think, now, of the times you've gone on vacation—alone or with friends or family. Remember the hours of planning? Figuring out the best time to travel? Whether to fly or drive? Which clothes to wear, which to pack? Were reservations needed? And, more important, how much was this jaunt going to cost?

That's the sort of preplanning you need to do now.

In the sample budget that follows, we explain the start-up charges and continuing costs of living sensibly, not lavishly, in New York or Los Angeles for six months with *no squeeze*. By that we mean that you should not expect, or need, to earn one cent during that time. We've offered specific figures to help you plan, but do remember to adjust for inflation since the publication of this book.

THE INITIAL COST

The first item to consider is what it will cost to travel to Los Angeles or New York City. This trip can be planned far enough in advance to allow you to take advantage of whatever bargain fares may be offered by the buses, trains, or airlines.

A SCOUTING TRIP

Ideally, you should plan a preliminary visit (with your family and/ or your potential roommate). High school seniors are encouraged to visit several campuses in order to acquaint themselves with various college communities and appreciate their differences, prior to deciding where they would like to apply for admission. Corporate personnel, when engaged or transferred, are shown all of the facilities of their soon-to-be new locale. If you've never been to the city before, such an exploratory trip makes very good sense.

New York and Los Angeles, while totally different in appearance and atmosphere, are two awesome places. Even the most sophisticated traveler needs time to absorb their impact. Yes, you will be dumbfounded by New York's huge tall buildings! Yes, in Los Angeles there is smog that you can see and flotillas of cars racing ninety miles an hour on the freeway!

Marilyn Bird, actress:

When I first came here to New York six years ago from Alabama, it was so intimidating. I am from a very small town and it's like this is the Land of Oz. I felt so tiny, like Dorothy. I looked at the Great White Way as if those were all a bunch of holy buildings. I know now that they're not; they are theaters, the places where we do our work.

Devote ten days or two weeks to discovering the places that are, or will be, significant to your life as a performer. See as much as you can of the city in the daytime: begin with a sight-seeing tour. Listen to the spiel of the tour guides and ask questions, and then venture out on your own. Scout for your locale—just as a production company would do when shooting sequences outside the studio. You are seeking the best background for you—and trying to effect a workable compromise between comfort and affordability.

Nor should it be necessary to squander thousands of dollars on this visit. This is not the time to indulge in the splendors of the Plaza or the Beverly Wilshire hotels, though you may wish to saunter through their lobbies. There are plenty of small hotels near New York's theater district (patronized by summer theater owners who come to New York each year to cast for their season) and in Hollywood that offer cleanliness and convenience at a modest price.

You can find out about them and get information on cultural attractions as well as maps of subway and bus routes by writing to the Convention & Visitors bureaus in Los Angeles (505 South Flower Street, Los Angeles, CA 90071) and New York (2 Columbus Circle, New York, NY 10019).

From the network of bed-and-breakfast establishments you can also find accommodations—often in the residential areas that may be just where you will want to look for an apartment—at reasonable rates. For information, write to the Bed & Breakfast League, Ltd., 2855 29th St. N.W., Washington, D.C.

An allowance of $80 per day should be sufficient.

RENT

Here, of course, is where the major chunk of your capital will go. Apartments in New York and Los Angeles cost more than they do in other cities.

Five minutes from the heart of Atlanta one can select a two-bedroom, two-bath apartment, with on-site swimming pool, garage, and even a health club for something like $750 a month. For that amount of money you *may* be able to find a studio apartment in Los Angeles, possibly large enough for two to share.

Try not to be shocked to learn that the same-size studio apartment can cost $900 a month in Manhattan. Or more. Or less. Depending upon the neighborhood. Neighborhoods affect the price of everything—even tomatoes. The neighborhoods we are talking about are decent, safe. And the apartment buildings employ a twenty-four-hour doorman or attendant. It is essential that you be able to come and go at odd hours: rehearsals and theater will keep you out late; job calls and auditions are usually early.

Most people share apartments. If you have friends or relatives already living in the city, they may have, or know of, a place for you. Someone from your school or town or club may also be moving to New York or Los Angeles to pursue another career: consider sharing your apartment with a novice lawyer and/or broker. If you are unable to find a roommate through these sources, you may wish to take advantage of notices on bulletin boards at the unions and wherever theatrical classes are given, personal ads in the trade papers, or by asking at the Actors Information Project (see chapter

4), once you've arrived in the city. Besides getting more space for less money, you gain the valuable sense of being with people who know and care about you. Life is not so lonely away from all the things you're accustomed to; good news becomes so much more pleasurable when it's shared; and the inevitable not-so-great times lose their aura of catastrophe, because the same sort of dumb things will undoubtedly happen to another member of your "family."

Barry Bruce, actor-dancer:

The first day I was here—I came from Lebanon, Tennessee —I got a job! There was a call for replacements for **Dreamgirls,** *and I went and got hired! I knew absolutely no one in New York, and I found a room at the YMCA on West Sixty-third Street. I was here six months before I was able to move into another place. One of the guys who was leaving the show sublet his apartment to me. I was able to keep that until I found my own.*

The frantic scramble for space in New York has, in large part, to do with the phasing out of rent control. Whenever long-term tenants, paying rents that controls have kept affordable, vacate their premises, landlords are allowed to raise rents to the fair-market level. The apartments then become rent-*stabilized*, and increases (according to numerical formulas that change each year) are permitted with each new lease.

A rent-controlled or rent-stabilized apartment that becomes vacated is considered lost to the Stratospheric Rent Monster, and performers are not the only ones who will resort to every conceivable strategy—be it sublet or share—to keep that from happening.

To further add to the complexity of this situation, apartments in newer buildings may be totally *un*regulated! For these, landlords are free to charge whatever they can get. The rent specified upon signing the lease becomes the amount due each month, for the duration of that contract.

While an apartment in Manhattan, within walking distance of the studios, theaters, and offices would be ideal, it is certainly not an absolute necessity. There are other boroughs, and plenty of performers enjoy living in Forest Hills, Jackson Heights, Long Island City—which are convenient neighborhoods in Queens; others rave about the bargains they've found twenty minutes away in Park Slope, Carroll Gardens, or Fort Greene—in Brooklyn.

Actors are even venturing across the Hudson River to New Jersey, finding in nearby Fort Lee, Rutherford, and Hoboken housing that is grander and far less costly than anything Manhattan has to offer. But there may be a drawback to living according to a train or bus schedule.

Actor-singer Richard Inguanti:

I can get to places in New York in less time than it takes many people who live in Manhattan. However, I am finding that I do not somehow get the opportunity to make connections with other actors. I am getting on the bus or train to come to New Jersey, while they are going out for coffee and conversation.

When you rent an apartment, you (and your roommate) will be expected to sign a lease, for one or two years. You'll also be required to plunk down one or two months' rent as security.

The situation in Los Angeles differs to the extent that it is basically a one-industry town, accustomed to a transient population of performers and technicians who come and go according to the film and TV industry shooting schedules. Furnished apartments are commonly available on a monthly basis. Studios will begin at $500 and go up. Some communities, such as Santa Monica, are instituting rent control. Again, prices will depend upon neighborhood, and in a city seventy miles wide, there are lots of neighborhoods. It is truly impossible to be near everything, which may be why your rental includes garage space for the car you will definitely need.

Albert Hague, Professor Shorofsky on *Fame*:

Of course, we have to drive everywhere. Luckily the place where I live is close enough to a shopping center for me to walk. So that is how I get my exercise. It is a mile each way. I've clocked it. In Marina del Rey, I am only twenty minutes by car from my studio. But when we had people to dinner, they complained because they live all the way over on the other side of the valley, near their studio. The wife said to me, "We wouldn't come out here if you weren't a star!" I hope she was kidding.

It's customary in Los Angeles, to pay the first and last month's rent in advance, plus a security deposit, and even a cleaning fee. You will not necessarily be required to sign a long-term lease.

SUBLETS AND SHARES

There are leases that provide for subtenants, but you may possibly make a private arrangement with the person who is living in the apartment, on a month-to-month basis, which leaves you free to leave as soon as you find a place of your own. Before you do business on the basis of a handshake, it's a good idea to get your privileges and responsibilities specifically enumerated.

■ RENT . . . . $500 TO $900 PER MONTH, WITH TWO ADDITIONAL
MONTHS AS PART OF INITIAL COST

IN AN EMERGENCY

If you find that you are totally without a place to stay or even park your belongings for a few days, consider the YMCA—in Hollywood at 1553 Hudson Avenue; in New York at 5 West Sixty-third Street. Both are centrally located. Their minimal accommodations are probably the least expensive you can find and will provide a brief respite until you make arrangements to share or rent space.

Jim Merillat, actor, composer:

> *I came here two days before my twenty-second birthday. I knew no one. It was my most miserable day. I found a room at the "Y" on Sixty-third Street. Without air-conditioning, because that cost five dollars more. The following day I walked into Joe Allen's (a famous theatrical restaurant) just to get the feel of it, and I was talking to someone who said, "I have a friend who is looking for a roommate!" So, I moved in with someone I didn't know. And, I lived there one year. It was a one-bedroom apartment on Ninetieth Street and Third Avenue. I paid half of $600 a month. I worked part-time at the Paris Health Club and studied.*

UTILITIES

Heat and water are supplied as part of the cost of renting apartments in New York and Los Angeles. Electric light, energy for cooking (either by gas or electricity), and electricity for air-conditioning are items you usually are billed for each month by the utility company.

■ ELECTRICITY...............................ABOUT $37–$50 PER MONTH

■ GAS ....ABOUT $8 PER MONTH

TRANSPORTATION

Los Angeles has been described as a sprawl of suburbs looking for a city. You can travel for hours along crowded highways, from one small community to another, and never reach anything that looks like the center of town. Headquartered in office towers or bungalows, production houses, networks, studios, and casting people are scattered in all directions.

Los Angeles does have a bus system, the RTD, as well as a number in the telephone directory to call for instructions on getting to your destination (as already noted, it's possible to request route maps from the L.A. Convention and Visitors Bureau). You could memorize one or two of Hamlet's soliloquies while waiting for the right bus to come along. They're great for seeing the town, but inefficient for actors hoping to accomplish serious job hunting.

The taxi meter drops twenty cents every few seconds, it seems. Rides of twenty-four dollars are not uncommon. It's pointless to think of this means of travel, except in emergencies.

Driving becomes the only sensible way to get from one appointment to the next. The low-cost car rental company, Rent-A-Wreck was born in Los Angeles. Their vehicles are far from decrepit, just a few seasons away from being new. In 1985, the monthly rental for a '78 auto was $475, plus insurance. Their new, lower-cost competitor is Ugly Duckling, offering (in 1985) a '76 Datsun at $375 a month, plus insurance. Drivers who wish to use newer vehicles will find them at the nationally advertised rental outlets; fees can go up to $1,000 a month, plus insurance. Lately the practice of leasing cars directly from local automobile dealers is becoming popular. In many cases the cost is lower and cars and service are better.

If you intend to stay in Los Angeles for at least a year, buy or lease the car where you live, from a dealer you or your family knows, and then drive (with all of your possessions in a rented van) to California.

The common wisdom regarding insurance is that one should opt for the maximum coverage, which, at least on the low-cost vehicles, runs from $60 to $80 per month. Considering the cost of gasoline and the great distances to be covered, most performers prefer small, economical cars.

■ CAR RENTAL.....................................$375–$1,000 PER MONTH

■ CAR INSURANCE ....$60–$80 OR MORE PER MONTH

For actress Lara Cody, living in the West Valley was less expensive than in Hollywood proper, but it cost her a great deal in gasoline and travel time.

My mileage used to be about 13,000 per year. Now that I'm more centrally located, it's down to about 4,000. At $1.15 a gallon at the self-serve gas station, that can make quite a difference. And, I had to change my oil and filter every 1,000 miles, which meant another thirty dollars each time.

My Hollywood apartment is only fifteen minutes from MGM or Studio City. In traffic I add five or ten minutes. And driving in the rush hours to appointments before ten or after four is the pits! That can cost half an hour of time.

To the cost of renting (or leasing), operating, and insuring your vehicle, you must add the daily expense of parking the car at or near each office you visit. Actors learn to carry a supply of coins of all denominations to feed the parking meters. Rates vary—here, too, it all depends upon the neighborhood.

■ PARKING ....AN ESTIMATED $20 A WEEK

One of the stops on your exploratory trip to California should be at the nearest office of the Motor Vehicle Bureau, to acquire a copy of the *California Drivers' Handbook* and the *Registration Handbook*. If you own your car, find out about the state's regulations concerning private vehicles. There are requirements for smog certification, registration, service and vehicle license fees, and a use tax. *Thomas' Book of Maps* is an invaluable aid.

New York, on the other hand, is a walking city, further enhanced by an elaborate subway system and dozens of bus lines. For the most part, theater, film, and television offices are clustered in the heart of Manhattan, which is about a mile wide at Forty-second

Street. The farthest outposts—the Astoria (Queens) Film Studios and the NBC Brooklyn TV Studio—are easily reached by bus or subway.

It's not unlikely that you might have a commercial audition at an advertising agency at Fifty-fourth Street and Third Avenue, which is on the East Side, followed by an interview for a play reading all the way west at Forty-second Street and Tenth Avenue, on Theater Row, and then rush to an acting class downtown on Bank Street in Greenwich Village. You can take buses and subways to all of these appointments, for a dollar a ride (and bus transfers are free).

Taxis, which should be saved for emergencies, start at $1.10, and drop ten cents each one-ninth of a mile. The average trip will cost four or five dollars.

■ TRANSPORTATION IN NEW YORK . . . .$50 PER WEEK

TELEPHONE

This is your lifeline to jobs, appointments, news about what's happening, and just plain gossip. Apartment sharers will simply pay their portion of the monthly bill, but having a new telephone line installed, now that Ma Bell has been splintered, may be complicated and costly. Unless you already have a poor record of payment with the phone company, at this writing there's no up-front security charge.

■ TELEPHONE CONNECTION . . . . FROM $57 TO $120 FOR INSTALLATION
AND ALLOW SEVERAL DAYS LEAD TIME

If your habit is to use the phone as an extension of your arm, your bill will be comparatively high.

■ TELEPHONE BILL . . . . ABOUT $60 A MONTH

Optional services such as Call Waiting (which tells you when a second caller is trying to reach you) and Call Forwarding (which allows you to transfer incoming calls to another telephone number) may be worth investing in. These will add to your monthly bill.

■ OPTIONAL TELEPHONE SERVICES. . . . . ABOUT $10 PER MONTH

And of course, you should investigate the low-cost long-distance phone services.

ANSWERING SERVICES

The twenty-four-hour-a-day, seven-day-a-week answering service devoted to the special needs of actors blossomed during the wonderful days of radio drama. The major services maintained direct tie-line telephones outside the door of every radio studio and in the CBS and NBC restaurants, so their busy clients could check in for messages during a rehearsal break or while waiting to grab a sandwich and coffee before dashing from a broadcast of *Our Gal Sunday* at CBS on East Fifty-second Street all the way across Fifth Avenue to Rockefeller Center for the first read-through of *Life Can Be Beautiful* on the third floor at NBC.

Most important, for business purposes, the services could be relied upon to deliver calls for auditions, rehearsals, and jobs. A call confirmed through one's answering service was recognized throughout the business as a commitment. It had the effect of a signed contract.

In addition to locating you quickly and relaying messages from agents, casting people, or friends, the service can be instructed to deliver crucial wake-up calls and function as a kind of appointment secretary. There is a charge (about fifty cents) for each call made in addition to the basic monthly fee. Reliable answering services advertise in all the trade papers.

■ ANSWERING SERVICE .... $12–$30 PER MONTH

TELEPHONE ANSWERING MACHINES

The actor selecting a telephone answering machine opts for the one-time purchase price over the continuing monthly service charge. Agents do not hesitate to say that they feel a certain frustration when they dial a performer's home telephone number and, instead of reaching their client, hear a recorded message—especially one in which the performer tries to be clever and offers heavy breathing, the fanfare from *Star Wars*, and jokes told in various dialects. On a heavy business day, that can work against you. Many casting people and agents prefer giving messages to a real person—the service operator, whom they may already know—rather than to a machine. And there is never a concern that the service will be out of commission, whereas machines have been known to break down.

If you decide that you prefer an answering machine, be sure you get a highly rated one, with a call-in beeper that *works.* Above all, call in to your machine *frequently.*

■ TELEPHONE ANSWERING MACHINE .... $150–$200

OUTSIDE CALLS

Remember that you'll need to make phone calls while you are out. For this you'll have to use a pay phone. Agents, secretaries, or receptionists do not take kindly to anyone tying up their lines and, essentially, doing private business on the company phone. (When you become a big money-maker for the office, this attitude may change.) Local calls to any of the five boroughs in New York are twenty-five cents; calls cost twenty cents in Los Angeles, but the local area is much smaller and calls to the studios are often charged as long-distance messages.

■ PAY PHONE COSTS .... $60 A MONTH

FOOD

Dining out may be the passion of the 1980s—and New York and Los Angeles boast fantastic restaurants at all price levels—but this is one adventure you should treat yourself to only occasionally. Let's face it, eating in restaurants is costly. So, if you've never mastered the technique of boiling an egg, consider this a marvelous opportunity to learn.

In Los Angeles and New York there are excellent markets offering fine fresh produce, in addition to all the cans and packages that you grew to love at home.

What cannot be overemphasized is the need to nourish yourself adequately. One cannot bear up under the rigors of a twelve-hour camera day on a diet of junk food and candy bars. Sharing meals with friends, roommates, or scene partners is a way to reinforce relationships while making certain that you take the time to eat well.

Treat yourself to a copy of *James Beard's Cook Book* ($4.95, paperback) or Uta Hagen's *Love for Cooking* or succumb to Rombauer and Becker's encyclopedic *Joy of Cooking*. Clip the cents-off coupons in the food sections of the newspaper each Wednesday; shop for specials; stock up on staples; make lists when you go marketing. Two people may expect to spend eighty dollars a week for food; living alone may be less expensive.

■ FOOD . . . .$40–$50 PER WEEK

Add to the costs of your food whatever you're used to drinking —beer, wine, or liquor are additional.

Then give yourself a separate category called Incidentals for the lunches, snacks, and after-theater and after-working or rehearsal meetings with colleagues and casting people.

■ FOOD INCIDENTALS . . . . $125 PER MONTH

ENTERTAINMENT

Movies, theater, ballet, and concerts represent more than diversion for you: they are opportunities to learn. You should try to see everything. Of course, with first-run films costing five or six dollars and theater tickets edging up beyond thirty-five dollars, this can be a costly assignment. Fortunately, you can get half-price tickets to theater, concerts and dance programs in both cities at the TKTS booths on the day of performance. Reduced-price tickets to Broadway shows, commonly called twofers, are available through local merchants. The Theatre Development Fund (TDF, 1501 Broadway, New York, NY 10036) offers theater tickets at cut-rate prices to those on its mailing list and sells vouchers that can be used at certain showcase and off-off-Broadway productions. Members of the Television Academy (NATAS in New York, ATAS in Los Angeles) who join the Cinema Club pay an additional fee, currently $80, to see new films at biweekly screenings.

For union members, free passes to plays on and off Broadway are frequently available at the offices of Actors Equity Association (AEA). To members of Screen Actors Guild, the Film Society offers the opportunity to see screenings of a number of new films at a reduced rate.

Audience Extras, Inc., is a unique organization operating in New York and Los Angeles through which people interested in the theater have a chance to see plays at reduced cost. For details, write to them at 163 West Twenty-third Street, New York, NY 10011.

Casting director Meg Simon advises:

If you can't afford TKTS, you can second-act some shows. At institutional theaters, like Manhattan Theatre Club, Playwrights Horizons, Circle Rep, and Second Stage, you can volunteer to usher for free. Aside from seeing the work, you meet other ushers doing the same thing. You involve yourself in a community.

■ ENTERTAINMENT . . . . $25 + PER WEEK

MAINTENANCE

The upkeep of your apartment, which we assume you plan to keep clean yourself, will require more time than money. Expect that whoever lived in the apartment before you may have left a mess, which you will have to scour away. To do this you'll have to purchase basic supplies such as a mop, broom, and household products.

■ INITIAL APARTMENT BASIC CLEANUP SUPPLIES $60

Invest also in a steam/dry iron, an ironing board, and handy items such as spot cleaners for the necessary daily touchups on your clothing.

■ IRON, IRONING BOARD, SPOT CLEANER. $75

Laundry (there's usually one in the building or nearby), dry cleaning, and shoe repair are other costs.

■ LAUNDRY, DRY CLEANING, SHOE REPAIR . . . . $50 PER MONTH

Marin Mazzie, actress, speaks of her first day in New York, three years ago:

The one thing I didn't expect was that I'd have to exterminate the apartment! We must've spent a fortune on roach bombs. I was terrified that if I went to sleep I'd get a cockroach in my ear. We also spent money on locks for the front door and gates on the windows. The apartment was on the first floor on West Forty-seventh Street. It was great to be in the theater district, and rent-controlled, which was lucky. The apartment cost $800 a *month. I figure my first day in New York I dropped $1,750 without batting an eyelash—that's including transportation, my share of the apartment deposit, the roach bombs, and the gates.*

IT IS YOUR BUSINESS TO HAVE . . .

Let us now take a cursory look at professional expenses. These are the choices that will affect your career. The reasoning behind all of them is given in chapter 2, "The Tools of the Trade." However, for the purpose of arriving at a realistic budget, we want to tell you what they are and approximately how much they should cost. See Table 1.

PROFESSIONAL ORGANIZATIONS

Membership in the performing unions is not a prerequisite for joining the Television Academy—the National Academy of Television Arts and Sciences (NATAS) in New York or the Academy of Television Arts and Sciences (ATAS) in Los Angeles. These organizations join to bestow the annual Emmy and Daytime Emmy Awards; local awards ceremonies are conducted by academy chapters throughout the country. Membership activities can be informative and may serve as opportunities to meet people working in The Business.

▪ NATAS OR ATAS ANNUAL MEMBERSHIP FEE............................$75

The same can be said of the American Film Institute (AFI), which is open to anyone interested in movies and offers numerous seminars and workshops, particularly in California.

▪ AFI ANNUAL MEMBERSHIP FEE $35

ON YOUR BACK AND IN YOUR CLOSETS

A performer really has two wardrobes—the clothing you wear to interviews and auditions (which we will discuss in chapter 9) and the outfits you wear in "real life."

TABLE 1.   Professional Expenses

Item	Cost
For the photos every performer must have, you will first need a photo session	$200–$600
Duplicating the pictures you select	$50 per hundred
Résumés	$10 per hundred
Photo-postcards	$25 per hundred
Trade papers	$20 per month
Mailing and postage expense	$1.50 per submission, $20 per month follow-up
Acting classes	$60–$375 for 3 months
TV commercial technique classes	$375
Singers' vocal coach	$35 per hour
Dancers' technique classes	$50 per card
Play scripts and sheet music	$3.50 per play $3.00 per song
Tape recorder (portable/ac/dc) and a color TV set	$60 and up $150 and up
Getting good TV reception may require cable TV	$20 per month and up
Cable TV installation fee	$50 and up
Union dues (Remember to inform your local or branch office of your change of address.):	
Actors Equity	$26 semiannually
Dues to AFTRA and SAG are based upon the previous year's earnings. We're using the lowest rate for this estimate:	
AFTRA	$28.75 semiannually
Screen Actors Guild	$37.50 semiannually
Talent directory listing. Union members are eligible to place their photo and contract information in professional talent directories:	
Players' Guide	$65
Academy Players Directory (3 times yearly)	$45

With casual clothing the order of the day everywhere—and nowhere more so than in Los Angeles—we doubt that you will need to plan on purchasing "real life" clothing during the first six months of your stay. Of course, New York winters can be excruciatingly cold, so if you don't already own a heavy coat and all-weather boots, you will surely need to buy them before the first snowfall. A good raincoat with a warm zip-out lining can be useful all year round; the classic trench coat, with its "I've just dashed in from the airport" look, is always in style.

■ WINTER COAT..UP TO $300
■ ALL-WEATHER BOOTS....................................... $50 AND UP

YOUR FABULOUS FACE

The way you look is, obviously, of vital importance. For both men and women, hair care is a necessity.

■ HAIR CARE .... $35 AND UP PER MONTH
■ IF YOU COLOR YOUR HAIR, ADD .... $100 PER MONTH

Bargain-hunting colleagues may suggest that you take advantage of free hair cuts, coifs, and coloring services available at beauty schools, salons, or cosmetic companies. We consider this a foolish economy. You have little or no control over what your hair will look or feel like. Spend the money and search around, so that you will always be sure you look the way you must—your best. Conversely, when you happen upon a talented stylist or colorist who somehow manages to make you look better than you ever looked before, take down that person's name, address, and phone number. Explain that you are a performer and that you may frequently need an emergency touch-up, trim, or comb-out. Make sure this genius wants to do the work.

Remember that all actors need *makeup* for stage work and for auditions.

■ MAKEUP...ABOUT $150 TO $200

CREATING YOUR NEST

The amounts you spend for furniture, linens, utensils, and appliances will depend upon your own sense of style, whether the apartment you find is already furnished and how well, or whether it is a pristine, empty space waiting to be transformed into your personal environment.

Some furnished apartments may be stocked with knives, china and glass, flatware, and an array of kitchen utensils, in addition to the expected sofa, tables, and chairs. Others may provide only the barest essentials to qualify as "furnished." Whatever the case, make certain that the bed you'll be sleeping on provides proper support. There are few things more aging to your face and body attitude or more conducive to slovenly posture and general poor health than the simple lack of adequate sleep. Even if space is tight in your apartment, there are sofabeds, sleep sofas, or convertibles nowadays with excellent mattress and spring combinations. Get the best you can afford.

■ SLEEP SOFA, SOFABED, CONVERTIBLE .... $500 AND UP

A traditional mattress and box spring may set you back $400; allow a bit more than half that amount for the mattress alone.

■ MATTRESS AND BOX SPRING..$400

Two sets of bed linens will allow you to use one while the other's being laundered.

■ BED LINENS...$60
■ TOWELS, BATH MATS, AND SHOWER CURTAINS........................$100

Canny shoppers will know that by taking advantage of furniture and white sales—usually held in January, May, and August—or by patronizing the discount outlets on both coasts they'll be able to save money on these purchases.

Other immediate necessities are a clock radio and a can opener —the foolproof, handheld kind.

■ CLOCK RADIO ....$20–$80
■ CAN OPENER .... ABOUT $5

Items you may not need to purchase but should have with you are grooming aids, such as an electric razor, styling/blow dryer, and hot rollers.

Some people will not travel without their beloved rocking chair, their stereo and record collection, their electric frying pan, or their food processor. One of the leading ladies on *Ryan's Hope* confesses that she is permanently attached to her microwave oven. Obviously these are personal choices. This is the time to make yourself aware of what you already have and what you need.

If furnishing your apartment is going to be one of your projects, there are less expensive ways to accomplish this than by heading for the nearest department store with your list. Bulletin boards— at the unions and wherever you take classes—almost always carry notices of objects for sale by owners who may be going on tour or relocating just as you are. Furniture finds are plentiful at Salvation Army warehouses and at thrift shops, auctions, and warehouse outlets. Flea markets are excellent sources of china, glass, and silverware. Frequenting these outlets can be fun, save you money, and serve as an opportunity to become better acquainted with your new hometown.

The amounts you spend for these items will depend on your taste and what you can afford.

HEALTH

Young people accustomed to perpetual good health may think that allowances for doctors' and dentists' bills and health insurance are optional expenses. That would be a mistake. Accidents happen; emergencies arise. And they inevitably occur when you least expect them and cannot afford them. Not all emergencies are threatening. But even slipping on a banana peel can lead to injury that is serious and painful and that can *keep you out of work* for weeks.

Until such time as you have worked under union jurisdiction and have become eligible for no-cost medical coverage (see chapter 6 "Understanding the Unions"), you must provide your own health insurance. If you're not now covered by Blue Cross, HIP, or some similar health organization, arrange for such insurance as quickly as you can, where you are now living. Once you have moved, you can inform the insuring organization of your new address.

If you don't already have one, apply for one while you are still at home. Several credit card companies permit family members to have separate cards issued in their own name; the bill will then be sent to the original card member (and you can send your parents whatever amount you've spent at the end of the month).

PROPER IDENTIFICATION

Two forms of identification are usually necessary when paying by check or when cashing a check and sometimes when purchasing an unusual or expensive item. A driver's license will be fine, as is a major credit card, a charge card from a department store, or a library card. Your Social Security card is *not* an acceptable ID—don't ask us why. Frequent travelers are accustomed to carrying their passport. As this valuable article is easy to lose and takes time to replace, we'd advise you to get all the other forms of ID as quickly as you can.

TABLE 2.   Where the Money Goes[a]

Item	Costs in New York	Costs in Los Angeles
Rent	$500–$900	$500–$800 $1,000–
Additional 2 months' security	$1,000–$1,800	$1,600
Cleaning fee	—	$50 and up
Gas and electricity	$58	$45
Transportation:		
Car rental (monthly)	—	$500 (approx.)
Insurance (monthly)	—	$60–$80
Parking (weekly)	—	$20
Gasoline	—	$1.20 per gallon
Public transportation (weekly)	$50	—
Telephone:	$60	$60
Hook-up	$75	$75
Outside calls	$60	$60
Answering service:		
Service (monthly)	$12–$30	$12–$30
Machine (one-time cost)	$160–$200	$160–$200

You should also have a complete medical checkup before y
embark upon this journey.

■ COMPLETE MEDICAL CHECKUP . . . . WHAT YOUR DOCTOR CHARG

Tell your regular physicians that you're moving—they may
able to recommend colleagues practicing in New York or Los A
geles. Friends, too, may know internists, dentists, gynecologis
chiropractors, podiatrists, and the like. Anyone with special pr
lems, such as allergies or blood, back, skin, or eye ailments, sho
ask for copies of all necessary medical records. The same holds t
for prescriptions for lenses and/or medication.

ARRANGING FOR CREDIT

Any person moving to a new location needs to establish cre
You want to be able to buy things without always paying for th
in advance and with cash. You will have to arrange for services
are delivered over a period of time, such as your rent, teleph
service, and others described earlier.

Because they do not usually have permanent employment—l
ing for work is the "steady job" in The Business—actors have
torically found it more of a problem than most people to estab
credit. You can circumvent much of this difficulty by making
arrangements ahead of time—ideally during your preliminary
You can do this by opening a savings account, preferably at a
located near your apartment. The simplest way to handle this
have a certified check drawn on your current account by your h
town bank for the amount you wish to deposit in your new b
A certified check is considered immediate cash; regular checks d
on out-of-town banks may take as long as three weeks to clea

Many savings banks, which pay at slightly higher interest
than commercial banks, offer checking accounts as well. You
need a checking account; pay by check whenever you can.
reasons for doing this are obvious: you should never carry
amounts of cash because money can be lost or stolen; also,
canceled check serves as your record of payment, useful fo
purposes and in case of any problem with your purchase.

Another method of payment, which gives you a record o
purchase and adds to your credit rating, is with a major credit

Item	Costs in New York	Costs in Los Angeles
Food and drink:		
Marketing (weekly)	$40–$50	$40–$50
Drinks—what you prefer	**	**
Incidentals (monthly)	$125	$125
Entertainment (monthly)	$100+	$100+
Trade publications: (monthly)	$20	$20
Photos:		
Sitting	$150–$600	$150–$600
Duplication (per hundred)	$50	$50
Photo-postcards (per hundred)	$25	$25
Résumés:		
Typing	$10	$10
Duplication (per hundred)	$10	$10
Mailing expenses:		
Manila envelopes	$18 per hundred	$18
Cardboards	$5	$5
Postage, per 8 × 10	$.44	$.44
Postcards, per card	$.14	$.14
Stationery	$18	$18
Classes:		
Acting workshop (per 13 weeks)	$60–$400	$75–$400
Commercial technique	$375	$375
Dance class (per card)	$50	$60
Singing	$35 per hour	$35 and up
Scripts/music	$3.50 per play $3 per song	$3.50 per play $3 per song
Hair care:		
Color	$100 up	$100 up
Cut and style	$40 up	$30 up
Cosmetics (for interviews/auditions)	$50 as needed+	$50+
Health club	$400–$900 per yr.	$400 up
Furnishings:		
Linens	$100	$100
Supplies	$135	$135
Laundry, dry cleaning, shoe repair	$50	$50

[a]No work. No union dues. Just normal costs for a performer. Can you afford to live in New York or Los Angeles?

EXTRA FRILLS

We have limited our list to those items we consider truly necessary. The allotted amounts are sensible, and not sparse. We'd like now to append a wish list of sorts—to show how you might augment your possessions, embellish your life-style—in the event that you enjoy a marvelous streak of good luck and find yourself with as much backing as you could possibly desire.

First, invest in a video cassette recorder, not merely to time-shift (tape broadcasts to view at other times), but to record your own performances and those of other good actors and to replay commercials that you think are right for you.

■ VCR, CABLE READY WITH A REMOTE CONTROL . . . . ABOUT $350

Once you've arrived and had a chance to get semisettled, a session with an image consultant, to determine your best colors, shapes, and styles, coupled with a consultation with a fine makeup artist, would be an excellent investment, for men as well as for women.

■ IMAGE CONSULTANT . . . . ABOUT $300

Membership in a health club, complete with swimming pool and lots of exercise classes, is a worthwhile investment.

■ HEALTH CLUB . . . .$600 TO $850 PER YEAR
■ MARTIAL ARTS CLASSES OR OTHER
SELF-DEFENSE TRAINING . . . . ABOUT $75 PER MONTH

Even though you are convinced that you sing *between* the notes and your dancing is fine for a person with two left feet, acquaint yourself with both disciplines, because in this business, you never know. Dance classes can be purchased by the month. Singing lessons are costly.

■ COACHING SESSIONS . . . . $40 PER MONTH
■ DANCE CLASSES . . . . $50 PER MONTH
■ VOICE LESSONS . . . .$35–$40 PER HOUR

And, to be able to keep your head in place with all of this excitement, you might want to visit an understanding therapist from time to time or find a clinic for much less.

■ THERAPIST . . . . $100 PER SESSION

As we said, these are extras, but they would be nice. . . .

THAT PERSON IN THE MIRROR

Starting to think of yourself as a business with categories of expenses and professional needs is certainly exciting. At this time many young people also begin to scrutinize themselves in mirrors that seem to magnify every slight deviation from perfection. They suddenly decide that what they really need is a new face—or at least a better nose or chin. The brown-eyed girl shakes her head, sadly, because blue eyes are what she knows she should have. Most of this self-dismay is a manifestation of fear of the unknown. It's merely an outburst of insecurity, a feeling that will subside. However, if your dissatisfactions are real and of long standing, do have them attended to before you set out. There are several reasons for doing so. The most practical consideration if you are contemplating surgical, medical, or dental work is the cost, which will surely be less where you are now than in either city. Then too, the physician you are now seeing knows you, your needs, and your temperament. You will also save yourself time and anxiety by arriving in New York or Los Angeles already looking your best.

To venture out on interviews when you are unhappy about your teeth, your nose, your hair, or your weight is to give yourself an unnecessary handicap: your concentration is centered upon what's wrong with you and whether or not the interviewer will notice. Yes, the interviewer will notice and either will note your deficiency on the back of your photo (bad teeth, needs to lose weight) or will tell you to come back when you have lost the twenty pounds. Why give yourself that pressure? Lose the weight! Get the hair transplants or your hair line improved or your eyebrows tweezed or that unsightly mole removed. Feel confident that you look terrific when you go out on that first meeting!

A GRAND TOTAL

As we indicated at the start of this chapter, a performer, like any other professional, needs to plan ahead for a successful career. *The best way to proceed is to be able to devote yourself totally to the task of getting interviews and jobs without worrying about supporting yourself, at least for the first six months.*

Once you've arrived and had a chance to unpack, you can pay attention to the real task, which is getting a job!

Chapter 2
The Tools of the Trade

You've found a place to live. You've unpacked your bags. The phone is hooked up, and you're eager to get started. As the sole proprietor of your one-person business, what you need now is customers and a way to attract them.

THE PICTURE AND YOU

If you were working in any other business, you'd hand out little calling cards with your name, company logo, and direct telephone number. In The Business, your calling card is an 8″ by 10″ black-and-white photo. Actors introduce themselves with a photo; they refresh contacts' memories with a photo. That picture *is you* to all the people you've met and hope to meet.

The picture must look like *you*. Not what you want to look like, your fantasy image; not what the photographer thinks you should look like, with extensive makeup and lighting tricks and fans blowing your hair. You. The you that is going to walk into the casting office or the agent's office.

Maxine Marx, vice-president, casting, for Cunningham & Walsh, Inc., notes the following:

What I look for is a photo that says, "Hi!" A picture that looks like you, friendly, open.

Casting people receive as many as five hundred pictures a day. Among all those faces, certain people are going to stand out—the ones who are using a good picture.

WHAT MAKES A PICTURE GOOD?

Naturalness is important. We are looking for real people. Isn't that what you see every day on television, at the movies, or in commercials? Even on stage, where distance allows us to be less specific, we're not transforming ourselves into outrageous apparitions; we are doing plays about people who are somewhat like ourselves.

Naturalness is reflected in your attitude—it should be open, friendly. Your shoulders should be relaxed. Your hands should rest in your lap, not cradle your cheek or chin. Your smile should be easy, not a clenched-teeth pose you held until the photographer released you.

Most important, warmth should radiate from your eyes—they are "the windows of the soul." They reflect you, your quality, the quality that gets you into the agent/producer/casting director's office.

Veteran casting director Mervyn Nelson says:

The first thing that I really look for is the eyes. *I believe all film acting is in the eyes.*

THE SIMPLE PICTURE TEST

Hold your 8″ by 10″ photo right next to your face and look in the mirror. Do you and that black-and-white image look like the same person? Does one of you look older, younger, tense, relaxed?

If your hair is blond, does the lighting make it appear bleached? Are you letting us see your dark roots? We don't want to—let it be a secret between you and your colorist.

Do you have freckles, laugh lines, or little puffs of skin under your eyes when you smile? Or has the photographer, aiming for the perfection of a 1940s movie still, airbrushed those out of the photo?

An outdoor photograph of Douglas Fisher (left) and a studio photo (right) show the contrast between outdoor location and studio lighting. Both retain the actor's natural warmth.

He did you no service. The lines, freckles, and beauty marks, the bumps on your nose—those will all be there when you walk into the office. If you are really concerned about puffy eyelids, dark circles, lines, bumps, crooked teeth, or other shortcomings, have them attended to by a plastic surgeon or an orthodontist *before* you have your photo session.

The lighting should frame your face and not hide it with shadows or harden your features or make you look as if you have a halo.

The background must never upstage you. Nor should we be distracted by dangling earrings or bold prints, plaids, or stripes. Sharp contrasts are also bad. Notice in Douglas Fisher's outdoor photo that there's just a hint of background. The plaid shirt he's wearing is of a medium value, and there's only enough of it visible to enhance the impression that this is a real nice guy smiling at us. It's an ideal commercial picture.

48

THE RIGHT PHOTOGRAPHER

Almost inevitably, the picture you have taken in Madison, Wisconsin, or Detroit or Peoria will need to be discarded when you are trying to make it in the major talent centers. It's not that local photographers are untalented; they simply do not have the frame of reference necessary to provide you with a photo that will do the job you need. Photographers in New York and Los Angeles understand what the business is looking for because they are part of it, they deal with hundreds of people, they know what's happening *now*.

Choosing your photographer is a major decision. Select the photographer as carefully as you would a surgeon. It is vital that you feel comfortable with and trust your doctor. So it is with your photographer. Your professional life is in his or her hands, after all.

Interview at least eight photographers before you make a choice. Examine their portfolios carefully. Do you like the work? Is the style so forceful that the actor takes second place? Sense where the photographer is coming from. Do you feel comfortable with this person? How does this person see you? Avoid anyone who seems to be giving you a lot of hard sell.

Find out, in advance, how long the photographer allows for each sitting. You want to be sure that you have all the time *you* need. Find out, in advance, how many shots are taken and whether you will be able to have a reshoot if you are not satisfied with the results of your first sitting. Find out whether the photographer uses a makeup artist or whether you will need to employ your own. Discuss the clothes you should bring to the session. Get the photographer's advice on necklines, collars, fabrics, and shades. Remember: whites and blacks make for bold contrasts, which are harsh and distracting. Find out, in advance, whether you will be receiving finished head shots *and* negatives, or just the final print. Find out, in advance, how many prints are included in the cost of the sitting and how much additional pictures will cost.

Photo session fees range from $125 to $600. Professional photographers advertise in the trade papers—*Back Stage* in New York, *Drama-Logue* in Los Angeles. We've included a list of those photographers whose pictures consistently seem to win attention.

TABLE 3.   Some Photographers Whose Work Is Consistently Good

Locations	Photographers[a]	
New York	Gerard Barnier	Ann Limongello
	Kathy Blaivas	Robert Newey
	Tom Caravaglia	John O'Donnell
	John Deane	Susan Oristaglio
	Dan Demetriad	Marc Raboy
	Nick Granito	Raffi
	Manning Gurney	James Savas
	John Hart	James Shannon
	Joe Henson	Betty Shirley
	Larry Lapidus	Lee Snider
Los Angeles	Kathy Amerman	Tony Rizzo
	Brad Brason	George Rodriguez
	Domonic	Buddy Rosenberg
	Scott Downey	Ron Sorenson
	Frank Edwards	Frank Teti
	Greg Gorman	Bob Vallard
	Roger Karnbad	Diana Whiteley
	Lennon	

[a]Consult the trade papers or the telephone directory for their current addresses and telephone numbers.

OUTDOOR SHOOTING

There are many photographers who prefer to work in natural light. This is particularly true in California, where climate and landscape are so conducive to outdoor photography. If you're more comfortable outside a studio, look for someone whose pictures share that same feeling. But be sure that this is really where you are at your best; if your hair frizzes when there's 10 percent humidity, stick to the studio shot.

SELECTING YOUR PHOTO

A few days after your photo session, the photographer will give you a set of contact sheets—pages of small prints of all the shots he or she has taken. Have a magnifying glass (preferably one with a light) so that you can see the contact prints clearly.

If there are so many good pictures that you cannot decide, try to get the advice of a casting director or agent. It is very difficult to see ourselves as objectively as we must for these choices. One terrific photo is really all that you need.

COMPOSITES

Full-face head shots are used for theater, films, television, and commercials in New York. The composite—an 8″ by 10″ that shows you in different outfits and with various props—is favored by commercials agents in Los Angeles. The photos you select and the costumes you wear should be discussed with your commercials agent. Do not attempt to put a composite together without direction.

Modeling agencies also require their clients to assemble composites. Again, these brochures are quite special and require the direction of the agent.

GETTING COPIES MADE

Once you have chosen the head shot that is really you, you will need to have it duplicated by a photo service. Take the photographer's finished print (and the negative, if it was included) to a duplicating service. Shop around. These businesses advertise in the trade papers.

Photos can be ordered with a glossy, matte, or semimatte finish. The semimatte finish is popular now. It has a very attractive, user-friendly, tone.

For a slight additional charge, you may have your name and telephone service number printed on the front of the photo. This is a good idea; pictures and résumés frequently get separated.

Order one hundred pictures as a start. The original and the negative should be returned to you. Additional reprints, when you need them, will therefore be less costly than this first batch.

You should also order one or two hundred *photo-postcards*. These are glossy photos printed on card stock. They are the size of a postcard and are mailed at postcard rates. Have your name and service telephone number printed beneath your picture.

If your photo session yields two absolutely marvelous shots that you love equally, use one for the 8″ x 10″ and the other for the postcard. Then you can get feedback about both pictures.

Your photos should be ready within ten days to two weeks.

THE RÉSUMÉ

To the back of your 8″ by 10″ photo you attach your résumé. Tips on writing a business résumé do not apply in the entertainment business: the résumé does not list information chronologically, and it does not state your career goals or salary expectations. It should tell us all about the work you have done and with whom you have studied.

The information should fit neatly on one page and should be arranged with a certain artfulness. You don't have to hire an art director, but the page should be neatly typed and easy for the eye to follow. Two examples are shown here.

Your name should be at the top; underneath give your *union affiliations*, if any, and the *telephone number* where you can be reached. If you have a professional answering service, write "(service)" next to the number. If you are using an answering device, write "(machine)" next to the telephone number. *Never include your home address or your home telephone number on your résumé.* Pictures are passed around to many hands and unfortunately may end up with some people whose interest in your career is questionable.

Vital statistics—your height, weight, hair and eye color—should be grouped together. If you sing or dance, tell us your voice type and the kind of dancing you do. It's not necessary to indicate your age range. That's an old stage habit. If we want an actor to look 45 years old, we will hire an actor who is 45 years old.

Now come *your credits*. In New York, the résumé lists *theater* credits first. Give the name of the play, your role, and the theater. If you've played a great many parts at one or two theaters, use a heading such as "Leading Lady, Forest Glen Theatre, 4 seasons, Representative Roles:" and select the most important plays. Next you list your *film* credits. Your *television* credits are third. Roles in well-known works should lead the list, as the sample résumés demonstrate.

RECOMMENDED RÉSUMÉ FORM (NEW YORK)

YOUR NAME
Union Affiliations

Service/Machine   Height:
Agent's name and phone   Weight:
                                                 Hair:
                                                 Eyes:

THEATER:

Broadway:	*Any Wednesday*	Dorothy	
	Cactus Flower	Receptionist	(understudy lead)
Off-Broadway:	*Ethan Frome*	Mattie	Cherry Lane Theatre
	Summer and Smoke	Alma	Stage 73
	Alison's House	Ann Leslie	Stage 73
Dinner Theater:	*Marriage Go Round*	Constance	Florida Palms
	House of Blue Leaves	Bananas	Palm Beach
Stock:	Leading Lady, four seasons		Falmouth Playhouse
	Twelfth Night	Olivia	
	Lysistrata	Casseiopia	
	Shadow and Substance	Thomasina	
	Streetcar Named Desire	Stella	
	Bell, Book and Candle	Gillian	
FILM:	*The In-Laws*	Mrs. Arthur	Pare Lorentz (Warners)
	The Wrong Man	Neighbor	Lawrence Heath (20th Century)
Industrials:	6 management training films	Instructor	Blue Cross
	Weigh of Life	Lead	Heart Association
TELEVISION:	*As the World Turns*	Julie Lester	CBS
	Texas	Mrs. Thomas	NBC
	Edge of Night	Prison Matron	ABC

COMMERCIALS: On camera and voice overs—list and tape upon request

TRAINING: Yale Drama School, M.F.A.
         Robert Lewis—3 years
         Uta Hagen—2 years

SPECIAL SKILLS: Fluent French and Spanish, pianist (classical)
             Dialectician

SPORTS: All racket sports; champion bowler (New Haven, 1979)

RECOMMENDED RÉSUMÉ FORM (LOS ANGELES)

YOUR NAME
Union Affiliations

Service/Machine   Height:
Agent   Weight:
Agent's phone: Hair:
                                                         Eyes:

FILM
The Heavenly Kid   Melissa (starring)   Orion Pictures
Porky's Revenge   Ginger (principal)   20th Century Fox
Cry Of The City   Reporter   Universal (1985 release)

TELEVISION
Miami Vice   Lana (principal)   "Home Invaders" NBC
Miami Vice   Got a Light Girl   "Rights of Passage" NBC
West Coast Women   Guest dancer   Selkirk Cable

COMMERCIALS
List and tape on request

THEATER
Anything Goes   Hope   Goodspeed
Life With Father   Mary   Bailey Hall
West Side Story   Chorus   Bailey Hall
The Fantasticks   Luisa   Parker Playhouse
Hello Dolly   Minnie   Tour 1983–84

TRAINING
Acting: Milton Katselas
         Broward Community College, theatre major (two years)
         Dillard School of Performing Arts (three years)
         School for Gifted Students in Arts (Summer study)
Voice: Richard Crawford (two years)
         Howard Ross (one year)
Dance: Jazz: Luigi, Jim Franklin, Ken Samuels, Debbie Rodenski
         Ballet: Randi Lefkow, Jerald Jaquith
         Modern: Revell Shaw

SPECIAL ABILITIES
Puppeteer, ice skating, cheerleading, horseback riding, aerobics

---

In Los Angeles, the preferred order is *film* first, then *television* and *theater*.

If you do *commercials*, state only whether you have been an on-camera and/or voice-over performer and whether you have a commercial reel or a voice tape. *Do not list the products.* Your local spot for Dazzle Toothpaste may be canceled three days after you meet the person who casts for Shimmer Toothpaste. That person may want to consider you for the upcoming Shimmer commercial. If your résumé says that you already have a toothpaste commercial, you will not be called to audition for a competing product. You will lose the chance at a job you're right for.

Your training should be the next category. We want to know where you studied, with whom, and for how long. Tell us about your awards—scholarships, fellowships—and about your degrees. For performers who have not done a great deal of work, this section is particularly important: experienced casting people know the teachers and the schools. A casting director who hasn't had the chance to see your work can at least have an opinion about the people you have studied with.

Here's what some leading casting people have to say about training:

Veteran casting director, Shirley Rich:

I believe in academia. There are wonderful theater departments in colleges throughout the country.

Agent Phyllis Black of the Fifi Oscard Agency:

When there aren't many credits I am most impressed with training.

Gene Blythe, head of casting for MTM Enterprises:

I don't care what they've done, but I do care where they did it. Training—how long you were with somebody. If they carried a spear at Long Wharf, it means more to me than if they played Hamlet at Orange County, because I know the process to get to Long Wharf.

Jane Alderman, Alderman and Andreas, Chicago:

I'm a great résumé reader, and they may have worked with somebody or studied with somebody I know.

Your special skills are listed next. By this we mean listing whatever languages you speak or dialects you do *well*; whether you're a concert pianist (or play any instrument reasonably well); whether you're an expert at anything—carpentry, sculpture, even twirling a baton. One young actress who'd just arrived in New York stated that she was a champion baton twirler. Her photo and résumé were seen, and read, by casting director Shirley Rich. The actress was hired to play a high school cheerleader and to stand-in for the leading actress in a film that Paul Newman was directing. It was her first professional job—a four-month assignment on a major film.

Sports skills such as diving, racquet sports, acrobatics, or karate get a separate listing. List the ones you do expertly. In commercials particularly, you'll be asked to perform a feat—such as diving off a high board—again and again for repeated takes from a number of camera positions. You may have to skate on an ice rink for several hours, jog all day, or serve a tennis ball expertly. You must be in superb physical condition when you list sports. Lying could be hazardous to your health.

PADDING YOUR CREDITS

There's a great temptation to embellish on a résumé, especially if you feel that your list of credits could be more impressive. Our advice is *don't*. This is a very small business.

Jane Alderman, casting director, Alderman & Andreas, Chicago:

> **People lie on résumés and I've always caught them. If people put down that they were in the national company of Evita, I have to say I don't think you were, because I cast it. I'd remember you.**

Mervyn Nelson:

> **You can't tell me this little girl in front of me with pigtails and a pigeon-toed walk has played Medea!**

INEXPENSIVE COPIES

Copies of your résumé can be made, cheaply, at any copying center that does offset printing. PIP, a nationwide franchise, does reliable work, quickly, and has a variety of papers to choose from. Select a weight that will stand up to a lot of handling and prints clearly. You don't have to use white paper—ivory or some other pale tone is attractive and generally costs no more. Order at least as many copies of your résumé as you do of your photo.

THEY GO TOGETHER

It is *your* job to staple, paste, or tape the résumé to the back of the photo. This may sound elementary, but performers have been known to hand them to the casting person separately—"This is my photo. And here's my résumé"—and then sit back as if it were part of the casting person's job to hunt for staplers, paste, or tape, and marry the two. Also trim the 8½″ by 11″ résumé to the same size as the 8″ by 10″ photo. Then your résumé will not shred or tear each time your photo is removed from the file for study.

THE GUIDES

Union members can, and should, be listed in two directories, *Player's Guide* and *The Academy Players Directory. Players' Guide* is the annual directory for stage, screen, and television. Since 1942 it has been distributed to casting people in every phase of The Business. Your entry includes your photo, name, union affiliations, contact (if you are signed to an agent), and service telephone. You may also include your significant credits. Founder Paul L. Ross is still the man behind the counter to whom you give your photo, entry form, and check. His wife, Marion, still visits each union and gives friendly advice to actors who cannot decide which are their most impressive credits. Deadline for submissions is in February of each year. The cost of an entry is $65 for a new listing; $30 for renewals.

For further information, contact: *Players' Guide*, 165 West Forty-sixth Street, New York, NY 10036.

Shirley Rich, casting director:

You'd be amazed at how many film directors sit with me thumbing through the Guide, sometimes for hours and say, "Oh, Shirley, what about this actor?" It's terribly important.

Juliet and Lester Lewis, agents:

When the Guide first came out, it was no more than half an inch thick and you knew everyone in it. Now, it's almost too heavy to lift.

The Academy Players Directories are published by the Academy of Motion Picture Arts and Sciences. Criteria are that you be a SAG or AFTRA member and represented by an agent. The directories are published three times a year. There are four editions, or categories: leading men and juveniles; leading ladies and ingenues; character men and boys; character women and young girls. Listings cost $15 per issue; $45 per year. The entry includes the performer's photo, name, contact phone, and agent. Credits are not given.

For further information, write: The Academy of Motion Picture Arts and Sciences, 8949 Wilshire Boulevard, Beverly Hills, CA 90211.

Performers in the South and Southwest have for the past eighteen years had access to the *Whitmark Directory*. Union membership is not a requisite for listing (Texas is a right-to-work state). The annual entry fee is $150, for which you may submit two photos, contact information, credits, and/or talent description. The fee also entitles you to a mention in the Whitmark monthly magazine.

For further information, write: Whitmark Associates, 4120 Main Street, Dallas, TX 75226.

If you decide to place your photo in any of the talent directories, be sure it is as good as the photo you're sending out to casting people. That means a current picture. The agent or casting director who sees your photo, calls you, and then doesn't recognize you when you walk into the office will wonder, "How long ago was that picture taken?"

RIP-OFF GUIDES

There are always ads or solicitations for publications promising to do more for the newcomer than the established guides can do. Clever entrepreneurs will offer to get information about their "personal" clients to "influential" people. Such ventures are usually rip-offs of one sort or another. A newcomer may enjoy feeling that some star maker is taking an interest in his or her career. But, the venture is just a money-making scheme for the person collecting the checks. Newcomers must face the fact that *they* are the only ones who can create interest in their career. And they have to do that by working hard for themselves.

With the advent of cable TV, the latest wrinkle in the scam is for a company to promise that, for a hefty fee, it will telecast performers' pictures on the public access channels during the day for casting people to see. An eager, unsuspecting performer may not stop to realize that casting people are in their offices, working, each day. They are seeing talent, in person, by appointment. The only audience for such a broadcast is the talent's family. That's not exposure you should have to pay for.

FINDING YOUR LEADS

Actors learn about job opportunities by reading the trade papers. *Back Stage*, which celebrated its twenty-fifth birthday in December 1985, has become the prime source of casting information for the New York actor and for the performer seeking work in regional theater. The heart of the paper, according to publisher Ira Eaker, is its coverage of commercials production, which generates billions of dollars each year—more than any other segment of the industry. *Back Stage* also carries ads for every industry-related enterprise.

For more than a decade, his daughter, Sherry Eaker, has served as editor of the Theatrical News section. She oversees all casting news and checks out all the notices:

Our peak months are March, for the summer stock season, and September and October, when the Broadway season begins. At those times we run 160 to 170 notices per issue.

At the start of each season, *Back Stage* lists anticipated productions; there is a monthly list of incoming films, with as much news about the production and casting staff as it is possible to garner. Each year, issues are devoted to off-Broadway theaters, regional theaters (and how to apply or audition for them), dinner theaters, and opportunities on cruise ships, in cabarets, in theme parks and amusement parks, and at outdoor drama festivals. In time for summer casting the paper publishes a directory of theaters, both union and nonunion, along with the plays they are planning to do and contact information.

In addition, there is news of interest to performers: columns on the doings in Equity, AFTRA, SAG, and NATAS (the TV Academy); columns with expert advice on monologues, auditions, and vocal mastery. Helpful to new talent is the paper's practice of reviewing new acts and small productions that will never be covered by the major critics. A favorable *Back Stage* review can often fill a tiny nightclub with local industry people—exactly the audience a fledgling talent is seeking.

Working actors may place a *talent ad*, at the special rate of $45 for four inches, including picture and credit or copy.

Casting notices for union productions, including EPIs and EPAs (Equity Principal Interviews and Equity Principal Auditions—see chapter 4) and Broadway replacements are carried at no charge; there is a fee for notices of nonunion productions, which are indicated by the abbreviation ADVT.

According to Sherry Eaker:

We also try to protect our readers . . . There are a lot of con artists out there. And every year there's a whole new crop of performers. Madonna says she got her first job through an ad she read in **Back Stage.**

Back Stage is on sale every Thursday. Single copies are $1. Subscriptions are available: $35 for 52 issues; $20 for six months. For further information write: *Back Stage*, 330 West Forty-second Street, New York, NY 10036.

Drama-Logue is to many actors the West Coast equivalent of *Back Stage*. It was founded about sixteen years ago by Bill Bordy, an actor who found looking for work in Los Angeles so difficult that he decided to establish one central source people could turn to.

The only advice I ever got was "Read the trades." Once in a while I'd see a little notice that so-and-so was casting a show. It never said what kind of show, whether it was union or not, or what sort of people they were looking for. By the time you drove all the way over to wherever the audition was held, you found out there was nothing in it for you, or they were charging a fee to audition!

Drama-Logue's staff, headed by another former actor, Lee Melville, covers theater, film, TV, and cabaret on the West Coast— San Francisco and San Diego as well as Los Angeles. There are pages and pages of casting notices, plus interviews with prominent personalities—actors, producers, directors, and probably most helpful to talent, casting directors. There is even a column on New York activity. It seems that everyone who teaches a course, runs a workshop, or takes a photo places an ad in *Drama-Logue*.

Drama-Logue is available each week on newsstands throughout the Los Angeles area and in the major production centers. Single issues cost $1.50; subscription rates are $36 per year; $21 for six months. For information on where you can purchase a copy, write: *Drama-Logue*, P.O. Box 38771, Los Angeles, CA 90038-0771.

Ross Reports Television was initiated in 1949 by the late Wallace Ross and is carried on by Jerry Leichter, its editor and publisher. He packs an enormous amount of information into this pocket-sized booklet. New York's advertising agencies, independent casting directors, TV commercials producers and packagers, talent agencies, and literary agencies are all listed, with information as to whether they will accept pictures and résumés, screen video tapes, accept audio tapes, or even answer your phone calls. Also included are the production personnel and casting directors for all the daytime serials (on both coasts) and for the New York prime-time musical and variety shows that employ dramatic talent.

The West Coast section lists all network prime-time programs and includes a directory of casting personnel, program packagers, and production facilities.

Easy-to-read symbols show at a glance which programs or offices have had personnel changes within the previous month.

Ross Reports, as everyone calls it, is published during the first week of every month. We suggest you buy one at least every other month, as there are constant personnel changes. Single copies, at

3.50, are available at the Drama Book Shop, 723 Seventh Avenue, New York, NY 10036; at stores listed on the back of each issue; at the membership department of AFTRA; or through the publisher, Television Index, Inc. Subscriptions are $30 per year; $16 for six months. A free copy of the current issue is given to the first 350 AFTRA members attending each semiannual membership meeting.

For further information, write: Television Index, Inc., 40-29 Twenty-seventh Street, Long Island City, NY 11101.

Theatrical Index is a weekly listing of play production—what's opening, what's on, what's in previews or rehearsal, and what's announced or projected for the future. For each show, the producer, the playwright, and the director are named, as is the casting director. Frequently there will be a brief outline of the play and capsule descriptions of available roles. Off-Broadway information is included, divided into the same categories.

The *Theatrical Index* is posted on the bulletin board of the Equity Lounge (165 West Forty-sixth Street, New York, NY 10036).

For information about subscriptions, write to the publisher: Price Berkley, 888 Eighth Avenue, New York, NY 10019.

Theatrical Calendar is similar to the *Theatrical Index*, except that this listing is published twice each month. It contains information about all Broadway, off-Broadway, and off-off-Broadway productions, current and projected.

For subscription information, write: Theatrical Calendar, 171 West Fifty-seventh Street, New York, NY 10019.

Theatre Information Bulletin, founded in 1944, is the oldest directory of theatrical production and includes details on regional theater productions along with news of Broadway, off Broadway, and off-off-Broadway. It is published weekly. Copies are available by subscription: $90 per year.

For information write to the publisher: Theatre Information Bulletin, 4 Park Avenue, New York, NY 10016.

Variety, Hollywood Variety, and the *Hollywood Reporter* may be the most famous of the industry's trade papers. *Variety* is available each Wednesday at newsstands in the theater district of just about any city that boasts a theater district. Its news is essentially about the *business* aspect of show business worldwide; its pages carry data on the grosses of movies, plays, record and nightclub acts, and television deals. *Variety* also reports on which executives have moved to which new offices with more or less power.

The paper is fun to read occasionally if only to acquaint yourself with industry jargon—"*Sticks Nix Hick Pix*" is one of *Variety*'s more famous banner headlines—and to acquire a sense of the tempo and scope of the business on an international scale. It is of minimal use to actors looking for jobs. A limited amount of space is devoted to casting news of theatrical productions.

Variety costs $1.50 per issue; subscriptions, at $75 per year, are available. Contact: Variety, Inc., 154 West Forty-sixth Street, New York, NY 10036.

Hollywood Variety and *The Hollywood Reporter* are daily publications that offer inside information on the intricacies of the business, chronicling as they do the comings and goings and the wheelings and dealings of studio executives, stars, and agents. Grand for gossip and an occasional read, they are of little real help to performers eager for jobs.

They are readily available at newsstands (and in the swanker hotel lobbies) throughout Los Angeles. Cost is 50 cents per issue for *Hollywood Variety*; 75 cents for the *Hollywood Reporter*.

Less well known, but extremely useful, is *The Motion Picture, TV, and Theatre Directory*, a guide to industry products and services. Between the listings of accountants, cameramen, and screening rooms, you'll find names and addresses of advertising agencies, casting consultants, and producers throughout the United States and Canada (as well as in Great Britain, Europe, and Japan). The directory is published semiannually; copies cost $5.95. NATAS members receive a copy at no charge.

For information, write: Motion Picture Enterprises Publications, Inc., Tarrytown, NY 10591.

ESPECIALLY FOR COMMERCIALS

As publisher Ira Eaker of *Back Stage* reminds us, commercials provide the largest source of income to performers and to the industry as a whole. To pursue this area properly, you may need additional tools.

Nick Granito

David K. Varna
as Mr. Jymm
ALL MY CHILD

Both of David Varnay's photographs illustrate the imaginative use of accessories. The leading man wears a hat.

The character prop is a marvelous comic touch.

Commercial Head Shots

The photo you choose as your best head shot should be fine for commercials. However, if you feel that you have a special character personality which is better suited to commercial copy, by all means have an 8″ by 10″ of that aspect of yourself. Notice the great difference in Douglas Fisher's photos, which were shown earlier in the chapter.

We do not mean to suggest that you take pictures of yourself with antic expressions, phonying delight over a paper plate, or wearing horn-rimmed glasses or a torn straw hat. That is caricature. In David Varnay's photos, the actor uses props effectively.

Videotapes

Videotapes of your work should be ¾″ professional quality video samples of professional work that you have done. Do not attempt to make a home video to distribute as your calling card. Whenever you shoot a commercial, ask the producer or the client for a copy of the finished commercial. When you have done three or more, have them assembled by a professional production house, into a reel, which you can have copied as needed.

Audio Tapes

If you have a distinctive speaking voice, with flexibility and range and have mastered Standard American speech; if you are a whiz at dialects; if you can come up with all sorts of trick voices and can do them consistently on cue, you may wish to be considered for *voice-overs*—announcers or characters who are heard but not seen on thousands of TV and radio commercials. A small cadre of performers have been extremely successful in this area. Herschel Bernardi has for many years been the voice of Charlie the Tuna for StarKist. Richard Widmark is the tough guy who assures us "nobody sweats the details like GM." To compete with them, and with the likes of Larry Keith, Tammy Grimes, Bob Kaliban, or Ruth Franklin, will require an *audio tape*. Ordinarily, this reel (cassettes too are beginning to be used for this purpose) is compiled of commercials you have already broadcast. If you're just starting out, you'll have to put a tape together from material that other actors have performed, or you may write your own copy *if you are good at that*. Listen to commercials, select those you feel you should have auditioned for, tape them (on your tape recorder), write out the lines, practice, and then go to a professional recording studio to have a reel put together. Sound studios advertise in all of the trade papers. The membership departments of the unions may know of studios offering members special rates. Interview sound houses just as you did photographers. It's important to feel comfortable and confident when you are putting your reel together: it will be another substitute for *you* in a casting person's office. Always start with the material you do best. The entire reel should be no longer than four minutes.

And you'd better equip yourself with a stopwatch, so that you can train yourself to bring in sixty, thirty, or twenty seconds' worth of copy *exactly* on time.

Larry Keith, who for more than seven years played the role of Nick Davis on *All My Children*, tells everyone that voice-overs allowed him to survive until that juicy part came along:

> *I auditioned for over a year before I won my first audition. It was for a cake mix. I did two spots, for which I was paid two times the $80 session fee, or $160. And then, a while later a check for $2,500 arrived, for all the uses. And I thanked my stars for SAG's contract! It was months before I won another audition. I was so low I couldn't see beyond the gutter. Which is how I happened to find a five-dollar bill in the street—that's where my eyes were. I took it as a sign my luck would change—finding money on Park Avenue. And, sure enough, it turned out that the spot I had just auditioned for was eighteen spots! For a soft drink. And I started to make a living.*

Bob Kaliban, Iowa born, RADA (Royal Academy of Dramatic Art) trained, and a former president of SAG–New York, is recognized by his peers as an actor who can do any voice you can think of. He does telephones, drops of water, stuffy noses. Bob's range is so wide that he no longer sends out an audio tape.

> *The people who use me know if I cannot do the voice they want, I'll tell them who can. Know what you can do. Be honest. It will work out for you in the long run.*

Body Parts

Yes, there is a definite need for lovely hands and beautiful, slender feet. If your hands or feet are photogenic, use a photo-postcard (of your hands or feet in an attractive, graceful position) with your name and telephone answering service number, printed below the picture. Be sure to tell agents and casting directors that you are looking for this kind of assignment.

Additional Trade Publications

To find out which advertising agencies create commercials for which products, consult the *Standard Directory of Advertising Agencies*, better known as the Agency Red Book, because it's bound in bright red. Published three times a year, in February, June, and October, it is as thick as the Manhattan telephone directory, contains information on approximately 4,000 advertising agencies—their more than 60,000 clients, account executives, creative directors, executives—and even includes the budget for ad campaigns. The latest copies of the Agency Red Book are available at public libraries and at the offices of AFTRA and SAG.

For further information, contact the publisher: National Register Publishing Co., 3004 Glenview Road, Wilmette, IL 60091.

The same company publishes a companion reference, the *Standard Directory of Advertisers*, which contains similar information on those corporations that advertise in print or broadcast media.

Other Publications

Advertising Age, AdWeek, Broadcasting, and *CableVision* are similar to *Variety* and the daily Hollywood trade papers in that they report each week on the business of the advertising business. You won't learn about casting from reading these trades, but you may see that an agency that appreciates your work has just won a new account. Good for occasional reading.

Handy Tools

If you don't know the territory, you need a map. As we have already suggested, you should be able to get these from the Convention and Visitors bureaus. Publications such as *Flashmaps: Instant Guide to New York* simplify the grid system and help you locate addresses. In California, everyone swears by the Thomas Brothers' *Los Angeles County Popular Street Atlas*. These are available in their respective cities.

When you begin seriously making the rounds (which we discuss in chapter 4, "Looking for Work"), you'll be able to plan your day efficiently if you invest in a *Geographical Casting Guide*—there's one for Los Angeles and one for New York. These guides cost $3.50 each and may be purchased in New York at the Drama Book Shop (723 Seventh Avenue) and in Los Angeles at Larry Edmunds's (6658 Hollywood Boulevard) or Samuel French Book Store (7623 Sunset Boulevard).

You've accomplished the first steps—had your pictures taken, ordered copies of your photo and résumé. You have your calling cards. Now let's discuss whom you're calling on.

Chapter 3
Buyers and Sellers

From your reading of the trade publications you will amass a collection of leads: names and addresses of producers, directors, agents, casting directors, and managers. You could sit down and in one great burst of energy send your photo and résumé to each and every one of them. A better way to proceed would be to learn first what it is that all of these people do and what they are looking for.

The eager newcomer tends to view all casting people as the modern-day equivalent of the emperor Nero—thumbs up, you're *in*, thumbs down, you're dead. In actuality, these people whom you wish to overwhelm with your ability can be divided into two major categories: they are either buyers or sellers.

AGENTS

Whether they confine their efforts to theater, films, television, or commercials, or are active in all of these areas, agents are *sellers*. They are in the business of selling their talented clients to the *buyers*—those casting directors, producers, and directors engaged in a particular project.

Actors, regardless of age, are frequently heard to moan, "Oh, what I really need is a good agent to get me a job!"

That's fallacious thinking. The agent cannot get you a job. Only you can do that. What agents can do is find out about jobs through their established contacts with producers, directors, and casting directors and through descriptions supplied them, at some cost, by an organization known as the Breakdown Service. The agents then try to find clients who are right for the roles being cast.

An agent can submit you, that is, mention your name and tell how terrific you'd be in the role, to the person or persons casting the project. If the person to whom your name is submitted agrees to see you, the agent will then arrange an appointment for an audition or an interview. If you win the job, the agent may then be able to negotiate salary and other terms, such as billing. The agent will be entitled to receive 10 percent of your earnings for that job *after you have been paid.*

This last is an important point. Agents work only on commission. Ten percent is the legal agent's commission. Never have anything to do with any person representing him or herself as an agent who asks you for a fee or any form of payment in advance. The agent gets paid only after the client gets a job and has received the check.

HOW AGENTS WORK

Talent agencies are franchised by the unions to submit clients for work in theater, films, television, and commercials. Some agencies specialize—an office may work only in commercials, for example. Others, usually those with several subagents, are active in all fields.

Some agencies work only with *signed clients*: a select number of performers whose work they know very well, whom they submit for all the jobs they may possibly be right for. There are offices that handle only *free-lance* talent. They will submit any performers whose work they know, for any jobs for which they think the actor may be right. The actors they submit are not signed to any other agencies for that field of work. There are also agencies handling *both free-lance and signed clients*. When none of their signed people is suitable for a role, they suggest free-lance performers whose work they know.

A performer may sign with only one agent at a time in any field. That is, you may have one agent for commercials; another agent may handle you for theatrical work; a third may represent you for films. If the office is large and active in all areas, you may be represented by three people within the same agency. The agreement you sign must state whether that is so. If you hear an actor say, "I'm with the William Morris office," that means the performer has been signed to a large, powerful agency and is represented by its staff in all areas.

Once you have signed with an agent, you do not free-lance in that area. You may, and should, continue to look for work on your own, but refer your contacts to your signed representative.

DO YOU NEED AN AGENT?

In New York the answer to that question is, "Not necessarily." It is possible to work as a free-lance performer in New York. In fact, many people believe that it is to the performer's advantage to do so. The agents you meet will almost invariably see you differently. One office may think you're perfect for roles described as the young executive type. Another office may categorize you as the down-to-earth, rural, homespun sort. You, of course, are certain that you can play both types of roles marvelously, as well as countless others. What you are looking to find, then, is representation that will be aware of all the things you do well. Until you meet that savvy agent, it's up to you to keep in touch with all the offices interested in free-lance talent. In New York, it is possible to get jobs without an agent (see chapter 4 "Looking for Work").

In Los Angeles, on the other hand, you definitely need representation. You need an agent for commercials *and* an agent for theatrical work, which in Los Angeles means TV and films rather than stage work.

The system in Los Angeles is such that you can barely get on a studio lot without a specific appointment from an agent with a casting director. However, agents in Los Angeles are willing to sign clients on the basis of a résumé and an interview.

Cricket Haskell, of the J. Carter Gibson office:

> *I love to see performers still working on their craft. I like to see current credits. If they are brand-new people, it would have to be their background. Then I look for a terrific personality and that "quality" within that comes "out."*

AGENCY REGULATIONS

Talent agencies are doubly regulated: they are licensed by the state, and they are required to sign franchise agreements with each of the unions in which they hope to find work for their clients. To obtain a franchise, the agent must have a certain amount of previous experience and a reputation in the business. The credentials are defined by the unions.

WHO BECOMES AN AGENT?

We polled agents across the country: the majority of them have previous experience as performers, directors, and/or producers and have worked as subagents for other, larger offices. Many of them have been in the business a very long time. Juliet and Lester Lewis run an office that employs four subagents. Lester remembers that he got his start in the business in 1932:

> *My brother sold a few jokes to George Burns at $25 a joke, which was a lot of money in those days. We produced radio programs. . . . In the early days of TV, I produced a weekly half-hour television show called* Hollywood Screen Test, *which gave Jack Lemmon, Grace Kelly, Cloris Leachman, and Marty Balsam their first crack at television. Then Betty Furness came into my life and asked me to represent her when she'd done a few commercials for Westinghouse. (Ms. Furness went on to become the first superstar spokeswoman.) I felt that in the commercials business a smaller agency like ours could compete against the huge agencies like William Morris. Today we represent more than a hundred clients in commercials, TV, films. Some of our clients have been with us for a long time, and we have personal feelings toward them. We are more like personal managers than 10 percenters.*

Juliet Lewis, Lester's wife and partner for more than forty years, says:

> *There is a chemistry and a delectable charge that comes from a really talented actor sitting across my desk. But of course, it*

is a matter of taste, too. And we do make mistakes. I turned down Eva Marie Saint for **Hollywood Screen Test.**

·Fifi Oscard, whose office now employs twenty-one subagents, went to work for no pay at a highly respected agent's office after her children started school:

And then, another agent, Lucille Phillips, offered to pay me a small salary. I went to work in her office. Later, when she retired, I took over the business. We are really looking for the same things now as we did then—a "look," something that makes you respond. I remember back then, a young actor came in. He was southern, very polite, and there was something about him that just blew everyone else away. His name was Zachary Scott. Well, a few years ago, the same sort of thing happened. A kid walked in the door and we just loved him, immediately. It was Matthew Broderick. We represented him until he went out to Hollywood to make a few films.

Richard Dunn, of the Los Angeles–based Brooke/Dunn/Oliver Agency, whose staff of four represents more than seventy signed clients, went from acting to a job as an NBC page, which led to a spot as a producer's assistant. He became a casting director, then directed and produced radio and television programs, among them the daytime serials *Love of Life* and *Guiding Light*.

Monica Stewart of the William Schuller Agency was a child model in the 1940s. After a successful career as a teenage model, she turned to agenting when she realized that she was never going to be tall enough to make it as a high-fashion model. Her background was "perfect for an agency that now handles about two hundred kids."

WHAT THEY WANT

We asked the agents what they look for in new talent. *Charisma, style, personality, uniqueness,* and *ability* were the words they used most frequently.

Dorothy Scott, of the Marje Fields Agency, put it this way:

> *The first requisite is talent. I like to be proud of the people I represent. I want them to be attractive and well groomed.*

The agent can pay the rent and the telephone bill only if and when the clients are working. Of course every agency wants the next new person who comes into the office to be a potential money-maker.

We asked agents what turns them off. The answers were almost unanimous: greed, egomania, ignorance, stupidity, sloppy appearance, overt aggressiveness.

Carmen LaVia, at Fifi Oscard's:

> *I am turned off by people who don't tell the truth. By people who don't treat me as a human being. Who somehow wangle my home telephone number and then call me at all hours, just to "chat."*

Barry Douglas, of the Barry Douglas Talent Agency, Inc.:

> *I hate dishonesty, insecurity, and the expectation that I will do their work. I love professionalism and energy.*

Meg Mortimer, ADM Associates:

> *What turns me off is anyone with an oversized view of himself and the attitude that I owe it to him to get his jobs.*

Mark Redanty, of Bauman Hiller and Associates:

> *I don't like actors with swelled heads. Especially those who have no reason to be so egotistical. They are usually self-defeating and don't get very far.*

THE RIGHT AGENT FOR YOU

Every performer would love to be represented by an agent who is dedicated, powerful, and willing to invest limitless time in the client's behalf. This may not always be possible to achieve, particularly when you are new in the business.

Certainly no reputable agent will really want to sign a client whose work he or she does not know and appreciate or whose potential he or she doesn't believe in.

You and the agent should be clear with one another about the contacts you are expected to make on your own. Be realistic. As we have emphasized, an agency only earns money when the clients are working, so there will naturally be greater incentive to make phone calls on behalf of a client whose earnings may be ten or more times what you can command. Therefore, it is sensible for you to continue your efforts to get yourself known to the potential buyers of your talents.

Clarify also how the agent sees you—as the upwardly mobile executive or the homespun hero or both. Try to find out whether the agent wants to hear from you about job ideas or whether he or she expects you to wait quietly for his or her calls.

Flip through the pages of *Players' Guide* and *The Academy Players Directory* to see whether the office handles clients you consider talent conflicts with your own ability. If you fear that there are too many people in the "stable" like yourself, discuss this with the agent. It may mean that you and the agent have different ideas of the way you register. Or it may mean that you should seek representation elsewhere. It may mean that the agent hopes to corner the market for a particular type, so that if young bride A is working, young bride B will be the next choice for a job or young bride C and so on. These are subtleties that must be discussed openly.

SIGNING WITH AN AGENT

First-time agreements—these are standard agency contracts, approved by the unions—may be for a period of one year. That should be sufficient time for you and the agent to test the relationship. However, each agreement contains an "out clause"—for you if you begin to suspect that the initial interest has cooled too quickly; for the agent if you in some way fall short of his or her expectations. After ninety-one days, if you have not had fifteen days of work, through the agent's submissions, either of you may abrogate the agreement.

MANAGERS

The personal manager is another type of seller who works with a very small group of signed clients. Managers are not franchised by any of the unions or regulated in any way.

Managers frequently work with agents, again with a smallish number they are close to, or they may sometimes go directly to casting directors, producers, or directors to get their clients' work seen.

Personal managers can be useful in guiding a career. They are expected to have a great many contacts with important, powerful people, such as packagers, studio heads, and executive producers. They charge a higher percentage of a client's salary than do agents—as much as 25 percent, over and above the agent's commission (if a job comes as a result of an agent's submission).

Yvette Schumer, who spent several years producing Broadway shows before turning to personal management, has represented Larry Keith, Nicholas Surovy, and Tony Award winner Christine Baranski:

The attention a manager can give is different from the attention an agent gives. It's like being a parent, a confessor. It's very personal. I think that is how people can become stars. But they have to be ready to work!

Larry Keith:

I feel that agents don't care as much about me as my manager does.

If a personal manager expresses interest in you, make certain that he or she has been in the business long enough to have amassed impressive connections. Ask for a client list, so that you can try to discover if the manager has a successful track record.

Like the agent, the manager should never demand any payment in advance. Managers' payments are commissions on work you have performed through their offices and for which you have been paid.

Effective managers will be known in the business. Any agreement you sign with a personal manager should be approved by an attorney—yours, not the manager's. When in doubt, inquire at union headquarters or ask a good agent.

HOW TALENT CAN BE DISCOVERED

The alert agent or manager does a great deal more than sit in the office, scan the Breakdown Service listings, make telephone submissions, and hope for an exciting new performer to drop off a photo and résumé. The good agent—the one you hope to sign with—is energetic in pursuit of talent. That means going to show-cases to see new talent at work and attending the graduation exercises of respected acting schools. It means leaving the confines of the city to see performances in regional theater, in summer stock, and at drama festivals.

Fifi Oscard, agent:

We discovered a skinny tall girl in an amusing improvisational group at the White Barn Theatre. Mary Steenbergen. She was so poor she was working as a waitress at the Magic Pan restaurant. We sent her to Paramount to meet Warren Beatty, and while she was sitting in the office, Jack Nicholson saw her. He asked if she was there to see him. She said no she was there to see Mr. Beatty. He asked if she'd mind seeing him after she saw Mr. Beatty! Out of that came the film Going South.

Jane Alderman, Alderman & Andreas:

My favorite story is when Stark [Hesseltine] and I went to the junior play at the American Academy of Dramatic Art. I think they were doing T. S. Eliot's The Cocktail Party. *A young, reddish-haired man in the background had very little to do, and he found a way to fill his moment. We were both riveted to him. Stark sent his card back, requesting a meeting. It was Robert Redford. There was something about his presence—doing what he was supposed to do—taking over in the best sense.*

A performer could not wish for more than the chance to be discovered working in a professional situation. For Marin Mazzie, her role in *Carousel* at the Barn Theatre in Augusta, Michigan, provided just that opportunity. The star of the show was the young TV-film actor Tom Wopat. His agent went out to Michigan for the opening and was promptly captivated by Marin's performance. The agent went backstage to see his client, made certain to meet Marin, and offered to represent her as soon as she came to New York! She made the trip at the end of the stock season—and is currently represented by the J. Michael Bloom Agency.

Richard Dunn told us:

I dislike the word discover. *I think an actor's talents are not well hidden from any pro. Discovering them is like sighting the World Trade Center. Somebody is bound to discover them. It's just a matter of timing.*

Agent Michael Thomas of the Michael Thomas Agency, Inc., tells this story about his early years as an actor:

Cyril Ritchard [the English actor] was a great friend and supporter. He had come to see me act in Connecticut and called his agent Milton Goldman to say that I was in the production, but there was an actor working with me who was superb and Milton should sign him. The actor was Alan Alda! Oh, well, Alan is an awfully nice fellow.

HOW TALENT IS *NOT* DISCOVERED

Legitimate talent agents and personal managers do not advertise in the Want Ad section of any newspaper or in the trade papers. An ad that solicits "new faces" for commercials, for modeling, or for films and then implies that experience is unnecessary and suggests that high salaries are waiting to be paid to the first people who answer the ad, is a phony.

Beware of any person who, representing himself or herself as an agent or manager, asks you to read sample copy for a dramatic scene or as a commercial test, who then agrees that you have "talent" but that it needs to be "developed," and who next suggests that you attend a particular school or study with a particular teacher to whom he or she recommends all of his "clients." Such a person is either a phony (getting a kickback from the recommended school or teacher) or a very stupid operator. In either case, such a person is *not* one who can be of value to your career.

Nor is talent discovered or eased along the path to stardom by means of the casting couch.

Carmen LaVia:

> *There are the people who, when you ask what time they'd like to come in and see you, say "Six o'clock in the evening." Then you know that they have a very wrong focus.*

Joseph Hardy, producer of *Ryan's Hope*:

> *Oh, that old myth about the casting couch. And that you have to put out to get work. And that someone's sexuality is going to be used for or against them. It is just a myth. It is not true, and what actors do is that they use it as an excuse. Honey, the reason you didn't get the part is that you're no good!*

CASTING DIRECTORS

The casting director is a talent *buyer* and your major link to the people who are in a position to hire you.
Mervyn Nelson:

> *The best casting directors are those who have acted. They know the problems that the actors have. Without this awareness, I don't see how they can do any casting.*

Gene Blythe, director of casting, MTM Enterprises:

> *An open mind is the most valuable tool that a casting director has. That makes the difference between being creative and being a hack.*

Ideally, casting directors go to see everything, remember all the good actors, and are willing to believe that a mediocre performance is not necessarily the actor's fault.
Mervyn Nelson:

> *You can't be a good casting director unless you have a heart big enough to understand all the people. You cannot be in judgment.*

Casting directors may have permanent positions—on the staff of an advertising agency, a network, a continuing show, working for a busy packager or production company. In such capacity they are actively engaged in seeking out talent and will frequently travel far from their home base to get a glimpse of it. They will be in touch with coaches at professional schools and directors of college theater programs. They will maintain contacts with agents and talent scouts across the nation and even pay attention to productions in foreign countries. They will also be interested in potential talents—the stars of tomorrow. Interesting talent is what they are after—able to grab an audience's attention and hold it, for thirty seconds, for two hours, or for the duration of a story line.

The *independent casting director* is a free-lance expert employed on a per project basis by the producer of a film, play, commercial, or other vehicle requiring talent. A free-lance or independent casting director may be involved in the initial casting of the core characters for a series or soap opera and then decide to hand the day-to-day casting chores to a staff casting director. The free-lance expert knows the available talent pool and will also go exploring for new performers. Possibly the major difference in the way they work is that the free lance is less likely to invest as much time in developing young people and will not feel the need to set aside time to meet actors unless there is a particular role for which to see them.

When she was on staff and involved with the continuous production activity of the Rodgers and Hammerstein office, veteran casting director Shirley Rich frequently held general interviews for actors she had never met. It was part of her job to be aware of promising new talent. Not only were Rodgers and Hammerstein the composer and lyricist of many of the American musical theater's greatest hit shows, they were also producers of straight plays (such as *The Happy Time*) and sent out touring companies of their successful shows. A great many actors were needed to fill all of those casts.

Now that she selects the projects she works on—films as well as theatrical productions and television series, Ms. Rich's procedures, of necessity, have changed:

In the theater, every time I have the EPAs I try to see everyone who comes in. Five hundred people a day. I see them all. I can't understand, when everyone reads the character breakdowns in

Back Stage *and sees the needed types and age ranges, why these people choose to see me, wasting my time and theirs, with a feeble, "But I just wanted to meet you . . ." The pictures they bring me may lie in a wastebasket or may be in a file for three years. So what is the point? Why don't they come to see me when there's something they are* right *for?*

Casting director Meg Simon:

Ideally you would like to audition many people for the role, but there isn't time. For Biloxi Blues *I saw well over two thousand people. In Chicago, I found an actor named Alan Ruck. He couldn't afford to come to New York and I couldn't afford to fly him in. I told him to find a way. He did. He got cast in* Biloxi Blues.

HOW THEY WORK

Whether on staff or independent, casting directors who work in the areas of television, theater, film, and commercials synthesize their personal impressions about each character, gathered from careful examination of the script, with the ideas they receive from the producer, the director, and the writer. Then they make recommendations.

Molly Lopata, casting executive at MTM Enterprises, *Remington Steele*:

We generally get a script about seven days before the production starts, and we'll have maybe three days of casting. The process involves the producer, the director, and the casting director. Ideally, we show them from three to five actors for each role. As the casting director, I feel confident that any of those people can do the part. Sometimes I'll get a script Friday morning and have a reading that afternoon at 3 P.M. That means I have about two hours to get my thoughts together and get the actors in for the parts. I've even cast on Sundays at times.

Betty Rea, casting director, *Guiding Light*:

I find out about major contract players from my producer, Gail Kobe, who has been an actress and a director and a teacher and who makes every effort to put people at ease and be constructive. I read about the roles in the script breakdowns. Each week I meet with the directors to discuss the noncontract players who will be needed. My assistant is told by them about the types and number of extras we will need. We try to be a month ahead in terms of casting. That is not always possible.

Maxine Marx, vice-president of casting, Cunningham & Walsh, Inc.:

You know with certain clients that there is a look that they want. Shampoos do not want people with dark hair. To the client that looks dirty.

Gene Blythe, casting director MTM Enterprises, *St. Elsewhere*:

I have seven to eight days to prepare. I read the script. I jot down ideas. I personally contact the files. I usually bring in at least two to three new people for each episode, whether or not I think they're right for the parts, so I can hear them read my words. The worst time I ever had was when we went through fifteen actors for a one-line paramedic role—to make sense of complicated medical jargon and still bring personality to it. When New York actors come to L.A., because of their training, those are normally the kind of roles I can zip them into. Right away they get a terrific credit, and it helps me out tremendously.

Independent casting director Meg Simon:

We read a script before meeting with the director. We talk about what they are looking for. Directors who don't know the talent pool are the most difficult to cast for, because they want to see all the available talent. Directors who know the talent pool will trust us. Peter Sellars [of the American National Theatre in Washington, D.C.] knows my taste connects with his taste and trusts my recommendations. I've worked with very few directors who didn't want to be inspired at auditions.

Feeling the constant pressure of time, casting directors must deal with certainties: there must be someone on the list of recommendations that everyone will agree on for each role. And yet, dissatisfaction can lead to innovative casting.

Shirley Rich:

When I was casting Taps, *two weeks to the start of filming we still didn't have Tim Hutton's roommate. I had been all over the country. Then Mary Harden [of the Bret Adams office] called to talk about a young actor named Sean Penn. She said he might not be what I'd described. The part had originally called for an attractive, sophisticated young man from a Park Avenue home, private schools. Well, in walked this sandy-haired kid, with the off-beat face, looking like something from Oklahoma. I talked to him, gave him the script, and he knocked me out with one of the most creative readings. I got excited and told the producer and director they had to see him. He wasn't what they had in mind, but they were excited by the reading. They tested him. We had to see if what he had in the reading would show up on the screen. It did. He got the part. They molded the part for him. And everyone who saw the picture couldn't help but notice him.*

Please remember, a casting director is *not* to be called a casting agent. It is a contradiction in terms. The correct terminology is talent *agent*, casting *director*.

THE HEAD HONCHOS

Whatever the casting director's recommendations, the final casting decisions must be approved by the executives in charge of the production.

In films they are the producer, the director, and the writer. Sometimes all of those positions may be held by the same person. And, in films, the entire production frequently relies upon the bankability of the star; all the rest is after the fact.

In soaps, if the show is owned by the network, they will be the daytime program executives, the producers, and the head writers. If the show is owned by Procter and Gamble, there will be a Procter and Gamble executive producer assigned to the show, the producers, and the head writers.

In commercials approval comes from the agency producer, the production house director, and the account executives, the art director, the copywriter, and the client.

In theater the decision makers are the producer, the director, and the playwright.

In made-for-TV films they are the producer, the writer, the director, and the network executives in the motion pictures division.

In a new series the final casting decisions are up to the network programming liaison executive, the producer, the directors, and the writer.

In episodes for an ongoing television series they are the executive producer, the line (episode) producer, and the writer.

Having separated the buyers from the sellers, it's time to set about meeting them.

Chapter 4
Looking for Work

Being an actor, even an unemployed actor, is a full-time job. Serious pursuit of your career involves developing your talents, looking for jobs, being able to perform them on cue, and packaging yourself correctly. It's a total commitment.

POLISHING YOUR SKILLS

Of course you can be born with a talent for acting, just as one may have a natural aptitude for sports, music, or even finance. In those fields we recognize that to compete as a professional requires training: singers vocalize morning, noon, and night; musicians practice for hours; athletes work out tirelessly under the guidance of a demanding expert coach; executives hone their business skills at seminars and management workshops.

Professionals endeavor to enlarge their potential by improving their technique; actors take classes. A good class develops and invigorates the "acting muscles": imagination, humor, sense memory, emotional range, style, movement, timing, improvisational facility, vocal variety, and speech. Class is where you stretch, where you learn how to analyze, understand, and enhance an author's material, where you refine your technique, so that when a director tells you to "do it again," you can repeat the moment—up to Take 45, if necessary.

Acting coach Flo Salant Greenberg:

An actor will frequently give a marvelous instinctive reading. The director will say, "That was a marvelous reading. I want you to do it again for Sam, the producer, who is coming in in ten minutes." And when the actor has to do it he is petrified. He has absolutely no idea what he did, because it was all instinctive. He has no idea what gave him that marvelous inspiration.

She recalls a conversation with Pat Hingle, who was then appearing on stage in *That Championship Season*:

I had a young actor with me and Pat said to him, "Young man, I want you to remember that at 9:38 every night I am delivering the same line in exactly the same way, at exactly the same tempo, because our stage hands' union is so strong that the curtain must ring down within thirty to sixty seconds of the same time at the end of every performance! And that involves technique! Professional technique."

Classes also put you in touch with other talented, creative people like yourself. They are the beginning of your own network—colleagues who know and respect your work, who feel comfortable with you, and who may remember you when they are involved in a future production. Class is where you may find the ideal stage partner, the other half of the act you've wanted to do.

Acting instructor Catherine Gaffigan includes this advice in her student guidelines:

Though deep friendships often develop [appropriately], the partnership arrangement in this class is a business relationship and should be treated as such. Your acting partner is not assigned to be a surrogate parent or a lover or to meet your emotional needs. Potential intimate relationships are wisely put on the back burner for the present.

The actor in New York or Los Angeles has the opportunity to work with some of the finest talents in the business: Geraldine Page, Michael Moriarity, F. Murray Abraham, Uta Hagen, Betty Buckley, Stella Adler, Helen Gallagher, Nina Foch, Milton Katselas, Jerry Stiller—these are only a few of the dedicated professionals who have so much to give and enjoy sharing their skills.

Prize-winning director Robert ("Bobby") Lewis, one of the founders of the Actors Studio, told the students who were ready to worship at his feet:

You know, in a good class the director learns something, too. I expect you all to teach me a great deal.

But the instructor's reputation should not be your prime concern. There's no benefit to you in studying with the chic teacher or the one whose class is supposedly most difficult to get into unless that person is someone whose work you respect, with whom you feel a connection, who demands the best of his or her students, and who seems genuinely interested in inspiring them. Try to audit a class first, or at least talk with the instructor. Check out the achievement level of the other students. Acting is like tennis: you get more out of it when you play with someone who's a bit better than you. If you are the best one in the class, leave.

Acting classes are generally operated on a month-to-month or thirteen-week basis. Schools offering a complete training course will usually require that you sign up for a complete semester.

Special Training

In addition to your acting or scene study class, you'll probably need workshops offering instruction in on-camera commercial technique and soap opera performance. While a background in acting is essential, the jobs demand different skills. It would be counterproductive to take classes in commercials and soap opera concurrently. Begin with the field that you feel offers you the most immediate opportunity. When you become expert in one, move on to the other.

Song and Dance

The performer who can sing and dance becomes a triple threat particularly on stage, because musicals employ so many more actors than do straight plays. For example, Bonnie Franklin's singing and dancing of the title song in *Applause* earned her a Tony Award and a subsequent career in TV.

Body movement is an essential element of the actor's training.

Movement is an element of character—as the writers of books explaining body language have understood. A dance class, therefore, may be more valuable than calisthenics for career purposes. And if you supplement your ability to "move well" with a knowledge of dance steps and combinations, you'll broaden your possibilities of work.

For a grand ball sequence on *As the World Turns* agents recently were swamped with calls for actors who could dance. The shows were complicated and required five days of taping. Two couples who seemed to understand exactly the kind of romantic ballroom quality that was sought became the focal point of each ballroom scene. None of the quartet had worked together before, or even met, but they were ideal dance partners, and the director quickly made use of what they could bring to the scenes.

For dance classes, which can serve as excellent fitness workout sessions, one can buy a card for a length of time or number of lessons. This is a relatively inexpensive aspect of your training.

Learning to sing can be costly. However, the trades frequently carry notices of less expensive music workshops. Consider trading lessons—offer your skill in another area to a colleague who sings.

Your Speaking Voice

The number of actors with slovenly speech is appalling. In what we laughingly refer to as real life, do strangers (not your family or friends who talk the same way you do and know what your sounds are supposed to mean) frequently ask you to repeat what you've just said? What's your name again? What was your address? This is, after all, a business of words as well as moving images. You make a lot of telephone calls in this business: before you can think of getting a job you need to ask for an appointment. And keep in mind that the hero must say, "I love you"; and the heroine must answer, "I love you too"; and the audience has to hear and understand every word.

Both Comden and Green's *Singin' in the Rain* and Kaufman and Hart's *Once in a Lifetime* deal comedically with Hollywood at the advent of talking pictures: there is consternation at the studio when it is evident that the he-man has the voice of a wimp and the femme fatale squawks like an irate peacock. What do *you* sound like? Does your voice match your look? If the voice you hear when you replay your recorded tape is not one anyone would care to listen to for more than three seconds, *run*, do not walk, to a speech coach.

Start practicing on your own: read aloud, slowly, for ten minutes, three times a day. Practice, practice, practice.

Cleanse your speech of localisms—intonation and pronunciation that announce even to a casual listener that you hail from up North, down South, or way out West. Aim for the general American sound of the announcers on national commercials or some of your network newscasters. When actors speak in any kind of dialect, they should be doing so for reasons of characterization, not because they always talk like that.

One of the many reasons British actors are so well regarded on this side of the Atlantic is that they are taught that the actor's vocal mechanism is an integral part of his or her instrument. And they are trained to read the words as the author wrote them. It is a pleasure to listen to them. Every word is as clear as crystal. Practice. Practice.

Books and Plays

The lives of well-known performers and the literature of the theater should be familiar to you. If you don't already have one, get a library card. Read plays—the entire work, not just the scene that may be assigned to you.

Uta Hagen, at a seminar for Equity members:

People come to me and say, "What should I work on?" I say, "Don't you read?" Musicians have jam sessions all the time. Why don't actors do that? Read plays, and when you find plays that interest you, start to work on them. We cannot stop practicing. You don't stop learning to act until you drop dead.

KNOCKING ON DOORS

Here is where the actor must switch from sensitive artist to energetic business executive. You are a door-to-door salesperson, and what you are selling is *you*. Obviously, the more doorbells you ring, the greater your chances of making a sale.

Sam Grey, actor:

> **When I was just starting out in Chicago, someone told me, if you make ten calls a day you are bound to get work. I made twenty.**

Send a photo and résumé to every franchised agent and subagent whose name you have read in *Ross Reports* or special issues of the trades.

SENDING OUT YOUR PHOTOS

You will need a supply of 8″ by 10″ or 9″ by 12″ manila envelopes, preferably with a cardboard insert. You don't want the post office to crumple your picture along with the rest of the mail. (Always write "Photographs, Please Do Not Bend" on the outside of the envelope.) With each photo and résumé include a *cover letter*. This is a short note introducing yourself. Mention the name of the person who may have suggested that you contact the casting director or agent, and request an appointment.

Now is the time to use every connection you have: parents, relatives, mutual friends, acting teachers, your college alumni. Be sure that the referral is legitimate.

Your stationery, while it need not be engraved by Tiffany, should, nevertheless, be attractive. Do not use a sheet of lined paper torn from a spiral-bound notebook or even a small legal pad. You are presenting yourself—via your photo and résumé and everything that goes out under your name—for consideration in your chosen career. You are advertising yourself. This is your first business call on a client.

The letter should be neatly typed. If that is an impossibility, a hand-written note will do, provided that your script is legible. Trying to decipher a scrawl is a turnoff. So is misspelling, improper grammar, or words that are used incorrectly. One actor's cover letter contained the line: "This is a funny *antidote* I heard the other day . . ." If you don't know that you're telling an *anecdote*, should an agent be willing to risk credibility by submitting you for work?

Make sure that you've spelled the casting person's name correctly. Mari Lyn, for example, and not Mary Lynne, Mariann, Mary Lou, Marry Lynn, or Merry Lynn. Be certain of the sex of the person: Lynn, Randi, and Carmen *could* be women, but, as it happens they are *Mr.* Stalmaster, *Mr.* James, and *Mr.* LaVia. It's your business to find out such things.

Mr. Carmen LaVia:

I get a note from an actor saying, "Dear Ms. LaVia, so nice to meet you at so-and-so's party last week!" Now, what am I supposed to think of that actor? Would I ever call him? Not on your life.

Next, go through your list of leads and find the casting directors who regularly cast shows. Send your photo and résumé and cover letter to them.

Advertising agency casting departments should receive a photo and résumé. If you have an audio tape or a video reel, mention that in your cover letter. Do not send them unsolicited.

Production houses with casting directors also get a photo and résumé and a cover letter. After about two weeks send a postcard as a reminder and ask again for an appointment. Be pleasant and positive; remind them that you sent your material to them a short time ago and ask when it will be possible to meet.

A telephone follow-up is not advisable because agents are trying to get work for clients they represent; casting directors are trying to accommodate agents and see people for specific roles. They don't have the time to talk with people they don't know. They will call you if they're interested. If you feel that you must call, be able to state succinctly what you want to ask and what you hope to say about yourself. This is not the time to stammer or be shy or giggle or sound desperate.

You will get one of three possible answers: your picture is on file—don't call us, we'll call you; call back in about two months; we see people at four o'clock on Thursday.

Note this response in your records.

KEEPING RECORDS

It is vital that you keep a file of all the people you try to see. Whether you use index cards, a personal computer program, or an accountant's notebook is immaterial. What matters is that you know at a glance *when* you sent a photo, to *whom*, and whether you received a *response*. As your career progresses, you will refer to the records for follow-up notes and phone calls and to remind yourself what happened at each exchange.

It is easy to forget that agents and casting directors are human beings with legitimate concerns beyond whether or not they are going to see you on Tuesday. Make a note that one casting director's son runs a French restaurant, that another's husband had a book published, that a third has been elected to an honorary position. It's something you might talk about *next time*. In doing so, you become a human being to the people to whom you are speaking. There is more to life after all than the next appointment, although it may not seem so at the time.

Jean Arley, producer of *Search for Tomorrow*, has been an actress, a casting director, and a producer of several shows for Young & Rubicam and CBS:

If an actor knew that I cast at a certain theater with a certain director, I'd be impressed and it would probably set me off on a boring anecdote while it gave him or her a chance to relax.

Financial Records

Because their income profile is so different from that of the general public, actors seem to be prime targets for income tax audits. We cannot overemphasize the necessity for keeping precise records —not only on your income, agents commissions, and tax deductions, but on every expense. Start now to train yourself to keep a daily account book, noting phone calls, meals (how much, with whom and where), clothing purchased for business occasions, travel, mailing expenses—the list is endless. Keep your receipts, too. As we noted earlier, paying by check is a way of recording expenses. As a careful record keeper, you are able to deal sanely with whatever changes occur in federal, state, or local tax regulations.

Don't think that your income is too small to attract the attention of the IRS. We know of performers earning $10,000 who have been audited. Precise employment records are necessary not only at income tax time, but in case you apply for unemployment insurance compensation. Qualifications differ from state to state, and change frequently. The local unemployment offices will let you know the current regulations.

GOING OUT

While you are conducting your mailing effort, continue to read the trades for specific casting news. If you see a notice for an *open call*, go! Open calls are held by casting directors, agents, producers, and/or directors when they need people for atmosphere *and* when they are looking to cast a very special role and have been unable to find anyone that the writer, the producer, and the director can agree upon (see the story of Punky Brewster in chapter 14). An open call means just that: is there anybody out there who can do this job?

Cast lists and character descriptions are almost always provided for open calls, EPIs, and EPAs (for EPIs and EPAs, see next section). Read the description carefully and try to look like what the production people say they want. Bring your photo and résumé and your additional materials—the tape, the reel, your scrapbook, your reviews. This is a chance to sell yourself; bring everything that you think will help you make the sale. You may not need it, or even get to use it, but you must be prepared.

 ### EPIs and EPAs

Actors Equity requires producers to set aside time for open casting. The members have the right to try to audition for every Equity production. The EPI is the Equity Principal *Interview*: on the day of the call, members sign up to be seen by a representative of the producer in the order in which they arrive. They hand in their photo and résumé and hope to be called back for an audition.

Meg Simon, casting director:

For **Biloxi Blues** *I had an open call where a thousand people showed up. Two of us worked on the stage. We accepted pictures and résumés. We made instantaneous decisions. We put the pictures in three piles: no, possible, and see. There were high possible and low possible. I called back one hundred. I hired Matt Mulhern from an EPI; he didn't have an agent. I had EPIs on* *the Jackie Robinson musical* **The First;** *nobody showed up. We notice minority actors don't come to EPIs.*

For the EPA—the Equity Principal *Audition*—the actor must come prepared with an audition selection: a monologue of two minutes or less. There is no limit to the number of people who may sign up, but only the first 115 are guaranteed to be seen on a day. There is no carryover of names. If you don't make it on the first day, you must come in early the next day and sign up all over again. Joseph Hardy, producer of *Ryan's Hope*:

> *I can almost tell after about thirty seconds or a minute whether the actor is right or not. So then it's up to the actor to keep me interested. The actor should find ways to keep me interested without losing the integrity of the material.*

Theatre Communications Group

The Theatre Communications Group (TCG) is the national organization for the nonprofit professional theater. Among its programs is a casting service, which identifies, refers, and presents professional actors for work in nonprofit professional theaters across the country. TCG holds general auditions for actors in the New York area. For further information, contact: Theatre Communications Group, 355 Lexington Avenue, New York, NY 10017.

Actress Patricia Elliott:

> *I auditioned at TCG and was seen by Gordon Davidson (of the Mark Taper Forum in Los Angeles). He said to let him know what I was doing, no matter where I was working.*

Other Places to Work

Almost every actor in New York has worked in one or more of the productions of Plays for Living, a division of the Family Service of America. These productions are original half-hour dramas that illustrate a particular family stress situation: alcoholism, a child's inability to read, stealing, lying, and the like. The plays are presented to parents' associations or similar groups in school auditoriums, churches, or meeting halls throughout New York City. Casts are small and usually double- or triple-cast to allow for jobs. Actors receive a small honorarium and usually are invited to share the coffee and cake served after the performance. Audience discussion follows, but by then the cast is on its way home.

While the payment received is minimal, the experience of adjusting to different theaters and audiences is invaluable. Some of the material is excellent for audition scenes.

To learn more about Plays for Living, contact: Family Service of America, 44 East Twenty-third Street, New York, NY 10016.

The Bedside Network is a volunteer service started by performers after World War II to present radio scripts for hospitalized veterans. Performers serve as professional directors, while the patients eventually become proficient enough after an evening's rehearsal to broadcast the script for their fellows. It's one of the favorite activities of AFTRA members.

For further information, contact: Bedside Network, 1841 Broadway, New York, NY 10019.

The In-Touch Network is a special radio station for the blind. Volunteers spend an hour or two reading into a microphone—the daily newspaper, news magazines, stories, almost anything of interest. This is a volunteer activity, and a marvelous opportunity for actors to improve their skill at cold reading.

The In-Touch Network is at 32 West Forty-eighth Street, New York, NY 10036.

MAKING ROUNDS

Trying to see agents and casting directors by knocking on doors has become difficult. Small offices, frequently staffed by women, must take security precautions: doors are locked to those without appointments. And yet we think it is always worth a try. If you are going out on an open call, an interview, or an audition, do take along a batch of photos and résumés (and manila envelopes) and call upon all the offices in the area. Even if no one will see you, you can always leave your photo, résumé, and cover letter, and note these deliveries in your records.

A SUPPORT SYSTEM

The Actors' Information Project, known as AIP, offers New York actors a new kind of support system, geared to helping performers with the business aspect of their careers. If this sounds like clever tips on record keeping, that's only a fraction of what AIP does. AIP's career consultants work with members on career planning, interview techniques, marketing strategies, and development of one's personal style. Intensive career workshops are presented throughout the year. AIP's computer services will store your résumé and target your mailing lists. Networking workshops make it easier to meet casting people and show them your work. At their centrally located offices, rehearsal space, rehearsal piano, and video equipment are available.

AIP is the brainchild of former agent David Rosen and actor-director–stage manager Jay Perry. Their own experience in the business convinced them of the need for a supportive environment where actors could discover what they need to do to be successful. Perry and Rosen say:

AIP is built around encouraging actors to set up their own personal business, which, if they're smart managers about themselves, allows them to win more often than not. It's not fun if you're pursuing your career in the "struggle aspect." That is not entertaining. Struggling actors are not entertaining. Desperation and anger at the business is not entertaining, and this is really the entertainment business. We are a place to come when they feel the roller coaster is starting to go down, so they stay in the game. If everything is measured against what that friend you went to college with is doing now, lose you will.

The AIP full-day business planning seminar contains a presentation section, in which actors take the stage, talk about themselves, and find out what aspect of their presentation—hair, personality, clothes, etc., is effective and what is not.

A Los Angeles branch of the Actors' Information Project is now in the planning stage. The New York center is at 311 West Forty-third Street, New York, NY 10036.

Added Assistance

Activities of the American Film Institute (AFI) in Los Angeles, the National Academy of Television Arts and Sciences (NATAS) in New York, and SAG and AFTRA include opportunities to meet casting people and others in the business. At the unions, workshops run by volunteers allow performers to see themselves on camera and improve their technique as well as their appearance.

PACKAGING YOUR PRODUCT

Every performer should attempt the personal evaluation touched upon in AIP's full-day seminar. Can you look at yourself objectively? What kinds of parts are you really right for? How are you presenting yourself? What impression do we get when you walk through the door? Does your voice match your look?

Try to see yourself as others—strangers—see you. The dark circles under your eyes may be a "family trait," but looking just the way your mother did when she was your age is not going to be useful to you in a close-up.

A young actress we know invariably got interviews whenever she sent out her photo. It was a terrific picture. She somehow didn't notice that the photographer had whited out the bags under her eyes. She never saw them when she looked in the mirror—she'd had them all her life. When the disparity between face and photo was pointed out to her, she invested in the simple cosmetic surgery that eliminated the unattractive pouches, permanently. Now she looks exactly like her photo; her boyfriend thinks it was a great idea, and she's getting more work opportunities.

If bags, circles, pouches, laugh lines, acne scars, birthmarks, or warts and moles are coming between you and your employment in television or films, why not have them attended to? You are selling what you look like.

Eyeglasses make a statement about the person who wears them. They are limiting to a performer. If you can't read a script without them, ask your physician about contact lenses.

Are your teeth straight? Is your jaw aligned? Advances in cosmetic dentistry make it easy to have a healthy-looking smile. Lauren Hutton has shown us all that unattractive spaces between our teeth can be masked instantly, with a removable flipper.

Jean Arley, producer:

I went to Lincoln Center to see a Molière play with Salome Jens. Her understudy went on. It was a girl named Faye Dunaway. I thought she was very talented and I said, "Hey, why don't you come up to the office? We're doing a lot of casting." She came up to the office and she had one problem. She was self-conscious; she never smiled. I said, "You're limiting yourself. What's the matter?" And she said, "I have these little pointy teeth." I knew my dentist was a whiz at caps, so I recommended him to her and she went to my dentist. Swell caps. We cast her in Hogan's Goat with Ralph Waite and away they went.

Knowing what colors look well on you is more important than which colors are fashionable each season. Place tones and shades of a color next to your skin until you can see for yourself which ones give you a glow and which tend to drain your color away. The glow is what you want. This is true of men as well as women. If you feel the need to be "current," use the color of the season in an accessory, such as a scarf or ascot, which you remove at interviews.

Pay attention to the shapes or silhouettes that look well on you. Flattering proportions can make you look taller and slimmer. Shiny, stiff fabrics don't move with the body and are unflattering. Large or very contrasting patterns, stripes, or plaids tend to be overpowering; aim for a subtle design that doesn't take attention away from *you*.

Wear attractive, comfortable shoes, especially in New York, where you have a lot of walking to do. Avoid spike heels and rubber soles, at least in interviews.

Examine the photos of actress Sydne Squire, who is generously sharing the story of how she arrived at her improved image:

I started taking business classes designed especially for actors. This was the first time I had been exposed to the business side of acting. I developed a marketing plan for myself, did visualizations, set up a card file on all the people I met, wrote thank-you letters and introduction letters, made rounds (even in L.A.). Spent time researching who I was, what shows I was right for. At the same time I was studying intensely with Milton Katselas.

I hired an image consultant—Susan Duffy—to help me. We met three times. The first was a consultation in which she told

These three photos show the evolution of Sydne Squire's "package." In this first picture, the contrasts are too sharp; her hair appears washed out; her skin has no tone; her expression is lifeless, unfocused.

The second photo shows some improvement, but the pose is too passive. Her features are undefined; the position of her arm is bad.

The most recent photo, taken after sage advice from an image consultant, has an intensity that almost leaps from the page. The look is perfect for the Los Angeles market, where Sydne Squire does most of her work.

George Gant

me my image was strong yet sexy, which I agreed with. She talked about things such as makeup with full mouth, light cheeks, strong eyes, soft on the face. Classy, expensive, beautiful. Executives, high-class call girls, strong women. I started to develop my concept even further. She told me to look through magazines, to look at image pictures. She told me to go into stores and try everything on. She even told me about specific stores.

The second meeting she did my makeup and showed me how to do it. She also talked about my hair, had me bring it back to my natural color, which was blond. At that time it was strawberry blond.

The third time she came to my house and went through my entire wardrobe. She would also have gone shopping with me, but I just couldn't afford it.

The results have been spectacular! I got some new head shots and postcards with my new image—which was really the image I had seen for myself all along. It was my concept, aided by Susan. I got signed by some wonderful agents and have been working a lot!

Seeing Yourself on Camera

A benefit of camera technique classes is that you can see your face as the camera sees it in motion. First-time reactions generally sound something like this:

"Oh, I didn't know I talk from the side of my mouth!"

"I squint! All the time!"

"My head's not on straight!"

Once you get beyond the initial shock, examine your performance and try to find what you like, what can be changed.

An actress we know had a perfectly straight nose that was too long for her facial structure and made her profile unattractive. She consulted a highly regarded plastic surgeon, whom she trusted. Her nose was reduced in size, in proportion to her face, and she felt fabulous!

A word of caution: when we speak about little nips and tucks, we are not suggesting that you set about changing your face. We mean to inform you that the slight defects which mar your on-camera appearance can be handled *conservatively*. We would not have told Jimmy Durante to get a nose job. If your face matches your personality, leave it alone.

Actors who start losing their hair frequently rush to cover their baldness with a part-time toupee or permanent hair transplant. The toupee wearers should realize that nature has now given them *two looks*, leading man or character.

How does your hair register on camera? Look at the photographs and see what a color change did for Marin Mazzie. As a general rule, highlights in the hair photograph better than does one flat shade. Think of a multifaceted diamond. This is not only a woman's concern. When his hair was lightened for a film role, Laurence Overmire found that his face took on an entirely new vitality; he exuded a "punk kid" quality that had never been evident in his

Marin Mazzie had an extensive résumé, but her photo was a hindrance. Notice her bleached hair and dark roots. The background is too dark. The triangle of white light in the upper right appears to be growing out of her head. The plaid in her shirt is too busy. The bright light washed out her skin tones. Marin Mazzie's new photo (right) is alive, healthy, brimming with vitality. Her hair has been styled and highlighted, but it is still recognizably blond. Her smile is real and her eyes light up the page. She recently made her Broadway debut in Big River.

Larry Lapidus

earlier photos, yet those were the kinds of parts he was very comfortable playing. He has decided to keep his hair lightened and get new photos.

YOUR INNER SELF

As you approach excellence in face, figure, technique, and appearance, remember to take good care of the inner person. Shiny hair, healthy skin, strong teeth, sparkling eyes, and an inexhaustible supply of energy come from proper nutrition. A schedule of interviews, auditions, classes, and rehearsals requires stamina. A balanced diet, rich in fresh fruits and vegetables, greens, and grains is essential. Candy bars or pills are not the answer for quick energy.

Plenty of people, including the biggest names, brown-bag it through the day, toting fruits, nuts, raisins, strips of carrot and green pepper, wedges of cheese. They do this, not because they are hypoglycemic or diabetic or to save the (high) cost of lunching in restaurants, but to take good care of themselves. This is especially true when you spend a full day at the studio or on location. It's impossible to predict what kinds of foods will be available in the vicinity. Catered shoots—which the crew always love to dig into—may not supply what you should be eating.

You are your package, after all. Keep it in perfect condition.

Chapter 5
Survival Strategies

"Oh, you're an actor! What restaurant do you work at?" is a line that's more true than funny.

Of the thousands of performers looking for work, almost as many thousands work at jobs outside the industry.

To pay the rent, utilities, and telephone bill, nonworking actors need survival jobs. We'd like you to view these secondary occupations rather as survival *strategies*. Consider what they can do for you beyond helping you to keep the wolf from the door.

THAT'S NOT MY TABLE

Restaurant work seems to be what everyone thinks of first. There's no commitment, no responsibility, and at the end of the evening you can gross a fair amount in tips. Swell. It's like a summer vacation job or working your way through college, again.

If you are able to get a spot at Orso, Fellini's, or Joe Allen's—restaurants that cater to a theatrical clientele—you stand the chance of meeting, or at least seeing, some of the casting people and agents whose offices you are trying so desperately to crack.

Mary Jo Slater-Wilson, casting director:

> *Please do not talk to me when I eat. I go to a restaurant to relax or to talk business.*

Many performers have been surprised to find that Joe Allen's *auditions* applicants for those choice waiting-on-table positions. There are a great many actors "between engagements," and the restaurant is in business to satisfy customers, not to provide actors with a neat way to make contacts.

If the tables you are waiting on are not at a theatrical restaurant, ask yourself, Is waiting on tables really what you came to the big city to do? The job is menial, demanding, tiring. We think you need more than that. We think you can go for alternatives that are rewarding, nourishing, that offer an outlet for your creative energy and give you a positive sense of self.

What kind of job should you want? One that will pay you a decent wage, add to your personal experience, and not tie you down to a schedule that's so tight you're merely trekking back and forth from job to home to job. If that is how you are spending your time, you don't have a survival *job*, it's your life.

What kinds of jobs do we suggest? The umbrella description is this: work that allows you to be creative, to enjoy a sense of your own accomplishment, and to be in control. Work that will not turn you into a drone with tunnel vision.

What skills do you bring with you? Can you type? Take shorthand? Do you have any skill as a word processor? You can register at any office-temporary agency in the city and even request assignments at offices related to the business. You will work on the days you choose, at networks, advertising agencies, production houses; you'll see what goes on in the industry and possibly learn while you earn. Or you can work the late shift at publishing houses and banking institutions, earning as much as $25 an hour.

Do you have a good eye, and can you spell? Magazines and publishing houses will employ you as a proofreader: again, you'll be in a pleasant environment, exercising a technique that you need as an actor, getting pay and appreciation.

Office-temporary agencies that like to hire actors—they are after all, so presentable, outgoing, and charming—advertise in the trade papers.

ON YOUR OWN

You can exercise greater control over your life by creating your own survival business. Like actresses Linda Boni and Catherine Rusoff, you might be an aerobics instructor. It's conceivable that you could turn that knowledge into the basis of a videotape; you could go on with it—we've all read stories of the personal exercise gurus who serve a select group of executive clients.

Jacklyn Zeman, before she signed her contract on *One Life to Live*, was the manager of an Elaine Powers slenderizing salon:

I scheduled my hours around my interviews, kept myself in shape, and became a very good manager.

We know an actor who is an excellent masseur. He has a license and a portable massage table; he has no trouble finding clients whenever he needs to replenish his bank account.

What are your hobbies? Photography?—why not take photos of other performers? Astrology?—you surely know what a constantly absorbing subject that is. One actor did "charts," free of charge, for the casting people he wanted to meet. He also sold his knowledge of the future on a consulting basis to the public.

Kerry Prep created his own singing telegram business. Preppy-Grams gave him the chance to perform every time he made a "delivery." He made use of his fine voice and his ebullient personality, got a lot of positive feedback, and built a list of enthusiastic clients in the business who call on his services repeatedly. He also established himself as a charming, talented, and *reliable* performer—and that led to acting jobs.

One actor runs a business that supplies party personnel—bartenders, waitresses, and even omelette makers. Everyone who works for him is an actor. Parties are always fun, the food is fine, and they generally take place in the evenings or on weekends—no conflict with the business.

Another actor fills the time between interviews with a job at a concert artist's bureau. "It allows me to get the nurturing I need."

On the back of her smiling photo-postcard, Elizabeth Popiel writes that in addition to acting jobs, she is available for carpentry work! Do you have any idea how welcome a skilled, responsible craftsperson is? Liz also designs jewelry and is an accomplished graphic artist.

Actress-playwright Bonnie Brewster acquired a knowledge of plants and flowers when she was putting herself through college. When she came to New York, she found part-time employment in the flower district and became expert at flower arranging. Her extravagant bouquets were delivered to each of the celebrities participating in the Actor's Fund's "Night of 100 Stars" celebration. She now has a long list of corporate clients, restaurants, and caterers. She notes, "Selling to clients is like acting, only you don't get the rejection."

Nancy Addison, Jillian Coleridge Ryan on *Ryan's Hope*, started a business designing hair ornaments. Some of Fifth Avenue's most exclusive shops were her clients.

Robin Strasser, Dorian on *One Life to Live*, refused to learn to type, because she didn't want to fall back on it. Instead she went to work in a boutique: "Selling clothes, to me, was a lot like acting."

If you like typing but have no wish to tie yourself to an office, you might consider typing résumés for other performers. You might get a part-time job answering the fan mail of one or more working performers.

What about becoming an image consultant? A makeup artist? A food stylist for commercials or print ads?

There are jobs that you can do at home, in your free time, such as telephone sales, free-lance writing, or coaching.

Richard Frank, a graduate of the Juilliard Acting School, turned his free time to good use by designing the *Starving Artists Coloring Book*. A publisher agreed that it was a great idea. Richard is happy with the royalty checks that arrive every six months. He now has a track record and a publisher eagerly awaiting his next book idea.

George Bouléy runs his own graphic arts company, Attitude. His audacious enclosure cards for gifts and flower arrangements are available in New York, Florida, California, and the New England states. He is now designing a line of greeting cards:

> *The company's success is a very important element in my life; it will be able to fuel my acting career.*

When he was starting in the business, John Allen quickly realized that there was no guide to *nonunion* summer theaters. He compiled such a reference, found ten friends who were willing to lend him $250 to get it printed, and sold it himself to other aspiring actors he met at auditions. The book, *Summer Theatre Guide from an Actor's Point of View*, is now enlarged and updated each year. Allen also publishes a theatrical newsletter, which is available by subscription.

Two actresses we know put the time between soap opera roles

to use by creating a theatrical tour business. They employed other performers as guides. Out-of-town visitors were thrilled to be in the company of the people they saw on TV each afternoon.

William Hickey has been teaching other actors and pursuing his own acting career for more than thirty years. Catherine Gaffigan and Kate MacGregor-Stewart are actresses who teach. Richard Peterson is an actor who became a dialectician: he helps foreign actors lose their accent and teaches American performers how to imitate them. Alice Spivak became a dialogue coach, a survival strategy that took her all the way to Australia working on a film!

A few seasons ago, macramé was very fashionable. It seemed as if there were wall hangings in every hotel room; restaurant ceilings were covered with pots of ivy hanging in macramé plant holders. Plenty of actors did very well tying those intricate knots. Are you interested in crafts? Do you knit, paint, crochet, do needlework? You can teach; you can take orders for hats, vests, pillows and possibly participate in crafts fairs all over the country.

Do you have a secret recipe? Are you an adventurous cook? The catering business beckons.

As you are already your own door-to-door salesperson, have you thought about becoming a part-time distributor of cosmetics, vitamins, pantry items? Suzy Lehman was very tentative about showing her friends the vitamins she'd bought from another performer. To her surprise and delight they became her first regular customers. Now her survival strategy allows her to rent a car and summer home, plan a vacation, and best of all, thanks to her success, she exudes confidence when she walks into an office.

Your survival strategy should be geared to enhancing your own estimation of self. The nature of the business requires that actors become adept at communicating on a person-to-person level. It's necessary to develop a manner that others perceive as charming, outgoing, pleasant, energetic, and confident. Try to capitalize on those attributes in your second occupation.

So, if at the end of all this you decide that you still want to be a waiter, be an energetic, attractive, smiling, *marvelous* one. Don't just wait, *serve!* Use the chance encounter with this or that executive as an opportunity to show that you are a terrific, attentive, excellent *waiter*. If you are good enough, they will want to know who you are and whether you can act.

Whatever you can do that is positive will serve you in every aspect of your existence. Work you loathe, work that is unrewarding, will taint your entire being.

Tony Call, Herb Callison, *One Life to Live:*

Whether you're working or not, you must have another stimulus, something that is fulfilling. To me this is a wonderful living, but not if I'm eating my insides out.

Think about it—you could be a taxi driver, going mad in traffic, never having time for lunch or a phone call, *or* you could take that same driving skill and become a chauffeur for a limousine company catering to celebrities. That, again, would put you in a place where opportunity can find you. You might even start your own limo service, using actors as your drivers.

Some time ago, one of the New York newspapers, in a feature describing the off-stage lives of actors who were a long way from being bankable names, told of an actress who began each day cleaning offices in a shabby part of the city, working with broken equipment, all alone. The description of her daily routine was unbearably sad. How, we wondered, could this young woman hope to succeed? Each day began on such a note of despair, it would take superhuman resources to rise above that daily dose of negative energy.

That is not the way to be an out-of-work actor. That's punishing yourself. That's not what you left home for. And if that is all you can do, stop and rethink your plan.

Take a year off from The Business, save every penny you can, see everything you can, learn. Then, when you've restored your own confidence in yourself, think about beginning again.

You don't have to be twenty-one to begin an acting career or even to continue it. You can begin at any age, so long as you give yourself a real chance.

Chapter 6
Understanding the Unions

Professional actors belong to three unions: Actors Equity Association (Equity), Screen Actors Guild (SAG), and the American Federation of Television and Radio Artists (AFTRA). The unions, in turn, are members of an umbrella organization, the Associated Actors and Artistes of America, known as the Four A's, chartered by the AFL-CIO.

In simplest terms, Equity has jurisdiction over performers and stage managers in live theater; SAG covers performances—movies and commercials—on film; AFTRA's jurisdiction includes live and taped television shows, soap operas, and commercials, radio, and recordings—its membership, in addition to actors, singers, and dancers, includes announcers, disc jockeys, sportcasters, and news persons.

In an arena that prizes individuality, where a performer's personal magnetism can be so captivating that it often overrides lack of technique or so dazzling that it may inspire an audience to forgive banal writing or insipid production, where the "powerful chemistry" between two performers can translate into a surge in ratings, the idea of performers belonging to a union may seem downright absurd. What, after all, can such free-spirited, highly distinctive artists have in common with the more or less anonymous people who deliver packages or work in offices or on assembly lines?

One essential feature is true of all of them—they all work for their living. And the work they do can be quite specifically defined. Moreover, the people who employ them, simply by virtue of the fact that they control jobs, are powerful and may even belong to power-enhancing organizations of their own. So, like seamstresses, bolt tighteners, steeplejacks, and countless others, actors (and singers, dancers, announcers, and news persons) have found that by forming a union they gain a certain measure of clout.

Through the process known as collective bargaining, representatives of performers (unions) and employers (networks, advertising agencies, and producers) arrive at agreements regarding performers' wages and working conditions. These contracts establish the minimum salary—or scale payment—for performances on stage, film, records, television, or radio. There are also agreements covering what is known as nontheatrical employment, such as industrial shows, educational or documentary films, and material recorded for purposes other than commercial broadcast.

Today's union members are the beneficiaries of the gains their predecessors struggled to obtain. The high unemployment rate notwithstanding, union scale (for a day's work in film, $361; for a principal on a soap opera, $357 for a half-hour show, $476 for an hour; for shooting a TV commercial, $333.25; or the weekly salary for a Broadway show, $700) would appear to be acceptable compensation. With health insurance, pension coverage, and COLAs (cost-of-living adjustments)—history-making benefits when they were first achieved—now perceived as inherent elements of the package, it's easy for new arrivals to think there's little or nothing a union can "do" for them.

Veterans become indignant at this attitude. Upon hearing the newest young leading man boast that his slightly overscale salary was evidence that the producer valued the spark his performance promised to add to the show, the matriarch of one of the long-running daytime soaps, an actress whose distinguished career has encompassed theater and films as well as television, raised her cultured voice so that everyone in the commissary could overhear. "Darling," she purred to the young man,

you would be working, gladly, for $5 without the efforts that all of us have put in for years! You think they're paying you all that money because they're in love with your blue eyes and your talent? Don't be a fool. They're paying you because a lot of actors who worked for a lot less money than you fought to get those minimums up to a decent level. You are riding on the shoulders of all those other people, and don't you ever forget it!

With her passionate words as our cue, let's take a brief look at the way things used to be and how they've changed.

A BRIEF HISTORY

Professional theater has existed in America since colonial times. President George Washington enjoyed the theater and helped to popularize playgoing; by the end of the eighteenth century there were functioning theaters in most American cities. As the managers were generally actors who had risen through the ranks to head companies of their own, relations between cast and manager were frequently close and personal. Years of tradition had defined the way an acting company operated and the actor's place within that unit.

In the boom following the Civil War, the development of transportation opened the country west of the Mississippi River, and the theater surged along with the rest of the nation's businesses. Productions that had previously traveled informally from one locale to the next were now routed along circuits dominated by chains of theaters. Booking offices were created to systematize the production and the financing of attractions, eliminate wasteful competition, and ease booking tangles. Stars such as Edwin Booth, John Drew, and Sarah Bernhardt received such acclaim that by the end of the nineteenth century acting had become recognized as a glamorous, rewarding profession.

In the years before World War I, the Theatrical Syndicate, a sort of superbooking office established in 1896, had become sufficiently powerful to dictate which productions played where, who would appear in them, and under what terms. The actor-managers, such as Joseph Jefferson, Richard Mansfield, Fanny Davenport, Minnie Maddern Fiske, David Belasco, and James O'Neill, father of playwright Eugene O'Neill (whom Eugene called James Tyrone in *Long Day's Journey into Night*) had to contend with a new species of theater citizen: the efficiency expert–manager, who knew nothing of theatrical tradition and cared less. To these businessmen, the actor was not the backbone of the theater but merely a necessary cost item on a balance sheet, to be obtained as cheaply as possible. That is not to imply that actors' salaries had previously been munificent—O'Neill tells us repeatedly that his father was a skinflint and that his mother's illness was the result of his father's penny-pinching; the man would not spend the money for her proper treatment. Surely Mrs. Fiske and David Belasco were dedicated to their own prosperity rather than their casts'. But one could sign a contract with them and be certain of what was expected.

These new people were constantly demanding concessions and inserting loopholes, writing a different agreement with each performer. There was no standard contract. Neither was there payment for rehearsals nor any limit to them: eighteen weeks was not an unusual rehearsal period for a musical, ten weeks for a straight play. As the theater was no less a gamble in those days than it is now, one might rehearse five or six months for a play that lasted only four performances and be paid only for the four nights of work—if at all.

Actors worked seven days a week, as many performances as the manager wanted.

According to the late Conrad Nagel, a film and stage star:

Stock companies doing ten performances a week—seven evening shows and three matinees—while rehearsing the next week's play each morning, were not unusual.

Salaries could be paid on any day of the week following performance—whenever the manager got around to it. The managers paid half salary for Christmas week, Easter week, and Election week regardless of business or whether or not any elections were in progress.

The centuries-old custom of two weeks' notice was erased; actors could be labeled "unsatisfactory" by a manager and dismissed; plays were closed with no warning at all. Sometimes the managers departed while a performance was in progress, taking the week's receipts with them, leaving the entire company stranded. The abandoned actors were often unable to pay for their lodging and had to sneak out of town, which may explain why so many innkeepers in stops along the circuit posted the warning, "We do not rent to theatricals!"

Many managers refused to pay transportation from the starting place, where the cast was engaged and rehearsed, to the opening town or from the closing point back home. So, if a show opened in Wilmington, Delaware, and closed in St. Joseph, Missouri, the actors had to buy their own tickets from New York to Wilmington and from St. Joe back to New York.

Performers were also required to supply their own costumes—a special hardship for the women in a company. The cost of elaborate costumes, which they could wear nowhere else, could be greater than the salary they received if the play unfortunately closed early in the run.

The actress Clara Morris wrote that at the start of her career in the 1870s, she was particularly proud that she was "gifted with her needle," and was able to rework the fabric of her gowns again and again, with no one in the audience realizing that she was, in effect, wearing the same dress she had toured in during the previous season.

Dressing rooms, usually in the cellar or way at the top of the building, were filthy, unheated spaces. They rarely had running water or sufficient room to set out makeup and hang one's clothes.

That was how matters stood in May 1913, when 112 performers—men and women—met in a hotel ballroom near what is now the site of the New York Coliseum and agreed to form the Actors Equity Association. They adopted a constitution, elected officers and a council (among whose members were George Arliss and Charles Coburn), and set about trying to achieve a standard contract.

Getting the managers to agree to their demands was a bit more difficult. Negotiations dragged on for six years! Finally, in the summer of 1919, the membership—now grown to more than 2,500—voted to strike. In this action they had the support of featured players and chorus people as well as stars—among them Eddie Cantor, Pearl White, Marie Dressler, Ethel Barrymore, and Ed Wynn. The strike lasted thirty days, spread to eight cities, closed thirty-seven plays, prevented sixteen from opening, and cost actors and managers about $3 million. During the strike period Equity membership increased to more than fourteen thousand.

In his book *The Revolt of the Actors*, Alfred Harding details the complexities of the struggle and its aftermath. It's fascinating reading.

Twenty years after the first Equity meeting, a handful of film stars met at the Masquers Club in Hollywood to discuss what could be done to improve their working conditions. Hollywood was turning out six hundred films a year, working six days a week, with no limit on hours. Actors could finish a day's shooting after midnight and be told to report back on the set at 9 A.M., which meant arriving at 7 A.M. for makeup, hair dressing, and wardrobe. Allowing for travel time meant a 5 A.M. wakeup call. Meal periods occurred at the producer's convenience.

Under the studio system, a handful of moguls controlled the industry. Contract players were property to be developed, groomed, and improved—and lent out to other studios at a profit.

One actress who'd been under contract to Metro Goldwyn Mayer says:

> *I was only in five pictures at MGM. By being lent and sent around to other studios and independents I made two dozen pictures in five years. My hair changed color in every picture. We had nothing to say about our appearance. We weren't asked, we were told.*

When the players were told by the moguls that they would have to accept a 50 percent cut in salary (nonstar contract players earned about $75 a week), talk about a union became serious. Articles of incorporation were filed on June 30, 1933. The eighteen founding members named Ralph Morgan president.

Within the year membership increased to two thousand. Eddie Cantor, who was one of Broadway's biggest stars and who had been signed by Samuel Goldwyn, was elected president.

Lyle Talbot remembers:

> *He gave us a big boost. I'll never forget the day we got a phone call from Eddie in Washington, D.C., telling us that we had been recognized as a labor union. He was a wonderful man, and very important in getting this guild off the ground.*

The contract proposals were for the following:

- An eight-hour day, with fifteen hours rest between calls
- Regular one-hour meal periods
- Sundays and holidays off
- Overtime pay
- Payment for transportation expenses
- Contracts in writing, with a copy of the contract given to the actor

• Continuous employment pay (Several days might elapse between calls for the same part, during which time the actor had to
be available and could not work for anyone else, but was paid only
for the days actually on the set.)

Four years later, in May 1937, the producers finally accepted the
guild's demands. The membership of five thousand had voted to
strike the studios. President Robert Montgomery, also a major star
who had been instrumental in establishing the guild, declared "the
victory of an ideal." Scale was $25 per day.

The last of the major talent unions to organize, the American
Federation of Television and Radio Artists (AFTRA) is the result of
the merger between AFRA—the American Federation of Radio
Artists, chartered by the Four A's in August 1937—and Television
Authority, TvA, which had been established in 1950. The merger
was effected in 1952.

In her entertaining book *Tune in Tomorrow*, actress Mary Jane
Higby tells us that, in the early days of radio, performers received
$5 for an hour-length program which they might have rehearsed for
two days. Sometimes performers were expected to work merely for
the glory of doing the show. When Barbara Luddy, a noted radio
actress, asked the producer of *Hollywood Hotel* how much she would
be paid for her appearance as the female lead on the show, she was
told, "You're not getting *paid*, you're getting *billing!*" It took great
courage for her to face a powerful producer and maintain that she
could not afford to work for nothing.

According to the late Conrad Nagel:

---

*Movie actors were frequently "invited" to appear on radio
shows to talk about their latest film. Then they'd do a dramatization of the picture, with four or five actors working for free.*

In New York and Chicago, small bands of performers, proficient
at reading a script and delineating a character, gained a foothold in
the industry and managed to do quite well. Some extremely versatile
actors played two and even three roles on the same show. However,
as more and more radio stations were licensed, more and more
performers joined the talent pool, and producers, whose ranks were
also growing, realized that someone was always willing to work for
less money.

Before long, according to Ted de Corseia, one of those first performers in the "theater of the mind":

> *Every agency was trying to do it a little bit cheaper. We'd spend the whole day rehearsing, with no meal breaks or even time for coffee, and end up with a check for $11.88 for the show and for the repeat [rebroadcast of the same show three hours later for stations on the West Coast].*

In his articles in *The New Yorker* in 1948, James Thurber stated the matter succinctly:

> *. . . before the American Federation of Radio Artists and the Writers' Guild were formed, the broadcasting industry took easy and cynical advantage of actors and authors.*

Fortunately, many stars, who had been down the same road with Equity and SAG, were among the earliest supporters of the idea of a union. At the first meeting of what was originally called the Radio Division of Actors Equity, some nominees for the board of directors were Eddie Cantor (who later served as AFRA's first president as he had done with SAG), Don Ameche, Jack Benny, Bob Hope, Bing Crosby, Edgar Bergen, Rudy Vallee, Dick Powell, Martin Gabel, and Helen Hayes.

Hearing that New York, Los Angeles, and Chicago performers had embarked upon the formation of a radio union, performers working at stations across the country wrote to the nearest headquarters requesting help in organizing their area. Within the year there were AFRA locals in cities across the country.

Management seemed to understand that AFRA's proposals for a code of fair practice benefited employers as well as talent: with standardized payment, rehearsal rates, and times, they could, in a sense, stop worrying about whether they were getting the biggest bargain and concentrate on getting the best work done. The first contracts between AFRA and the networks were signed in July 1938.

HOW THE UNIONS WORK

Equity, SAG, and AFTRA are unique among labor organizations in that they are governed by the members. There are differences in their specific structures, but essentially they are run by councils or boards of directors whose elected members are volunteers and serve with no remuneration. The policies determined by these bodies in weekly or monthly meetings are then executed by a staff of paid executives.

Contract demands are formulated by volunteer committees made up of performers active within each field. Their proposals for wages and working conditions are presented to the union's highest governing body—the annual convention or meeting of elected delegates. At the convention the proposals are accepted, rejected, or modified. The executive staff then attempts to negotiate the demands with management.

... AND WHAT THEY DO

While the unions cannot get any performer a job, they protect all performers in their relations with employers. By negotiating and then policing their contracts, the unions guarantee minimum salaries and the conditions under which performers will work.

Working conditions include such things as length of rehearsal, meal periods, place of rehearsal (you cannot be made to rehearse in an unheated barn in the wintertime), time between calls, manner of transportation, and performer safety. This last is a new concern as movies and TV films (and even daytime serials) seem increasingly to search for outrageous situations and locales in which to deposit their leading characters: the pressure upon performers to be courageous good guys and perform their own stunts can be heavy, and trained persons are required to be on location to perform all of those feats.

Union representatives regularly visit studios, production centers, and location shoots to make certain that contract provisions are observed and that union members, whose dues have been paid, are being employed. The field reps also deal with any member complaints about the day's work. These are handled with absolute secrecy as to the identity of the performer; no actor who voices a legitimate complaint need ever fear reprisals.

In long-running situations, such as theatrical productions and TV serials, an elected cast member, the deputy, serves as liaison for the cast, the union, and the management. Members bring concerns about the show to the deputy; management, when it feels a performer is acting irresponsibly, brings that to the notice of the deputy.

The union contracts also guarantee that you will be paid within a certain time after your performance; otherwise a late payment penalty is invoked. You should not ever have to call an employer to find out when or if your "check is in the mail." In certain instances, AFTRA and SAG receive and distribute the payments for session fees and reuse. Residuals for rebroadcast of programs and commercials now form the bulk of the earnings of SAG and AFTRA members.

While it may seem obvious nowadays that recorded material *is* a performance, winning reuse payments was difficult. Many people thought that if session fees were set high enough, performers should not expect to be paid for work they'd already been compensated for. At that time it was inconceivable that programs would be rerun for decades, as they seem to be now. Nor was there such density to commercials; ten-second, twenty-second, and thirty-second spots were nowhere on the horizon.

Of course, it was already known that certain former stars whose films were played constantly on Saturday mornings received not a cent from those uses and were living in poverty. The late George Reeves, the actor who played the first Superman/Clark Kent in the half-hour weekly TV series filmed in the early 1950s, suffered because years later, when the children of America were watching him every afternoon, he was receiving no income from any of the stations carrying his show. Yet he was so identified with the role that he was unemployable! Times do change.

The life of a performance, in commercial or program material, is now protected through a system of use and reuse fees. The unions maintain departments devoted to processing residual checks and monitoring reruns of recorded material. Recent developments in the fields of cable, pay-TV, and videocassettes indicate that the principle of payment for performance will be increasingly important.

Hardest fought for and possibly their most significant achievements are the unions' pension and health plans. These are totally financed by employer contributions of a specified percentage of each player's salary, original payments and residuals. The pension plans thus manage to offer a modicum of financial security to retired performers based upon their earnings and length of employment. With group medical coverage (and life insurance), for which members qualify by earning a certain amount of money within the union's jurisdiction each year, performers, like other Americans, are freed from the terrible fear that unexpected medical expenses will bankrupt the family. The funds are jointly administered by representatives of industry and the unions.

The unions also regulate the business relations between actors and talent agents. Union members may not be represented by any person or firm not franchised by the union in which the agent hopes to be able to get the actor work.

National and local publications inform members about all union activities. The publications also publish lists of franchised talent agents, incoming productions, and performers who have residual checks waiting, and they frequently call attention to pending legislation that will affect performers.

ADDRESSING THE ISSUES

Union concerns reach beyond money matters. It was a committee of SAG that first monitored TV commercials and then agitated for a change in the way women were portrayed in them. "We do other things besides the laundry," their report stated.

Equal employment opportunity committees of the three unions have pressed for better minority representation in casting. In this they fortunately have had the support of many in management. When a feisty young woman attorney was being written into the story line of *The Edge of Night*, it was the agency casting director who asked the producer of the show, "Does this character have to be white? I've just seen a fine black actress named Micki Grant who could do the job." His nod meant that Ms. Grant auditioned for and won the role.

Still another SAG committee, reporting on rip-offs by phony talent agents, provided sufficient documentation to the office of the attorney general of New York to effect a crackdown on the offenders and create the office's warning brochure for the industry.

With each new contract negotiation, the unions press for greater access to casting information and for member preference at auditions. Equity has managed to require that producers conduct Equity Principal Interviews (EPIs), at which a representative of the production must be present to receive photos and résumés from Equity members who sign up for an appointment. This procedure has been augmented by the Equity Principal Audition (EPA), which further strengthens the contact between performer and producer.

Through its Memorial Foundation, AFTRA offers several scholarships to eligible members and/or their children. These grants were established in the memory of past union leaders. Some are available for any course of study; others are expressly for persons interested in performing arts, labor relations, or music.

INCOME TAX ASSISTANCE

One of the most successful membership activities is a program initiated by the late Michael Enserro, a very good character actor. He saw that people in the business had special problems in making out their income tax forms because of the sporadic nature of their work, because they worked for multiple employers during the year, and because they had unusual deductions. He set out to provide tangible help, in the form of Volunteers Providing Income Tax Assistance (VITA). At first, Michael Enserro was a one-man committee, working each spring at Equity's offices. Now, the work he began is carried on in his name, at Equity and AFTRA, by a growing committee of training volunteers headed by Conard Fowkes.

CREDIT UNIONS

Performers have always had difficulty establishing credit. Banks, in particular, viewed them as irresponsible folk and refused to consider them for loans. One of the leading actresses on a daytime serial, who'd always paid in full for everything when she bought it and had been advised to establish credit, was told by a bank officer that, as her show could be canceled the next day, she could not borrow $800. The program is still on the air. She wonders where the young man has gone.

In 1961, Conrad Bain—you know him from *Diff'rent Strokes*— and Theo Bikel were the instigators of an effort to protect their fellow actors from this prejudice. Through their efforts, and with the support of the membership, the Equity Federal Credit Union was established. Within a few years AFTRA in New York and, later,

AFTRA and SAG jointly on the West Coast, followed Equity's example.

Says Arthur Anderson, a past president of the Equity Credit Union:

> *Of course, actors are still interviewed. We do have to know that the money can be repaid. But at least you are interviewed by someone who understands the sort of life you lead.*

LOCAL AUTONOMY

Union branches, or locals, are free to engage in whatever membership activities the body wishes and is willing to finance. AFTRA locals in Boston, Chicago, Miami, Philadelphia, and Washington/Baltimore distribute talent directories to the industry. Miami, Boston, Philadelphia, and Washington/Baltimore maintain Casting Hot Lines. SAG and AFTRA in New York have each invested in fine audio and video equipment that members who pay a small annual fee may use to improve their skills. The fees have paid for the cost and maintenance of the equipment. Member volunteers also teach others the fine points of soap opera, voice-over, and commercial technique.

In other cities union members are able to arrange for seminars, weekly rap sessions, workshops, showcases, or outings that allow members to get to know one another and to network.

And, of course, all of the union offices offer the essential members' bulletin board, where one can learn about apartments, equipment, classes, scenes, possible roommates, car rentals, jobs, lessons, or even whose adorable pet needs a new home.

EQUITY LIBRARY THEATRE

Without doubt, the best example of union activity aimed at helping performers get work is Equity Library Theatre (ELT), which has been a showcase of members' musical and dramatic talents since February 1944. The list of players who have been seen in the more than four hundred productions that have been mounted since that first performance (of two one-act plays—*Shadow of the Glen* and

Fumed Oak) reads like a list of Who's Who in Show Business: Anne Jackson and Eli Wallach, who appeared together in the Tennessee Williams one-act play *This Property Is Condemned* (1945), Jerry Stiller in *Men in White* (1954), and Anne Meara in *Maedchen in Uniform* (1955), Jane Alexander in *Royal Gambit* (1963), Danny De Vito in *DuBarry Was a Lady* (1972) are but a handful.

ELT's managing director, George Wojtasik, points with special pride to two alumni—Sherman Hemsley and Georgia Engel:

Their path was almost the same. Direct. Sherman appeared in our 1969 production of **Purlie Victorious,** *which immediately led to his being cast in the same part in the musical version of the show,* **Purlie.** *From there he went immediately to a role on the Archie Bunker show and then to the spin-off, his own show,* **The Jeffersons.** *Georgia did* **Lend an Ear** *that same year, which got her into Phyllis Diller's tour of* **Hello Dolly.** *While the show was in L.A., Georgia took a dance class, where she met Mary Tyler Moore and got a role on* **The Mary Tyler Moore Show.** *Just like that.*

WHAT MEMBERS DO

We have gone into some detail about what the unions have been able to achieve for their members. There is a reverse side to this picture: what the members are obliged to do—not for the union per se—but for the professionalism of the whole.

Actors must do their jobs to the best of their ability. Actors must be on time; actors must be prepared to work; actors must abide by the contracts they have signed. Actors must know what their responsibilities are. Actors must comply with union regulations. Actors must let the union know where they live and can be reached (so they can receive those hard-won residual checks in the mail).

It's fine to know that an employer can be penalized for late payment of your session fee or for failure to break for lunch within five hours of your original call. You should know that performers also can be disciplined, and have been, by their peers. Stars have been fined for failure to honor contracts. Actors who have jeopardized productions have been called to account for it.

No one is too talented to abide by the rules.

Like civilization as a whole, The Business is a complicated mechanism, delicately balanced. It only works when we all respect one another and do our jobs. To do your job, you have to know what it is. Get all the information your union has to give, study it, and abide by it. When you don't understand something, ask. And if you feel strongly about it, contribute. Join a committee. Volunteer.

Larry Keith has been president of the New York branch of SAG for five years:

> *I wanted to help. I felt it was important to do so. The business had been good to me. And I am very glad, because I know there were times when what I said helped us to avoid confrontation, which would've hurt everyone.*

BECOMING A UNION MEMBER

The simplest way to join Equity, SAG, or AFTRA is to get a job in their jurisdiction. A signed contract with a legitimate producer, saying that you are engaged for such-and-such a role in such-and-such production at whatever salary, immediately confers upon you the status of professional. You will then be required to pay the initiation fee and first six months' dues.

However, there are other ways to get your union cards. Let's see what they are.

AMERICAN FEDERATION OF TV
AND RADIO ARTISTS (AFTRA)

AFTRA is an open union. Any actor can sign the membership application and pay the initiation fee—which is established by the local. New York and Los Angeles are the largest AFTRA locals; their initiation fees are $600. Dues, which are paid semiannually, are on a sliding scale, based upon the previous year's income. As a new member you'd pay the lowest amount—which in New York is $28.75 semiannually.

Under the Taft-Hartley Law it is possible to do your first AFTRA job and then work in TV or radio for up to thirty days without joining the union. After that, membership becomes compulsory.

SCREEN ACTORS GUILD (SAG)

If you have been a member of either AFTRA or Equity for a year, and have worked as a principal at least once in either union, you may apply for membership in SAG. If you have not been a member of either of the other unions and now have a commitment for a role as a principal in a film, a commercial, or a filmed television show, you will be accepted for membership. You must bring a letter from a signatory producer or the producer's representative stating that you will be playing a principal part in a specific picture.

SAG's initiation fee is $600, plus the semiannual dues payment of $37.50.

ACTORS' EQUITY ASSOCIATION (AEA)

If you have been a member of either AFTRA or SAG for a year or more and have performed work comparable to Equity principal work, you will be eligible to join Equity.

Since 1978 it has been possible to earn a membership card by means of the Equity Membership Candidacy Program. Under the program, nonprofessional actors are allowed to credit fifty weeks of work in participating Equity theaters toward AEA membership. This work does not have to be at one theater, nor must it be consecutive. The program is in effect at dinner theaters, Equity resident theaters, Chicago Off-Loop theaters, and in resident and nonresident stock theaters throughout the country. One of the great benefits of the Equity Membership Candidacy Program is that by the time you have *earned* your union card you have acquired experience and built a résumé: you are qualified to be in the company of professionals. As many as ten weeks of the fifty may be spent doing technical work. Membership candidates at stock companies may also receive credit for weeks as production assistant to the stage manager.

An Equity membership candidate, after securing a position at a participating theater, must register for the candidacy program. This is done by completing the nonprofessional affidavit (supplied by the theater) and sending it to Equity, along with a $50 registration fee payable to Equity. The fee will be credited against the initiation fee, which is due upon joining the union.

Once you've accumulated fifty weeks of work, you have five years in which to join Equity. If you get a job at an Equity theater, you will now be required to join the union.

Equity's initiation fee is $500. Basic dues are $52 per year. Members also pay working dues: 2 percent of gross earnings from Equity employment. If you earn less than $5,000 under Equity jurisdiction in any year, a credit of 25 percent of your working dues will be applied to the following year's basic dues. The maximum amount of earnings subject to the 2 percent working dues is $100,000 per year.

YOUR "PARENT" UNION

You need not pay full dues to all three unions at the same time. By an informal arrangement among the unions, performers who are more active in one union may pay full dues to that organization and pay less than the full amount (generally half dues and initiation fee) to the others. The union you pay full dues to is your "parent" union.

If you think that you are not going to be active in a jurisdiction for six months or longer (you may sign to tour with a play for a year or more and therefore be unable to work in TV or films), you may elect to take a temporary withdrawal from AFTRA and/or SAG. At that point you will not be required to pay dues to those unions, but you will, of course, be paying full dues to Equity. Equity will be your "parent" union. If you go on location for a period to shoot a film, you may temporarily withdraw from Equity; your "parent" union will then be SAG.

The important thing is to remember to apply for temporary withdrawal and not simply let your unpaid union dues accumulate. This oversight may lead to a fine and may even endanger your membership status. Similarly, once you return to your home base, remember to reinstate yourself as an active member.

TRANSFERRING MEMBERSHIP

Performers who join a union in one area may simply apply for a transfer to the branch or local of the city they will reside in. You may be required to pay additional dues to meet the scale of your new local.

SHOULD YOU JOIN THE UNIONS?

We cannot overemphasize that being a member of Equity, AF-TRA, or SAG will not automatically bring you a job. Nor does union membership guarantee that you are going to get a job. Your only guarantee is that as a union member you will enjoy the same benefits and protections as all other union members *when you work.*

A discerning casting person will be able to tell from your résumé whether you have merely purchased that union card or whether you've earned it.

If you are really new to the business, have not had a great deal of experience in any area, and have few contacts among professional people, you should think seriously about whether it is essential or even advisable for you to attempt to join any of the unions at this time. Understand that as a union member you will be prohibited from working with nonprofessionals. Amateur groups, community theaters, or school groups may be the very places you should be turning to for the experience you need.

It would be ironic if union membership prevented you from learning how to be a versatile performer.

THE JOBS: WHAT THEY ARE AND WHAT THEY PAY

Actors have always worked wherever there was an audience to watch, to laugh or cry, to applaud, and it was hoped, to toss a few coins. Nowadays actors' performances are on stage, film, and television.

The official language of all contracts is, as you can imagine, extremely detailed. Some codes run to hundreds of pages. This overview aims to show, quickly, what kinds of jobs exist, what they are called, and what you can expect to earn when you land them. In all cases, you should check with the union for the fine points.

IF YOU WORK ON THE STAGE

Broadway

For a Broadway show, the minimum—scale—payment for *actors, singers,* or *dancers* is $700 per week (until June 30, 1986, when the current contract expires).

Chorus people who say lines or have a specialty number receive $15 per week additional pay.

Dance captains receive an additional $120 weekly.

Understudies who are cast members receive $33 per week additional pay for each role understudied, plus one-eighth week's salary each time they perform the role. Understudies who are *not* cast members earn the minimum $700 weekly fee, plus one-eighth the week's salary for each performance they play. Such performers may be signed to understudy as many as three roles without additional payment.

Rehearsal pay, $700 per week, is the same for all performers, even those working on an overscale contract (unless otherwise negotiated).

Dramatic plays may rehearse up to eight weeks. Musicals may rehearse principals nine weeks, chorus ten weeks. If rehearsals last longer, performers then receive whatever performance salary they have negotiated.

For example, the cast of *Forty-Second Street* numbers fifty-six Equity members. Of that number, four are stage managers, twelve are principals, and forty are chorus singers and dancers, who may also speak lines or play small parts but who do not play characters that are identifiable.

Remember, we are giving you minimum payments. Actors and stage managers with a long list of credits negotiate higher salaries.

Touring Companies

Rates are the same for *touring companies* as they are for Broadway. The producer is responsible for transportation of the company and for the maintenance of sets and costumes. Because performers are required to pay for their own accommodations—and maintain their original apartments—there is an additional payment of $67 per day or $469 per week while on tour.

Special Production Contracts

The special production contract covers theaters with seven hundred seats or less. The lower minimum salary, which is allowed, may be increased, based upon the gross. Scale, in such theaters as the Ritz on West Forty-eighth Street in New York, is $430 per week for a dramatic play, $545 for a small musical production, $580 for a full production musical.

Off Broadway

Off Broadway blossomed about thirty years ago in small theaters away from the immediate Broadway theater district. These theaters were places where a writer of noncommercial or experimental plays could enjoy a low-budget production and try to find an audience, freed from the commercial pressures of Broadway. At the same time, off Broadway provided opportunities for new performers—talented people who had no reputation to risk and who didn't mind working for little more than carfare. Jason Robards and Geraldine Page are two stars whose lives were changed after they appeared—Robards in *The Iceman Cometh*, Page in *Summer and Smoke*—in productions mounted at a defunct nightclub in Greenwich Village by a company calling itself The Circle in the Square.

Today, established players are just as eager as the rest of us to be seen in an off-Broadway play that just might settle in for a run or even make it to a Broadway house. *Hurlyburly*, David Mamet's 1984 Pulitzer Prize–winning play, moved from Chicago with its cast of seven name performers directed by Mike Nichols, to the Promenade Theatre on West Seventy-sixth Street and Broadway before chancing it at the Ethel Barrymore Theatre on West Forty-seventh Street. Of course, other productions are quite content to remain in the house where they first won acclaim. New York's longest-running show, *The Fantasticks*, is still charming audiences at the little theater on Sullivan Street where it opened more than twenty-six years ago; *Little Shop of Horrors* has played more than four years at the Orpheum on Second Avenue, a theater that could not be more perfectly suited to the production.

The off-Broadway theater contract relates salary to the size of the theater and potential audience. Minimum for theaters of 100 to 199 seats is $225 per week; for theaters of 200 to 250 seats, scale is $275; for 251- to 299-seat houses, scale is $320; for 300 to 350 seats, scale is $385; for 351 to 499 seats, scale is $435. Rehearsal pay is the same as minimum salary. A five-week rehearsal period is permitted. Stage managers, as in Broadway shows, are paid a bit more money.

Off-Off-Broadway

Off-off-Broadway has recently come into existence in response to the increasing costs and commercialism of off Broadway. These productions, often given in lofts, basements, and hotel function rooms, are usually presented for a limited number of performances. Under the Showcase Code, which allows for an admission charge of no more than $6, actors are reimbursed for their expenses, which is usually no more than their carfare. Under the Funded Non-Profit Theatre Code, admission of $8 may be charged and performers may be paid a small salary, which, again, is based upon the size of the theater, potential gross, and number of performances. The smallest contract is for $72 for twelve performances. Minicontract salaries may be negotiated for twenty-four performances in the largest of these little spaces. Many of the houses on Theatre Row, Forty-second Street, west of Ninth Avenue, seat fewer than a hundred people.

Regional Theater and the LORT Contract

Regional theater now employs the largest number of professional actors. As of this writing, there are more than ninety members of the League of Resident Theatres (LORT Contract). You'll find them listed in this book's Appendix. Among them are the prestigious Mark Taper Forum in Los Angeles, the long-established Barter Theatre in Abingdon, Virginia, the Guthrie in Minneapolis. More and more productions are originating in these theaters, away from the scrutiny of theater critics. After they have ironed out their kinks, these productions frequently move to New York, with enormous success. Chicago, Louisville, and Washington have given us three Pulitzer Prize winners: *The Great White Hope* began at the Arena Stage in Washington, D.C.; *'Night, Mother* was first produced at the Actors Theatre of Louisville; *Hurlyburly* premiered at the Goodman Theatre in Chicago.

Salaries at LORT theaters are based upon seating capacity and potential gross of the theater. They range from $321 to $401 a week.

Stock Production and the CORST and COST Contracts

Summer stock can be the actor's best training ground. Learning and performing ten plays in ten weeks forces you to grow, widens your range, sharpens your skills, and teaches you how to work in front of an audience. There are still a number of resident companies, employing at least six actors. In this contract—the Council of Resident Stock Theatres (CORST) Code—salaries are based upon theater capacity and potential gross—they range from $341.88 to $408.08 per week. No per diem is paid in these theaters.

There is also a COST Code, for the Council of Stock Theatres—producers of *nonresident stock*. At these theaters, they either produce their own packages or book productions, usually starring well-known TV or film personalities in well-known plays, which travel to a different theater each week. There are two classifications: small productions, paying $380.50; large productions, $414.58. Per diem is paid for these jobs.

The producer is responsible for transportation and for the maintenance of sets and costumes. The actor is required to pay for hotel accommodations, food, and all other personal expenses.

Musical Theater

There is an outdoor musical theater contract for the large theaters in St. Louis, Indianapolis, and Kansas City. Minimum is $399.25 plus per diem.

Resident musical stock theaters, in Milwaukee, Pittsburgh, Fort Worth, and Sacramento operate under a contract that pays $421.35 plus per diem.

Dinner Theater

Salaries at professional dinner theaters are based upon their restaurant capacity. Current scale is for petite theaters, seating up to 279, $257.75; small, from 280 to 399 seats, $294.50; medium, from 400 to 599 seats, $362; large, from 600 to 1,000 seats, $376. Rehearsal pay is the same as minimum performance pay. There is no per diem allowance.

Many dinner theaters and stock theaters are located in resort areas where room rates go sky-high during the vacation season. Performers who are required to pay for their own accommodations under these contracts are not supposed to spend more than 20 percent of their salary for lodging. Managers must arrange for space their players can afford or make up the difference between 20 percent and whatever the cost is. Performers should ascertain what their living expenses will be before they accept such bookings.

Children's Theater

This code is called Theatre for Young Audiences and covers about fifty professional companies. Theaters that run on a weekly basis pay $220 per week. Companies with other schedules have the option to pay per performance, which may be $37, or $25 for a neighborhood performance.

Industrial Shows

These are productions paid for by a corporation and performed for an invited, nonpaying audience, such as company employees, dealers, or buyers. Many stars, especially those who have become identified with the client's product through TV commercials, work in industrial shows.

Corporations have lately begun to cut down on such spectaculars in an effort to economize, but industrial shows remain among the better-paying assignments in live theater. Actors working two weeks or more earn $675 per week. Actors working one week earn $844. Those working fewer than seven days are paid a daily rate, $241 for the first day, $121 for each day after that.

Industrial shows frequently travel for four to six weeks. Transportation and housing are provided, as is a per diem of $45. Stage managers, as is usual in all contracts, earn a bit more.

Letters of Agreement

To encourage the development of professional theater, Equity's staff endeavors to work out special agreements to fit the peculiarities of each situation. Workshops, where director, cast, and writers work in a very fluid relationship, may ultimately result in full-scale productions. Some of these, such as the Broadway hit *Dreamgirls*, may provide jobs for many people long after the original seed work has been done. The attempt is made to nurture the effort while at the same time protecting those whose talents are contributing to the venture.

And there are other contracts, designed for other types of live performance. Equity invites inquiries. Each production has a life of its own; things are always in a state of flux. Most of Equity's reps have worked in the industry; there are actors, stage managers, company managers, box office people, and lawyers among them. Their experience, therefore, is practical. As we have already suggested, all contracts have fine points; ask questions before you sign.

IF YOU WORK IN FILMS

Motion picture work is covered by the SAG contracts.

Theatrical Films

Actors engaged for a day of shooting on a picture being made for theatrical release are called *day players*; they are paid a scale rate of $361.

If the actor is engaged for the week, scale is $1,256. Scale is the same for blockbusters or duds, for extravaganzas, or simple stories. Cost of a film doesn't affect scale payment.

Release of the film to TV means that performers will receive an additional percentage of their salary each time the film is shown. Those percentages will depend upon the cost of the film and the terms of the deal.

Films for TV

Films made for prime-time television, the once-a-week half-hour, hour, or two-hour shows aired between 8 P.M. and 11 P.M., pay the same daily rate as theatrical films, and they also have a *three-day contract*. Minimums are as follows:

- $915 for 30- to 60-minute shows
- $1,077 for 90- to 120-minute shows

Extras are paid as follows:

- $102 for a half-hour show
- $130 for an hour show
- $159 for a 90-minute show
- $186 for a two-hour show

Special business is the term for performers who don't have lines but who do some action demanded by the director that figures in the continuity of the show. They are paid as follows:

- $181 for a half-hour show
- $224 for an hour show
- $255 for a 90-minute show
- $291 for a two-hour show

If you work in a TV series and are guaranteed a certain number of performances out of each thirteen shows, here is the scale, per week:

- $1,455 per half hour
- $1,687 per one-hour show
- $2,278 per 90-minute show
- $2,912 per two-hour show

David Varnay, an actor whose work has him commuting frequently between New York and Los Angeles, reminds us:

What you are paid for doing a show is only part of what the job will eventually be worth to you. If the show is aired, it will definitely be repeated during the summer season—so, that's doubling your salary. If the show goes into syndication, you get a little bit more, and if there are also foreign replays, you get a few dollars more. And anyway, in L.A. no one works for scale, that's only the place to begin negotiating from.

TV Commercials

Television commercials are covered by both AFTRA (tape) and SAG (film and some tape) contracts.

For an *on-camera principal*—a recognizable person who may or may not have lines to speak, scale is $333.25 per day, or per commercial if more than one spot is filmed in one day. *Voice-over performers* (those who are not seen, but whose voice is heard) are paid $250.60 per spot.

In commercials, most performers do work for scale—even stars, because they stand to make so much more money if the commercials get a great deal of use. Residuals, payments for additional showings of the performers' work, are computed according to tables that take into account the size of the market (potential audience), number of uses within a thirteen-week period, whether the commercial is a *wild spot* (seen during station breaks and the blocks of time between discrete programs) or a *program spot* (shown within the body of a show).

Extras, persons who are not identifiable, who are used to suggest the environment of a restaurant, an airport, or a bank, for example, are paid $232.37 for the session, which is commonly referred to as a *buy-out*. If, during the day of shooting, direction makes you identifiable—you are shown relating or reacting to a product or the commercial copy about it—you are *up-graded* to the category of principal and receive those residuals.

Hand models, whose exquisite fingers are seen using a product, earn $332.30 per session. Extras and hand models do not receive residuals.

Exclusivity

It should stand to reason that if you are seen or heard extolling the virtues of Salad Dressing A, you cannot work for any of its competitors—Salad Dressings B, C, D, E, or F. To do so is to have a *product conflict*. Performers may not do competing products in any category. An actor who does allow conflicts may be sued for damages by the first client. If the sponsor—Salad Dressing A—also wishes you not to work for as many as three additional products, which are not in the same category, the sponsor may purchase additional exclusivity by payment of 50 percent over scale. To have your services absolutely exclusively, he or she will have to pay you double scale, or 100 percent more. These terms may be negotiated more favorably for the performer.

Educational/Industrial Films

The contract for nontheatrical films, such as material used in training and motivational films, has a much lower scale. *Day players* earn $275; *three-day players*, $688; and *weekly* contract people earn $962. *On-camera narrators* or *spokespeople who play themselves* receive an additional $225 for the first shooting day. *Voice-over people* are paid $225 for the first hour; $65 for each additional half hour. *Extras* are paid $91. Additional clauses in the contracts offer protection in case the material is later broadcast.

IF YOU WORK IN TELEVISION

Taped television shows are usually covered by AFTRA contracts. In some cases, the work may be done at a SAG facility, under SAG jurisdiction, but the terms remain the same for all practical purposes.

Daytime TV Serials

Actors on a daytime TV serial fall into three categories. *Principals*, or *day players*, are recognizable people playing a role, speaking scripted lines. Scale is $357 for a half-hour show; $476 for an hour show. Actors who play *contract roles* will receive anywhere from $500 to $900 a show, depending upon negotiations between the show and the actor's representative. *Under-fives* are nonspecific people, such as maître d's, bank tellers; they speak fewer than five lines and are paid $169 for half-hour programs; $200 for hour shows.

One example of a soap star who was upgraded from an under-five is Jackie Zeman, of *General Hospital*, who has this to say:

I was hired to do an under-five on **One Life to Live.** *I played a waitress. At the time Jameson Parker was on the show, playing Brad Vernon. I had a two- or three-line exchange with him in a restaurant, and out of that the producer had me come back two weeks later to do the same part. But this time it was three pages of dialogue and the contract came after that.*

Extras, the people in the restaurant, at the airport, at the party, are paid $97 for a half-hour show, $124 on an hour show.

Prime-Time Dramatic Programs

Prime-time dramatic programs, such as *Kate and Allie,* pay the same in AFTRA as they do under SAG. *Day players* earn a minimum of $361. *Three-day players* earn the following minimums:

- $915 for half-hour and hour shows
- $1,077 for 90-minute and two-hour shows

Extras earn the following:

- $102 on a half-hour show
- $130 for an hour show
- $159 for a 90-minute show
- $186 for a two-hour show

Extras who perform special business, that is, action required by the director for the continuity of the show, are paid as *under-fives:*

- $181 for a 30-minute show
- $224 for a 60-minute show
- $255 for a 90-minute show
- $291 for a 2-hour show

Actors who speak at all are paid as principals.

Nondramatic Shows

Nondramatic shows using actors, such as *The David Letterman Show* and *Saturday Night Live,* pay as follows:

Time	Principal	Under-Five	Extra
60 minutes	$490	$224	$130
90 minutes	$618	$255	$159
2 hours	$747	$291	$186

Included in all of these program fees are a set number of rehearsal hours to be used within a set number of days. Rates for additional rehearsal are $11 for extras, $16 for all others. Overtime is paid at $24 per hour, $16.50 for extras.

Wardrobe Fees

If you perform in your own clothes, you are paid a wardrobe fee of $10 per garment for daytime clothes, $25 for formal wear.

Educational/Industrial Material

Rates are the same as those for educational/industrial films.

WHAT ABOUT RADIO?

Work in radio comes under AFTRA's jurisdiction. Anyone who listens to an AM or FM station quickly realizes that opportunities for actors exist in the dramatized radio spots—commercials—which interrupt the music, news, sports, talk shows, and call-in programs.

Actors in commercials recorded for radio are paid a session fee of $125.10 per spot. Residuals are based upon a formula that takes into account the potential audience and use of the spot.

Nonbroadcast audio is material designed for corporate or educational use. The great body of this work is straight narration by a single person. Scale is the same as for voice-over performance on industrial film or tape.

Job opportunities in radio exist primarily on the local level for announcers, newscasters, disc jockeys, and sports reporters. Nevertheless, radio programming is so inexpensive, and there are so many small stations, that anyone with the imagination and capacity to create even a one-minute program for which a local station might conceivably find a sponsor should see this as a challenging area. Think about it. A subject that strongly interests you may also be of interest to a great many others. Is there any aspect of it that you might base a continuing program on? Think about it. Use your tape recorder. In this business, you never know . . .

THE PHONOGRAPH CODE, FOR ACTORS

With the recent interest in recording books for consumers to listen to as well as publishing books for them to read, it is sensible to look at AFTRA's code for the spoken word on records or tape. Scale is $84 per hour, or per side. A *side* is defined as five minutes of recorded material. So if you were to perform twenty-five minutes' worth of material, you'd be paid five times $84, or $420; if it took longer than five hours to do the work, you'd be paid $84 per hour.

LOCAL OPPORTUNITIES

As we pointed out earlier, holding a union card is synonymous with being a professional. A level of experience is assumed. If your own experience is limited, you should be on the lookout for ways to acquire the proficiency you will ultimately need.

Kathleen Noone, Ellen on *All My Children*, says:

I needed to learn more about acting. For thirteen years I worked in different rep companies. The theater was my home. I was in the wings of the Cincinnati Playhouse in the Park doing Shaw's **Heartbreak House** *when I realized I'd had enough of this. I decided to stay in New York, and two months later I had a job on* **All My Children.**

For stage work investigate local stock companies, community theater groups, acting companies at local theater schools, children's theater, and nearby dinner theaters. Yes, you may be expected to hunt for your own props or wait on tables *and* play the lead in the play of the week, but if that's the only way you're going to get on a stage, why not chance it, at least once?

Maureen Stapleton, winner of an Oscar, an Emmy, and two Tony Awards:

I have been in this business for forty years, and the moment that really stands out, the high point, was that first summer, when we all chipped in to be at the summer theater in Blauvelt. Herbert Berghof, who was teaching at the New School, along with Stella Adler and Erwin Piscator, had found this abandoned theater—Greenbush was the name of it—and he kept telling all of the people in all of his classes that they could do it. That it was possible to run a theater by ourselves. He said he would help in the beginning—and for the first play, he did—after that we were sort of on our own.

We all chipped in $150. What a lot of money that was at the time. I don't remember how I ever got it. I know I was working at the Hotel New Yorker as a part-time receptionist, telephone operator, whatever. And we all lived in the barn. It had two halves, and the girls were in one room, the fellas in the other. I learned a lot that summer.

If there are schools offering courses in film production or communications, those students will undoubtedly be required to produce *something* on film as a class assignment. Working with them will give you an opportunity to learn about camera technique.

To attract feature film and television production, every state has established at least one motion picture film commission. The staff may be able to give you a clue to incoming projects with jobs for local talent. The commissions are listed in the Appendix.

It is frequently possible to work as a narrator or spokesperson for local merchants or businesses or the public relations firms serving them.

Seeking and landing jobs in your community allows you to gain experience and to build a résumé, and brings you into contact with people as energetic as yourself who also share your dream. That's how you start to build your own network.

Maureen Stapleton:

My first job, after we came back from Greenbush, was as understudy to Beatrice Straight in Playboy of the Western World. *One of the actors in that company had found out about the opening and said to me, "You've got to call, you're right for it." Well, I was scared to death to go up for anything! And he pushed me into a phone booth. And I said I didn't have a nickel. So, he gave me his nickel. And he forced me to make that call and ask for an appointment. Well, somehow I got it!*

Tony Award winner, Patricia Elliott:

I was working at Harvard, in the news office. The people around me were all involved in the theater. I asked if anyone could audition. They said yes, and that's how I got my start. I have been passed along from one job to the next. People would see my performance and say they'd want to use me in something. My whole career is about networking.

The best advice was given to me by Gordon Davidson of the Mark Taper Forum and Shirley Rich. They both said, "Whatever you are doing, write and tell me. Tell me where you are. Even if you don't hear from me, let me know what you are doing." And I have taken that to heart, and I do that with everyone I have met.

Part 2
The Breaks

I never got a job I didn't create for myself.
—Ruth Gordon

Chapter 7
Interview and Follow-Up

Before you get to work on a stage or in a studio, you will need to succeed at two other kinds of performances: the interview and the audition. Interviews and auditions are the givens of the industry. Or at least they will be until you become so well known that the mention of your name as a possibility for a role triggers an instant: "Oh, yes, just the one we were thinking of." And even at that level you will be invited to "take a meeting" because "Sweetheart, they just want to meet you."

Meetings by any name are interviews, and in Los Angeles they're auditions.

The interview is a chance to be seen, at last, by people who can help you. And, yet, not everyone sees interviews as opportunities.

Lester Lewis, veteran talent agent:

Most actors when they come into the office are so damned nervous they can hardly respond. I've had actors read for me and their hands are shaking. I tell them, "Look, we're not the enemy . . . yet! Just relax."

Why the terror? This is not a screening process. Agents and casting directors do not sit at the entry to the industry, like admissions officers waiting to stamp you Untalented and tell you to go away. They want you to be *mahvelus, Dahling.*

Of course, how marvelous you appear to another person will depend upon innumerable conditions that you cannot control: the size of the office, whether they are active in the area that offers the most activity for you, whether you look like the agent's brother or mother-in-law and what those relationships are like, whether the series you might have been right for has been cast, canceled, or put on hold. You cannot possibly know about such things, nor could you change them if you did.

Here is how some agents describe the you they want to see:

Richard Dunn:

> *I am impressed immediately by an actor's vitality, friendliness that still possesses a quality of reserve, that gives an air of mystery. So many come to an interview with such a desire to be liked they are not interesting. Mostly a feeling that the actor knows who he is as a person and what he has to offer.*

Doug Johanson, APA:

> *A great look, an impressive education, and a great personality.*

Robbie Kass, agent:

> *I look for commercial appeal and potential, talent, and the sure feeling that they are good, honest people.*

Meg Mortimer, ADM:

> *I look for talent, a sparkle, training, and a commitment to constantly growing as an actor. I also feel that actors should have a clear idea of their potential and where they are in their career at this particular time.*

Greg Villone, Peggy Hadley Enterprises:

> *I work with a lot of young people (eighteen to thirty). They have to be hungry, I mean really want a career. You can tell in a ten-minute interview if someone really desires a career in the entertainment industry.*

Phyllis Black, agent:

> *We respond to people who are comfortable with themselves, with their own skin.*

Tex Beha, STE Representation, Ltd.:

> *I want a prospective client to have common sense, self-aware-ness, understanding that show business means that this is a busi-ness, willingness to learn all aspects of the business and to be prepared for any and all auditions.*

The interview, then, is a meeting at which both parties can get some idea of whether they like one another and whether there is any possibility of a relationship at this time or in the future.

BEFORE THE MEETING

Do you remember how, as a teenager, you would prepare for a party where you expected to meet Mr. or Miss Wonderful? How you went about getting that paragon to ask you for a first date? Remember the determination? The research? Was he interested in football? You learned who Doug Flutie was. Did she like ballet? You came up with tickets for a recital. And before the grand occasion, all the time spent planning what to wear, how to look. Anguished hours over earrings and matching lipstick and nail polish; aftershave and the right shirt or jacket. Remember the excitement, the pent-up energy, the expectation? The electricity!

Bring that concentration, that fervor and anticipation, to your interview planning.

Find out as much as you can about the person you are going to meet. Your scene partner, your roommates, someone in your circle may be able to give you a clue. Your instructors should surely have some information that can be helpful.

Small warning: try to latch onto positive information. Negative comments, such as "So-and-so is a pain, or a fool, or only likes people who went to Yale, or has no taste," are personal responses from that person's meeting. It may have been a bad day for both people in the interview. Put such data way back in your forget-it file. Or try to turn it around for positive use, as "I think Yale has produced some superb actors, directors, and writers. I wish I'd had the chance to go there."

Rehearse what you are going to say about yourself that is relevant. We don't intend you to launch into a speech about everything you've done since you were in the sixth-grade play, like a machine spewing words until the nickel drops down. But practice is the only way to attain ease with answers to questions like, "Well, what have you been doing?" or "Tell me about yourself," or "How did you enjoy working at such-and-such theater?" or "What parts have you played?" Don't trust yourself to think fast on your feet. Improvise the interview with your friends, your network. With all of your information on the tip of your tongue you can listen and answer intelligently and even show that you have a sense of humor.

Practice shaking hands. It's amazing that this perfunctory gesture can present a problem. Why does this vibrant, healthy person have a handshake like a dying fish? A bone crusher is equally undesirable.

Decide what you are going to wear; make sure the outfit is clean and fresh: sew buttons, remove spots, press creases. Think of this experience as though you were going to a party and meeting the host or hostess for the first time. For men that means you should wear a jacket, slacks, and shirt; the tie is up to you. Women should wear skirts or dresses; slacks make us wonder if you have terrible legs.

As we have explained, clothing for interviews and auditions should flatter you and be appropriate for The Business. Color is important. It enhances your complexion. What you wear also indicates to us how you see yourself: upscale—which means higher income, suburban, more sophisticated (think of Lincoln commercials) or middle American (Ford or Chevy commercials). Watch programs and commercials and learn. See where you fit in. Apply that awareness to your choices.

Plan your day so that you have plenty of time to arrive, relax, comb your hair, check your face, and so forth. All the things you would do if you were visiting another person in real life.

If you have several appointments on the same day, make every effort to allow sufficient time between them. Be more than realistic, be generous. On a day that you have your time planned tight, to the minute, you will more than likely be caught in traffic, have to wait to see your first contact, spend more time than you anticipated in the agent's office because he is on a long-distance phone call or because he may ask you to read or because he may want to introduce you to the others in the office. Allow yourself the leeway to deal positively with these things. You cannot concentrate properly on interview number one, if a part of your mind is worrying about dashing to appointment number two, and possibly being late to appointment number three.

Bring a supply of photos with your résumé attached and your photo-postcards. Ask for the agent's opinion of these. "Oh, so that's your picture, eh?" doesn't tell you very much. Bring your tape and your reel if you have them, though you should not expect the agent to review them at that time. He or she may also be interested in your portfolio of pictures of yourself in recent stage productions. That will give you the opportunity to talk about what you have done.

Be prepared to perform your monologue or whatever material you use for a solo audition.

Be prepared to read copy. Be prepared to show what you can do in the equivalent of an audition. That's part of what the agent is looking to see.

WHEN YOU GET THERE

Look around. Notice the paintings in the office. Get a feel for the atmosphere. Is it musty, dusty, or full of verve? Listen. Are the phones ringing? How are they answered? Do you sense an attitude of respect? Politeness? Would you want these people to represent you? It's a mutual decision, after all.

The agent will conduct you to his or her office or desk area within a large office room, and you two will proceed to get to know a little about one another. The agent will explain his areas of activity and where he sees your greatest potential.

WHAT CAN HAPPEN

The very best thing that can happen, and what everyone hopes for, is the equivalent of "love at first sight." Your originality, dynamism, and talent will wow the first agent you meet, who will introduce you to everyone in the office and immediately telephone a casting director who agrees to see you right away.

That's possible.

Actress Carol Emshoff:

It was a fluke. I happened to meet the agents who were then setting up their own office. At that moment a call came in for a narrator for an educational film. So they sent me, and I got the job. Then there was something to do about Emily Dickinson, and I got that. And I got a radio demo [demonstration] spot. All in the same week. They signed me, and I have been with the same agency for thirteen years.

It is also possible that the agent will not be able to visualize you in any of the projects he or she is working on *at that time.* In that case, you will be ushered out with the admonition "Keep in touch."

Between those extremes are lines such as: "Let me know when you are doing something, I want to see your work"; "I'd like you to come in again and meet so-and-so, please keep in touch"; "It's been nice meeting you, give my regards to so-and-so [the person who suggested you get in touch]."

That all adds up to *keep in touch,* which is exactly what you must do.

No one will say to you: "Are you out of your mind? Go home, you don't belong in this business!"

You may get a referral to a friend or colleague at another office, at an advertising agency, or at a production house, or a referral to meet a casting director.

At the end of the day, note all of this in your record book, and prepare for your next set of appointments.

MEETING A CASTING DIRECTOR

As we explained in chapter 3, "Buyers and Sellers," casting directors may be on the staff of an advertising agency, a network, or a production company, or they may be independent consultants who work only on projects going into immediate production. Part of your preparation is finding out who does what.

Advertising agency casting departments, such as the one presided over by Maxine Marx at Cunningham and Walsh, want performers for the commercials the agency creates for its clients. The Agency Red Book will tell you who these clients are. At the interview, you will be very impressive if you know what accounts the casting director casts for.

Some sponsors use "real people"; some products use only beautiful people or models; some employ ethnic or character types. If you believe that you are exactly right for a product the agency handles, mention that to the casting director.

Your preparation for the interview will otherwise be the same as for a meeting with a talent agent: photos, résumés, tapes, reels, your portfolio, and a conversational attitude plus a lively appearance.

It is doubtful that you will be asked to audition any of your own prepared material, but the casting director may offer you a piece of current commercial copy—especially if you fit the description of a spot they are working on. Take the time to analyze the material (see chapter 9, which deals with auditions, and part 3, which will help you with script analysis), and give it your best.

When you talk to a *network casting director*, whose job it is to cast daytime serials, you are expected to know the shows on that network. You should also know the difference between prime-time soaps (which are broadcast once a week, in the evenings) and daytime soaps (five times a week, in the afternoon).

If you are meeting a *soap opera casting director*, know the show that person casts, the names of the leading characters, and the names of the actors who portray them. Certainly you should take the time to watch the program so you understand what is happening and are aware of what the show looks like. If you are unable to do that, purchase a copy of *Soap Opera Digest* and read the plot synopses. Meeting the casting director for any *series* requires that you bone up on that show. Can you seriously expect to work in TV if you don't know the medium? An interview may lead to an audition, later.

Casting directors who work in theater and films are independent consultants. Your interview with them is preliminary to an audition for a role in a specific production, which you must try to find out about. The theater interview will usually require you to perform your own prepared material: monologues showing two types of scenes or two kinds of characters. Some casting directors want to see you do a classic piece and a contemporary selection. You should be preparing these as part of your personal homework. Don't suddenly dash to the library or bookstore to find a piece to do the next day.

Casting directors on films are less interested in what you do with other writers' material: they only want to see what you can do with the script at hand. Writers and directors sometimes try to maintain the secrecy of a project, but you and/or the agent who submits you, want you to know all you can about the film, so that you can behave confidently. Who are this casting director's steady clients? What had this writer done before? Did you see it? Did you enjoy it? Who was in the cast? Is the director's name familiar?

CREDITS

Get in the habit of paying attention to the opening and final credits of films and dramatic shows. Movies, series, and TV films always credit casting directors as well as writers and directors. Get to know who those people are. They are all working in a business you want to be part of.

Then, when you meet someone like Reuben Cannon, you will be savvy enough to say something like, "I so enjoyed *Roots*. It's my all-time favorite miniseries."

HANDLING EMERGENCIES

Despite your careful preparations, the unexpected can happen. Emergencies occur: your wallet may be lost or stolen; a pipe bursts in the bathroom; you sprain an ankle; you've got strep throat or the flu. You may get a flat tire and find yourself stranded on the highway. Don't panic. You are not missing the one opportunity of a lifetime. Do the best you can—call the casting director as soon as you are able and try to reschedule your appointment. Call your service and have them get in touch with everyone you were to see. That is normal behavior.

What is *not* sensible is to get up from your sick bed and head for the office, on crutches, or with your box of tissues. We really cannot tell anything about you, let alone your work, when you're unable to walk, when your eyes are tearing, or when you're sneezing and spraying the office with your germs. That's a disordered sense of priorities and does you no credit.

Emergencies occur on the other side as well. The interviewer's baby may be sick; there may be an office emergency; an actor's sudden illness may require an immediate casting replacement. Again, it's a disappointment, but life's like that sometimes. You and the casting director will set another time to meet, and all will proceed as if the delay had never occurred.

FOLLOW-UP

Between the time of your initial interview and your audition or your call for a submission by the agent, there is usually a space of time, frequently a large one. You fill that in two ways: with personal work—on yourself, on your technique, on relationships and with the follow-up—the creative pushiness designed to keep you in the minds of the agents and casting people.

Shortly after the first meeting, a nice-to-have-met-you note would be in order. Report on whether you've followed any suggestions or advice the agent or casting person may have offered. Thank them for their time and attention and hope to see them soon again.

After that, your most effective means of follow-up is the photo-postcard. As we've already mentioned, your face, name, contact, and telephone number should be easy to see. Send your postcards every two weeks or so. Include a brief message; tell what you've been up to, pass on a witty line.

Actor Charles Frederickson:

Sending cards is a way to get on their Rolodex. I knew no one when I came to New York. It took me ten months to get my first job, on As the World Turns. *I kept at it, sending cards every week to all the people I'd seen or wanted to see. Now I think I can estimate that if I send out forty cards I will get a call.*

Mary Jo Slater-Wilson, casting director, *One Life to Live*:

There are, what, eight soaps a week which tape in New York? That means eight cards a week you send to casting directors. Is that too much to do to get a job? I call that being a business person. There are people who work every week.

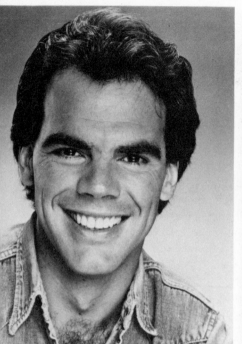
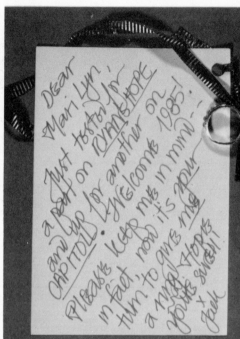

Roy Blakey

Jack Staub enhanced his follow-up photo imaginatively.

Yes, of course, if you are artistic or innovative you can come up with a marvelous caricature or an amusing gimmick. The ring Jack Staub attached to his card was the kind you'd find in a party favor. The idea was a charming attention-getter. The cards John Zarchen uses are conversation pieces; two are shown here.

Promotional items, such as pens or desk calendars bearing your name and phone number, can be useful, too, and seem to be favored by performers who concentrate on voice-overs.

Whatever your choices, the thing is to *keep in touch*, regularly, pleasantly, respectfully, and with the understanding that establishing yourself in anyone's mind is going to require a bit of time. <u>Persevere</u>.

The back of John Zarchen's card lists some times when his work could be seen on television.

This is another appealing photo follow-up from John Zarchen.

Chapter 8
Finding a Vehicle to Showcase Your Talent

"Call me or send me a flier when you're in something! I need to see your work!"

Every day actors hear this mandate from agents and casting directors.

They also hear, "Don't invite me to a turkey!"

No matter how wonderful you think you are in a showcase, remember that casting directors and agents are observing the possibly mediocre portrayals of your fellow cast members as well. If you stand out because you have no competition, reconsider inviting anyone to see you.

If from the first days of rehearsal your instincts tell you this is not going to be a rewarding experience, get out of it. There is no stigma, no blot on your record, no blacklist for trusting yourself and making the right career choice. Especially when you are receiving no financial compensation.

The rehearsal period and performances should be an enjoyable process and provide opportunities for paying jobs. Be sure that the producer and director guarantee advance publicity and that invitations or fliers are available at least two weeks prior to the opening night. The program should contain your brief biography and contact information—agent or telephone answering service number. If the cast prefers not to have their numbers printed in the program, your management should be sure that casting directors and agents receive a contact sheet with this information. Some showcases offer packets of pictures and résumés to industry VIPs. Some have sign-in books for them, so that the cast members can follow up by sending them their pictures.

You can discover the better showcase theaters in the Arts and Entertainment guides of your Sunday papers, in *New York Magazine*, and in other such publications, because the listings are free. We recommend that you attend performances at theaters whose choice of play strikes a creative chord. You may be able to open some doors by volunteering to work as an usher, in the office, or behind the scenes. Your hard work and dedication might lead to an audition for a future production.

There are also groups that sponsor staged readings of new plays. They don't have too much rehearsal time and may only be performed once for a specially invited audience—possibly potential backers. The playwright gets a chance to hear his or her words and discover where revisions are necessary. If the play or musical moves from there into production, you may have a chance of reprising your role. It is advantageous to leave favorable impressions with writers.

It used to be extremely difficult to get cast in a Broadway play. Today, it is just as tough to be cast in an off-off-Broadway showcase.

Veteran talent agent Juliet Lewis:

One of the saddest things that's happened in the business is that the entire industry is so hipped on names. Anyone with a Hollywood credit—from a small role in a TV series or a film— has a better chance of making it. Showcases used to be proving grounds for new young actors on their way up. Now they're proving grounds for those who have been in front of a camera and need to have the reassurance of treading the boards in New York.

THE ENTREPRENEURS

Actors on both coasts have discovered that if they raise the money to rent a space and finance publicity and refreshments, they can be their own "angels." Having control of the casting process ensures that there will be the same level of experience and professionalism. You will avoid the possibility of being placed on the bill after three boring scenes and losing part of the industry audience.

The actor-produced showcases are consistently of better quality. Some actors have become producers because they find the control and the challenge more creatively fulfilling than the performing.

Gregory Drambour and Tom Nichols coproduced an evening of scenes and gave it continuity with a movie theme. We think that their flier is an excellent example of showcase promotion.

The format of the scene showcase guarantees industry attendance. For approximately ninety minutes, twenty actors can showcase their talent. The time is usually from 6 P.M. to 7:30 P.M., with wine and cheese being offered before the show. Your acting ability can be assessed by an equal sharing of focus, which occurs in a ten-minute scene, as opposed to a tiny part in a full-length play.

We have attended scene nights where it was obvious that very little attention was paid to packaging and direction. To avoid that, here are some suggestions:

- Be sure you appear confident.
- If an inept director is your curse, turn it around. Reblock the scene and enlist the aid of a "third eye" you respect.
- Choose your wardrobe carefully. It should suit the character you are playing.
- Select a scene to which you feel connected. You might even write your own material.
- Don't try to stretch from A to Z in ten minutes. Don't force the emotions.
- Be sure your scene partner is as good as you.
- If you have an affinity for comedy, do it. We want to be entertained.
- Avoid scenes by Gorky, Chekhov, Strindberg, Ibsen ("Not another Hedda Gabler!"), and the popular American playwrights whose works have been overexposed.

ONGOING GROUPS

In addition to actors who produce their own showcases, acting teachers will sponsor special scene nights for the industry to view their students. Graduates of professional theater training programs, such as Carnegie-Mellon, Southern Methodist University, and the American Conservatory Theatre, produce plays and staged readings, possibly written by fellow alumni. They have studied with the same teachers, worked with one another as an ensemble, and share the same vision.

This is an attractive program for an actors' showcase.

Performers from the same state join forces in the competitive marketplace and can create exciting projects. That is how the Nebraska Ensemble Studio Theatre (NEST) got its start. Suzy Wurtz, a cofounder of the group, discussed their development in an interview for the Omaha *World-Herald*:

In Omaha I had a lot of competition, but there were only a few people really serious about acting. Here the competition is really stiff.

We did a lot of sitting around talking about that and complaining, and then it was like Mickey Rooney and Judy Garland—"Let's do a play!"

They got a couple of scripts from a playwright who has received his doctorate at the University of Nebraska-Lincoln. For the sets they contacted a native of Wayne, Nebraska, who was known in New York and worked on the staff of the George Street Playhouse in New Jersey. Cast members were University of Nebraska degree holders and actors who had worked at dinner and regional theaters in Omaha. They had special buttons made that say, "You don't have to be Nebraskan to love NEST."

It is estimated that most struggling new theater groups can fail within the first couple of years because of lack of organization rather than lack of funds. Ms. Wurtz said:

We were already a year old before we decided to be legal. We're still small, but we are creeping up. In New York City, just to have someone say "Yes, I've heard of that Nebraska group" is really something.

An off-off-Broadway company called the Actors Collective got its roots in an acting class. Perry Jon Pirkkanen and a group of his scene mates from the Strasberg Institute decided to produce plays. They were very idealistic and did not realize how long it would take to accomplish their goal:

What started out as a nucleus of twenty people became seven. We discovered that everyone wanted starring roles rather than working for the ensemble. We also produced some very bad plays. We now concentrate on revivals of rarely produced plays with merit, and original plays.

We rent a space for six months. Company members sell ads for the program at $100 apiece. If they don't sell an ad, the $100 comes out of their own pocket.

Writers will come to see our shows, which the press has consistently praised, and offer to submit plays for our consideration. Directors will attend and talk with us about future projects. We have created a theater family that we can work with on a steady basis. I clean toilets for the people on stage and they do it for me. No one is better than anyone else. We are from different backgrounds and from different levels of experience and teachers. We have control over the material and share a pride in our accomplishment.

Mr. Pirkkanen also recommended an organization called Volunteer Lawyers for the Arts, which offers free counsel on incorporating and acquiring not-for-profit status. He advised that if you become a member of the Dance Theatre Workshop you will get a free press kit that contains names and addresses of listings editors, radio contacts, and free-lance reviewers—an invaluable networking aid. When the group takes off, a press representative can be hired. He is also convinced that the indispensable member of your staff is the stage manager who oversees the organization of rehearsal and performances.

THE ONE-PERSON SHOW

Over the years on stage and television, we have seen famous actors and actresses perform one-person shows. We can cite Henry Fonda as Clarence Darrow, James Whitmore as Harry Truman and Will Rogers, Julie Harris as Emily Dickinson, Hal Holbrook as Mark Twain, Pat Carroll as Gertrude Stein, and Oscar winner Ben Kingsley as Edmund Kean.

Lecture bureaus and agents for concert attractions book lesser known actors at universities and community theaters with their presentations of the lives, loves, and letters of such luminaries as Sarah Bernhardt, Oscar Wilde, Edith Piaf, Sophie Tucker, Groucho Marx, and Louisa May Alcott. They are challenging and ultimately important acting *tours de force*.

Actress Leslie Ayvazian created her own show around different pairs of shoes. She would see pink cowboy boots in a store window and create the person who would wear them. The show is called *Footlights,* and a review in her brochure states: "In the sequined heels of her prom night, Leslie Ayvazian welcomes the audience to their fifteenth high school reunion. She immediately starts us on a fascinating journey." In sixty minutes she creates eight characters from the feet up, characters who span a wide range of age, experience, and outlook. She is in control. Whenever she can, she talks to children and encourages them to use their imagination. She has received unanimous praise throughout the country.

If you research a life that you want to portray for public approval, you have the wherewithal to do it. Some graduate schools afford degree candidates the opportunity to create a solo vehicle for their diploma.

There are scores of subjects in the arts waiting to be given a new life. Getting your production together may take several years, but the effort is worth it if the show pays you enough to survive and allows you creative freedom.

SHOWCASE PROTOCOL AND FOLLOW-UP

Agents and casting directors might not care to attend showcases that are not in Manhattan or in relatively safe areas. Remember, there are a lot of women in the business, and you might induce them to attend if you offer to see them to a cab after the show. Don't offer them expensive gifts or limo rides. That smells of payola and suggests the showcase may not be great, only well funded.

In Los Angeles, having to drive long distances to some remote section of the city or to the San Fernando Valley might prevent a good industry turnout.

We all work long days and sometimes long nights when there are casting crises. We want our time to be spent productively. If the program is more than two hours long, do not expect us to stay to the end. If you don't appear until the second act, make sure you inform those you invite what time you make your entrance.

If a casting director or agent has made a reservation for a specific performance, the management should inform you of it. There should be some extra courtesy extended—specific seats could be roped off with their names clearly designated.

The performance begins before the play starts. The environment, the welcome, the comfort of the seats, the leg room in the rows, the proper ventilation, the box office attitude, and the ushers all contribute to the enjoyment of the showcase.

When the run has ended and been acclaimed, send notes to the casting directors and agents who attended, thanking them and requesting an interview. Response is totally contingent upon their individual needs. You may have been wonderful, but the agent has four like you, or the casting director is not currently working on a part that needs your physical description and type.

Don't give up. Send postcards periodically, reminding them that they saw your work and should keep you in mind for future projects.

Chapter 9
Audition, Call-Back, and Screen Test

Auditions are performance. They are your chance to show, in however many minutes you may be allotted, what you can do with a particular piece of material.

Robin Strasser, Dorian Lord Callison, *One Life to Live*:

> *I didn't do well at auditions. I had the "clutch" problem. The more I wanted it, the more I got in the way. The voice didn't project and I didn't know proper comportment. What I learned was, Don't walk into an audition as the means to an end to get a job. Leave all that aside. Look at it as an opportunity to perform. I love performing. I played a game. I would say, "This is already my part. It may be for only five minutes, but it's my part."*

Shirley Rich:

> *It is an extraordinary experience. If you walk into a room and see eight people . . . and they all have something to do with this film, it can be intimidating, difficult for an actor.*

Judith Light:

> *Keep your sense of humor at an audition. Remember, underneath the nervousness is excitement, the real child in you is excited. Excited rather than nervous.*

Bob Kaliban:

At RADA (the Royal Academy of Dramatic Art) they instilled in us the awareness that no one can do it the way you can. You are the best you. You have to prove to them that you are the one they should want.

Maureen Stapleton:

The people hiring you need to know that they've made the right decision. Eli [Wallach] and I must have auditioned fourteen times for **The Rose Tattoo** *before they decided to let us do it.*

GENERAL RULES FOR DRAMATIC AUDITIONS

Every audition situation will have its own peculiar conditions. However, these dos and don'ts will help you to avoid the most frequently made mistakes.

Don't do heavy, climactic scenes. Moments that are truthful are more effective than screaming scenes.

Don't choose an excerpt from a play that has been inextricably linked to a major star, unless you are certain that you can do it much, much better. Examples are *American Buffalo, Beyond the Fringe,* and *Nicholas Nickleby.*

Don't show the audience how hard you are working. This leads to strained neck muscles, tight throat, furrowed forehead, vocal strain, forced laughter, and false emotion. When you are pushing for effect, your timing is off, your partner is forgotten.

Don't choose to do a British character, in a British play, by a British author, unless you do a British dialect with integrity and skill. The same is true of any play requiring a dialect; do it well or do something else.

Don't confuse your comedic monologue with a stand-up act. Christopher Durang's *Actor's Nightmare* is a trap piece: we laugh at the man's nightmare because he makes it *real.* Therefore pushing is unnecessary.

➔ *Don't* choose a scene partner whose performance is weak or dull.

Your performance will not look better by comparison. The other actor will only pull you down and ruin your timing.

Don't be general, either physically or emotionally. Unspecific gesturing or a tentative delivery with eyes cast down signifies that you have lost your focus on the scene and will lose your audience's attention.

Do realize that we want to know you through your auditions. Therefore, the audition begins when you enter, cross, come down, and introduce yourself. How you introduce yourself and your partner is part of the audition process.

Do pay attention to what you wear. How you dress is part of the character you are creating. It is part of the audition. Think about your shoes: jogging soles squeak on floors and rugless surfaces; they do not afford you any grace of movement. Thin spike heels make clicking noises. Any clothing that inhibits your movement or calls attention to itself is inappropriate.

Do choose material that you can connect with—emotionally, physically, and intellectually. Understand your own limitations. We all have favorite musicians, composers, and novelists, and we have playwrights with whom we feel truly comfortable.

Do pick a selection that will let us know who, what, where, when, and why. We don't want the climax, we need the setup. We want a sense of self and place. Ask us to imagine with you: who are you? to whom are you relating? who are you supposed to be?

Do know the moment before, the moment after. Be aware of your transitions.

Do connect with your material, the audience, your partner, your self, your space.

Do relate to someone when you perform a monologue, a duologue, or a dialogue (see part 3, "Script Analysis").

Do make specific choices, physically as well as emotionally. Your body must know what it is doing, and your vocal and interpretative choices must be connected. All parts of you must work together.

Do allow a transitional "beat" between two audition selections. Use a costume accessory: a scarf can become a shawl; a headband can become a tie; a cane can become a rifle, and so forth. You can roll your sleeves up or put them down. Make use of a belt. Take your shoes off. Think these moments through. Unify your performance.

Do choose a scene partner who is a strong performer, whose energy will give you something forceful to react to. You will look better.

Do deal in specifics. One terrific physical choice can make the whole monologue or scene come together.

→ *Do* bring sexual confidence to your performance. Mind and body work together.

Do investigate plays that were written before 1970. Know the whole play and bring a sense of the whole to the part that you are doing. Keep finding ways to keep it fresh. You should never get bored with it.

Do embrace your nerves. Be in control. The emotional connectors are the springboards from which everything else flows. Inner truth means we don't see you working.

Do watch out for *mood*. It is *doom* spelled backward.

SCENES WE NEVER WANT TO SEE AGAIN

Key Exchange	*Feiffer's People*
Beyond Therapy	*Split*
Loose Ends	*Cheaters*
Lone Star	*They're Playing Our Song*
Private Wars	*Say Goodnight, Gracie*
Laundry and Bourbon	*Scuba Duba*
California Suite	*Lovers and Other Strangers*
Chapter Two	*Bad Habits*

SOME MONOLOGUE SUGGESTIONS

A Social Event by William Inge
Julia by Alvin Sargent
The Man Who Disappeared by Ken Campbell
A Thurber Carnival by James Thurber
Confessions of a Female Disorder by Susan Miller
Geniuses by Jonathan Reynolds
History of World Drama by Ann Hudgins
Watch Over Me by Marie Whittey
Hooters by Ted Talley

In Fireworks Lie Secret Codes by John Guare
Diner (film script) by Barry Levinson
Coup/Clucks by Jane Martin
Chocolate Cake by Mary Gallagher

COMMERCIAL AUDITIONS

Some actors have for years looked down on commercials as a less-than-legitimate way of earning a living. What an unfortunate attitude. Doing a commercial *well* can be as challenging as making a feature film. Some of today's successful film directors got their start in commercials: Michael Cimino, Stan Dragoti, Richard Donner, Richard Lester, Lawrence Kasdan, and Howard Zieff, to name only a few.

As is true of any other material, commercial copy can be brilliantly or poorly written, with most of the work falling between the two extremes. You may think the copy is poorly executed; the concept may strike you as pure corn. Don't judge the material. You must believe in it 100 percent and never for one second let on that you don't.

You have to motivate and justify every word you say. If there are no written words, you must make every action and reaction believable. As a trained actor you should be adaptable to sudden changes in direction. Your job is to create a life in thirty or sixty seconds. There is no time to wait for "inspiration." You are expected to bring that into the audition with you.

Have at least three different approaches to the material. But be selective about these directions. They should never upstage or interfere with the integrity of the material. If you are clever and imaginative enough to take a risk and it pays off for you, *bravo*! You deserve the job.

Your audition for a commercial usually takes place in the advertising agency recording studio. Your performance will be recorded —on video or audio tape. These studios are small and usually crowded with the cartons and cue cards from the many projects that the staff is working on concurrently. The demonstration package of *your* product may not be on hand, however. You will have to mime using it. This is where training, concentration, and sense memory become important.

Arrive early. Get your copy of the script; ask if there is a storyboard—a cartoonlike illustration of the way the action proceeds. Isolate yourself so that you may work privately on your audition. Go to the nearest restroom to practice without interruptions.

Treat the script you are given as your own property. Mark it, make notes to yourself—whatever helps you do your best. If the script is more than one page long, remove the staple that holds the pages together, so that you don't waste time turning pages, which is difficult to do.

The audition begins the moment you meet the casting director, who will usually explain to you what they are looking for. If you don't understand, ask questions. When you are ready to begin, you will be instructed to "slate yourself." That means you say your name directly to the camera or microphone. This introductory moment is also part of your audition. Use it. It is not invisible time. We don't wish to see you transform yourself from dull to sparkling before our eyes. That's like showing us how hard you're working. Just be sparkling from the moment you get your cue. You are meeting the client at that instant.

Here is Bob Kaliban's advice on commercial auditions:

The first thing to remember is that you are there to sell the product. Your job is to help. You create, you re-create, you lend a little something that they have no idea they wanted, until they hear you do it!

The writer hears it one way, his way, in his ear. The account exec, the sponsor, each of the people involved in the job hears it in his own ear a certain way.

You have to be a good listener. Listen to the writer, the account exec, all those people, the actors you are working with. All of this colors your performance, your approach to the words.

The words will speak to you. Fresh. Smooth. Natural. You will have a different sense of those words and how to say them than anyone else. Sight reading is what this is all about.

Don't limit yourself. Don't think you can't do whatever job it is. I got an announcing job because I read opposite another actor, and then he read opposite me. Take every opportunity to do the best you can. They will call you back if you have done a good job.

Another thing actors frequently have to contend with at commercial auditions is the Polaroid snapshot. Some clients like to see pictures of all the people who have auditioned for their spots, in addition to seeing them on camera, to looking at their photos and résumés, and to hearing the audition tapes. Use this as another chance to show yourself at your best. Practice your instant dazzling smile. You might try to help yourself by having your roommate take a photo of you, at home, in the outfit you're going to wear to the audition, and bring that with you. You may feel more relaxed and look better. There's no guarantee that the casting director will accept your snapshot, but isn't it worth a try?

CALL-BACKS

Rarely does one win a role through one audition. There is a second session, which occurs after the unlikely prospects have been eliminated and the choice has been narrowed to five or six candidates, any one of whom could do the job very well. This is the call-back.

Your task in a call-back is to repeat your performance—same clothes, same hair, and same delivery, but perhaps an almost imperceptible bit sharper, better. Your concentration should be focused on the material, selling the product and being what they need to do the job. Winning the call-back usually means that you have an excellent chance at the job.

DAYTIME SOAP OPERAS

Like commercials, daytime dramas have been held in low esteem by many performers. To the thousands of people who work on them, this condescension is inexplicable. Soaps offer actors challenging work at salaries they enjoy.

Nowhere else does an actor have the opportunity to play a wide range of emotions while working with the sharpest professionals in the industry. Soaps avoid the formula plots and predictable resolutions of conventional series; they have shied away from the excessive violence that pervades prime time; because story lines heighten the kinds of problems and concerns middle-class viewers have—

with a dollop of fantasy added for occasional change of pace—soaps have attracted and maintained loyal audiences.

Watching a soap for the first time is like walking into a movie theater in the middle of a film: you don't know quite what is happening, which may be why media critics never catch on to soaps. With repeated viewing, the relationships are sorted out and the quality of the performances becomes evident.

Soaps are for actors who love to work. They are the electronic equivalent of a repertory company. Rather than playing different roles in a series of plays, the actors here stretch by playing the same character thrown into a range of situations.

On soaps, performers may progress from extras to under-fives to day players and, frequently, to contract roles.

Gillian Spencer, Daisy Cortlandt on *All My Children*:

> *I've seen actors as extras who then become under-fives and then come in to audition for parts. I know. I sit and watch extras on soaps. If I see an interesting face or someone does an interesting bit, I make a note to find out who the actor is, and I have a file now. The business is eating up faces, and you're always looking for someone new.*

Day player auditions usually take place in the casting director's office for the producer. A brief character description is provided by the casting director. Concentrate on the character clues and the meaning of the scene.

Remember, the audition starts the moment you enter the room. You are not invisible while you engage in some sort of preparation that the casting director and the actor who will be reading with you are not meant to share. That's the work you should be doing while you are in the reception area.

Relate to the other actor as if he/she were Olivier. Never play to the casting director. Endow the lines with your individuality, your sense of self.

Mary Jo Slater-Wilson remembers how Brynn Thayer was cast as Jenny Vernon on *One Life to Live*:

> *She had been doing commercials and was sent by her commercial agent for a role in the show. She wasn't right for that*

part, but I put her in the file of actors I might cast some other time. When the part of Jenny came up, I remembered her, we tested her, and she got the part. There was something about her that stood out—a beauty, an inner glow. It wasn't great acting. She has come so far. She has talent, works seriously. She has grown. But at the outset, it was her look—classy, sophisticated, urbane—that landed her the part.

The casting director and producer will make the decision. There are no call-backs for these roles. If you are selected, you will be called and told when to report to the set or to the costume designer for the show. If you are not selected, keep in touch. If you were submitted by an agent, try to get feedback on your audition.

Major Roles

Candidates for contract parts go through a lengthier process. Their interview with the casting director is followed by a reading of the audition scene, which they receive a day or so prior to the audition. No one is required to learn lines at this first reading, but a deep knowledge of the material is essential. While a character description is provided, the actor should try to create a personal history of the character (often called a back story). The more you create a life for the character, the more you will have to play in the scene.

Jacklyn Zeman, Bobbi Spencer on *General Hospital*, talks about her audition for her current role:

Uta Hagen, in her book Respect for Acting *(which I read once a year) has a section in the back of the book about writing a background for every character. I always do that when I am auditioning for something. For this part I think they wanted a horn-rimmed-glasses intellectual. Her name was originally Barbara. Well, that didn't say anything to me. I asked the producer, Gloria Monty, if, for me, the name might be Barbie. She said, "No, no, let's make it Bobbi!" Well, that has a bit of a bounce. I got my whole image of the character from that!*

Your success at the first reading will be rewarded by a call-back attended by the producer.

Betty Rea, casting director, *Guiding Light*, remembers how imaginative use of a prop helped an actress win a contract part:

There were six or seven females for the final call-back on the part of a recording studio executive in her early thirties. The actress who got the part gave the most wonderful audition. She was playing in Desire under the Elms *at the Long Wharf Theatre, in New Haven, Connecticut. She had to bus down to New York and was an hour late. I told her not to worry, that we'd put her on at the end. She entered, dressed in a pants suit, carrying a Sony Walkman and wearing the earphones. She started the audition with her back to us, listening to the music, and she took her time. It was the most wonderful lesson in how to audition.*

The Screen Test

Here is your ultimate chance to convince the producer, the writers, and the network executives that you can do the job better than anyone else. It is also the most difficult time to remember that, although they already love you, they want to scrutinize your work under the lights.

For this on-camera audition, you will arrive about three hours early, for makeup, hair, and wardrobe. There will be a period of blocking the action of the scene with another actor—the one with whom you will be playing on the show. This is the closest approximation of the working conditions of the actual show. There will be a run-through and then, lights, camera, action! and your scene is taped. Of course it is difficult to relax under these conditions. Added to the stress is the fact that screen tests are sandwiched in between the run-through and dress rehearsal of the day's regular episode or tacked onto the schedule at the end of a long day.

Kathleen Noone, Ellen Chandler on *All My Children*:

My audition for the role of Ellen occurred on a rainy day. I was supposed to be the mother of a seventeen-year-old daughter. I was actually thirty-one. I walked into the makeup room. The actress playing the daughter was sitting there, and except for one other woman in my age range, everyone was older. I saw one gal and I thought, "Oh, she's so much prettier than I, she'll get it." I told myself all the things that wouldn't get me the role. So, I decided to have the best audition and have fun. When I got the role, I cried, I just couldn't believe it.

The prototype for the role of Felicia on *General Hospital* was someone like Linda Darnell or Jacqueline Bisset. The ingenue who actually won the part, Kristina Malandro, is more in the Doris Day tradition. The producer saw, in Kristina's beauty and freshness, the *longevity* she needed for the show's major story line. The amount of "Aztec blood" running through her veins was greatly diminished.

Being Ready for the Break

With increasing frequency actors from all parts of the country and from Canada are brought to New York to audition for major roles in daytime TV. What an opportunity! What a fabulous break —for an actor who is prepared.

One such performer failed to qualify for a second call-back, and a sympathetic casting director reviewed the audition with him. Although the script had been sent to him in advance, he had not learned it. Nervousness made his voice flat and uninteresting. He had made no specific choices about the moment before the scene starts—he hadn't decided whether the character had been having a nap or having lunch. He didn't know anything about the other people mentioned in the scene, although all were regular characters on the show for which he was auditioning. Nor had he taken the time to watch the show before he flew to New York to read for the part. He *had* decided that he was not comfortable with the script as written and so had paraphrased the speeches. It was suddenly clear why this young man was eliminated from the competition. He had not done his homework.

Out-of-town actors must surely experience a subconscious response when pitted against New York actors. They may believe that they are not part of the mainstream. They may worry that they are not yet ready to compete in the major market. They have come from a small pond and haven't set up housekeeping. They are not bona fide and have got to be nervous and intimidated, with a network soap opera producer staring at them during a reading.

The dream has become real, and the reality is nerve-shattering.

But if the out-of-town actor is sufficiently prepared, has a foundation, knows how to analyze a script, is comfortable in any situation—then he or she is ready to assume the awesome responsibility of a principal role in theater, film, or soap opera.

AUDITIONING FOR A TV SERIES

In prime time everyone auditions—even for the three-line parts. Producer and director participate in these auditions. If the part is important enough, approval of other executives may be necessary. Call-backs are rare and will depend on the size of the role.

Gene Blythe, casting director MTM, advised:

If you have an audition, don't make it the sole part of your day. Be coming from somewhere or be going to some place. Look clean and neat. <u>Don't dress for the part</u>—allow some imagination for the director's process. Don't give them everything. Even if you have memorized it, they don't need to know you've got it down. Use the page. <u>Make them think you're prepared, not finished!</u>

Judith Light advises:

It's important to keep your sense of humor at an audition. I used to say, "Look, I don't want to waste your time or bore you. So, if what I'm doing isn't what you have in mind, please let me know and I will try something else."

Leading Roles

Landing a leading role in a prime-time series entails interviews, auditions, call-backs, screen tests, *plus*. The plus is the unknown factor having little to do with talent that may get you the job. You have seen TV series recast parts during the season or from one season to the next. On *Cagney and Lacey* three actresses have played Christine Cagney; two actors have played Mary Beth's husband, Harvey.

A great many people are involved in these decisions. When they all agree that you answer all of their separate needs and they can trust you, you will win.

ROLES IN FILMS

Your audition will come as a result of your interview with the independent casting director working on the film or that person's knowledge of your work.

If the part is small, you may be engaged right from that first audition. Actors trying out for pivotal roles will be called back for a screen test.

In a screen test for a film, a prime-time series, a miniseries, or a movie for TV, the casting director will rent studio time and actors will be made up and have a hair stylist in attendance. Most of the time there will be an off-camera reader. The camera will be on you throughout the scene. Your close-up—how you project the character and yourself—is the test.

Auditioning for a role in a film is decidedly a low-key affair, bearing no relation to the gaudy circus atmosphere generated by motion picture promotion companies in order to sell tickets. Of course, there is always excitement at the prospect of working, possibly with a director of great reputation or with a star whose talent, or profile, makes you giddy. But whether a film will be a hit or a fiasco, no one can guess at the start.

Composer Albert Hague's audition for the role of Shorofsky in *Fame* was an appointment he almost didn't keep. Winner of a Tony Award for his score for *Redhead*, he divided his time between working on a new musical and coaching musical comedy performers.

One of my students auditioned for Fame *and heard that they were looking for an actor to play the music teacher. He said to somebody, "You should see my music teacher." Whoever he talked to must have listened, because I got a call to meet the director. At first I thought they wanted to talk to me about writing the music for the movie. But no, they wanted me to act in it!*

Work on the film, which was shot in New York, took only a few days. He enjoyed the new experience, found the people charming, and thought no more about it. When the movie became a major hit and was quickly sold to TV as a series, he was asked to recreate his role for television.

The result of that has been amazing. Who would have thought we'd be going on for so many seasons? The show is seen everywhere—and I can truly say that I am known all over the world!

At age sixty he has embarked upon a second successful career.

THEATER AUDITIONS

Casting directors for theater companies planning a number of productions in a season will want to see your prepared audition material. New productions will want to see how you deal with the script at hand.

Your assignment is to be heard and to bring to life the person the writer and director have in mind, or better still, to show them someone they haven't thought of but who is perfect for their production!

No matter what you audition for, go with your vision of the role.

FACTS OF LIFE

We cannot ignore the fact that some producers and directors are rude, ungracious, and into power trips. If you are not what they are looking for, on sight, they may ignore you as if you were not there.

Take your place on that stage and hold your ground. Never let rudeness get you down! Rise above it.

The Casting Anecdote

This story was told to us by an actress friend of the performer to whom it happened:

The scene is the reception area of a Los Angeles television production company.

An audition is being held for the part of a *nurse* in a prime-time made-for-TV movie.

Seated in the reception area are the casting director and several actresses she has called in to read for the role. Almost all of the actresses wear nurse's uniforms, which they have rented for the audition. (In New York you would wear a tailored dress or a plain blouse and skirt.)

The door to the producer's office opens and out comes the producer. He is tanned, trim, and wearing gorgeously tailored gabardine slacks and a silk shirt that is open to the waist, revealing several gold chains around his neck. He greets the casting director and surveys the assembly of women, who are looking at him, smiling.

He seems to recognize one of the actresses. He snaps his fingers, pointing at her, and says, "I know you! You're . . . you're . . ."

She tells him her name.

"Yes, that's it. And I used to see you on . . . on . . . on . . ."

She tells him the name of the show.

"Yes, that's right. And you were a . . . played a . . ."

She tells him she played the role of a doctor.

"Yes, that's it! You were a doctor!"

He wheels upon the casting director.

"What kind of casting is this?" he asks. "How can a doctor play a nurse!"

————Dissolve to black————

Chapter 10
Congratulations! You've Got a Job!

"Dear, they want you to do it."

Seven one-syllable words and it's hallelujah time. You are going to be a working actor. You've got a job!

If this glorious message means that you've been selected for a part in a stage play, you will be signing an individual contract, which we discuss in chapter 12, "They Want You to Sign a Contract." This chapter is about work in TV and films, which is a bit different.

Actors whom the casting director has called directly—usually the extras and under-fives—will generally confirm with the assistant the date, time, and place of the *call* (the industry term for day of employment).

If you've been submitted by an agent, that office will give you your call and will then confirm your acceptance of the call with the casting director.

In either case you will be asked to pick up a script at the production office (or the studio), and you'll be given the name of the wardrobe person to talk to about what you will wear on camera.

WHAT ABOUT MY CONTRACT?

The standard contract will be presented to you on the day of shooting soon after your arrival on the set. At some time during the day the production assistant will collect the signed forms, and your copy will be mailed to you or given to you at the end of the shoot. Simple.

174

WORKING WARDROBE

Costumes are created or rented for special events—historical scenes or fantasy or sci-fi sequences. But for the normal life depicted in commercials, soap operas, and most nighttime shows, designers are happy when any performer's wardrobe is suitable for the scene; that saves the production shopping time and rental expense. The actor gains a wardrobe fee for each garment used, plus the comfort of wearing something that fits well.

Before she became costume designer for ABC's *All My Children*, Carol Luiken had designed costumes for opera companies all over the world. As a favor to a friend, she did the costumes for a short-lived play, which was seen by very few people; but among them was Jean Arley, then producer of *Love of Life*, who asked Carol if she wanted to do a daytime serial.

Carol Luiken's advice to actors in regard to wardrobe is this:

Actors should be aware that the place they will most likely work is in commercials, and for those they have to think of Middle America. The clothes to wear are those for a housewife, husband, young, attractive, a middle-of-the-road, classic look. Not expensive.

It's easiest for women to do with a skirt and blouse. A simple shirt look. For men it's slacks and a shirt, with or without a tie, depending upon the product, of course.

This look is hard to find in New York and Los Angeles stores, which are all trying to be upscale and trendy. Brooks Brothers exemplifies the look, and in catalogs, it is L.L. Bean.

When you bring clothes, bring choices!

We asked what belongs in the working actor's working wardrobe. She suggested:

For the ladies, a number of blouses so you can have variations on the housewife look. Definitely a dark skirt so you can play a waitress. Everyone in a soap is always going to the local restaurant. An evening dress, because there are several party scenes on soaps each year, and they need extras. It should be pretty, but not too glittery. That can catch the light and shine way out of all proportion. And the fabric should not rustle—like taffeta—because that makes noise when you move.

Men need a tuxedo, a navy blazer, and gray slacks. A business suit is being used now, too. Shirts should be in pale tints—blue or pink, but not white. Women shouldn't wear white either; it leaps out at the camera and makes for difficult contrasts. Come to think of it, nowadays a gal should also have a jacket for the young executive look.

You will usually describe your clothing to the wardrobe person and then be asked to bring the best-sounding outfits to the studio at the time of your call.

YOUR PREPARATION FOR THE DAY

If you have words to say, learn them.

If you interact with any of the running characters on the soap, watch the show, so you know to whom you will be talking. If you have any questions about the character, the scene, or the words, which were not answered at the audition, make notes to yourself to ask the director during rehearsal of your scene. Wait until the director tells you what he wants; the director may have anticipated your query.

The night before, make sure everything is clean and in wearable condition. Pack the garments in a lightweight suitcase or wardrobe carryall. Don't plan to do that in the morning; it will inevitably take longer than you expect, and you'll risk being late for your call. Pack everything that you will need. That includes shoes, mirror, personal items, your comb and brush or whatever you use to do your hair. Prepare your healthful food to get you through the day. Yes, there is a lunch break, but you may need nourishment before that time.

Check the weather report. Try to anticipate any emergency, and set your alarm early enough to go about your morning tasks without insanity.

If you feel that you may be catching a cold or a sore throat, take care of yourself! Nothing prevents a professional actor from appearing at a job. (If this were your senior prom, would you stay home?) Bring your vitamins, cold remedies, tissues, and nose drops with you and be as unstressed as possible.

On the morning of your call or the night before, wash and set or blow-dry your hair so that it can be shiny and healthy-looking. Yes, there is a hair stylist on the set, but the stylist's first responsibility is to the principal players. Every project also has one or more makeup artists, but be ready to do your own face, in case they are extremely busy.

Ask your service to give you a wakeup call; alarm clocks have been known to fail. Get a good night's sleep. We'll see you on the set.

Chapter 11
Your First Day
on the Set

Kristina Malandro, Felicia, *General Hospital*:

Coming into the show I thought that memorizing the lines would be the most difficult part, but that thought process soon becomes second nature. Making the scene work, making it real within the context of my character, becomes the most important factor. Being on the show is basically painful, frustrating, exhausting, heartrending. I love it.

Our day on the set of *All My Children* began at 7:15 A.M. The actors who had the early call were signing autographs for a fan who said she'd traveled thousands of miles to snap their pictures outside the studio that rainy morning. The ABC guards told us it happens all the time.

DRY REHEARSAL

Upstairs in the large, gray-and-white, fluorescent-lit rehearsal room, director Jack Coffey has arranged folding chairs and card tables to represent Benny's Place. The actors playing Robin McCall, Greg Nelson, Benny, and his wife, Donna, take their positions and begin the first scene. Seated opposite them at a long table, the A.D. (associate director) notes the playing time of each page of the script. The director tells the actors where to move and when; they write his directions on their scripts and continue. He calls camera shots, saying, "We're on *you* now. Let's have a little sarcasm here," or "Dry your hands, you've been working with chemicals." The actors nod without stopping the action or the words. They know the words; they carry scripts to mark the moves and changes.

After the second run-through of the scenes at Benny's Place, the director says, "Thank you, people." The actors take this cue to head for the coffee urn.

The director sets the chairs and tables for another scene. Over the PA system the A.D. pages the next trio of actors.

This part of the day is the *dry rehearsal.* All the scenes in one location are rehearsed in a block twice through regardless of where they fall in the sequence of the script. Two hours are allotted for the dry rehearsal. Director Coffey says, "We can stagger arrival calls and try to give the people who worked late yesterday an extra half hour of sleep."

A veteran of TV's Golden Age, Jack Coffey started as a cameraman, advanced to technical director, and then became director of *Somerset* (an NBC soap that was canceled when *Another World* expanded to ninety minutes). He has been a director for fifteen years, has been with this show for nine. His work on today's script was done many days earlier. Copies of his plan were distributed to the other departments—lights, camera, props, etc. "I see it all in my head before the actors get here. I give them the blocking. It's up to them to motivate what I give them."

Yet his experience has taught him to offer a reason for each move. He tells Dottie: "You're disgusted with him, that's why you walk away, up to the dresser!" "You want her to turn around so you can tell her to her face," he says to Greg.

Done with the scenes in Bob and Hilary's apartment, he sets up the See Spray Motel with Dottie and Tad. Coffey wants humor in their scene, even though she is furious with him, and they are delighted to give it to him.

As each location is struck, the actors are released to go to their dressing rooms to rehearse privately, to wardrobe, to hair and makeup, knowing they are due on the studio floor at 10:00 A.M.

Two day players have been waiting quietly in the seating area. The director now explains the floor plan to them, gives instructions where to move within the set. Both have dialogue with principals of the cast. Introductions are made. One actor, an under-five today, is tall, good-looking, has been in New York ten years. He sends postcards to the casting director every week. He has worked on this show before, but not with this director.

Jack Coffey changes a line and tells the actress who must play with David Canary, "Cross down on cue. I want your walk to him to be about something, not nothing, understand?" She nods and smiles; Canary asks him, "Why don't I get on my knees to plead with her?" And Coffey says, "Good, you do that." Canary practices the moves with her.

Producer Jacqueline Babbin comes in to say good morning. She tells us that this is not a typical day: there are twenty-four principals, thirty extras—for atmosphere in the See Spray Motel, Benny's Place, and scheduled to arrive late in the afternoon, a group bringing their own formal clothes to work in a gala movie premiere scene, in a brand-new theater lobby set. ABC's newspeople Katie Kelley and Joel Siegel will portray themselves in the scene. They are called for 5:30 P.M. In addition, David Canary, who plays a dual role, has a scene with his other self, which will be taped after everyone else has been released. For rehearsals of that scene, an actor Canary's size and coloring stands in for the other role. This actor never appears on the show.

Consequently, *All My Children*, which generally tapes each show in sequence, will work out of sequence today. Everyone expects it will be a long day. Susan Lucci/Erica Kane has three costume changes, with hair changes, too. She wants to be assured that the taping will be stopped until she is ready. "If we rush it, something may go wrong." Director and producer give her a nod and a pat on the shoulder. Mark La Mura/Mark Dalton, overhearing, rushes to them asking, in an expectant stage whisper anyone can hear, "Oh, is she going to be naked in this scene?" He is chased away with a playful spank. He chuckles, and that becomes his running question of the day. Coffey plays along with him, answering, "No, Mark, not today," or "No, Mark, I erased that from my notes."

WALK-THROUGH

At ten o'clock everyone is in the studio, ready for a fast walk-through of the action. This is the first time the actors run the show in sequence, and run is practically what they do. The purpose of this part of the rehearsal is to acquaint the camera crew with the sequence of scenes. The actors suddenly see, however, that they will have very little time between costume changes.

The general feeling is that they are lucky this difficult script has fallen to Jack Coffey, who is the director with the most technical skill. Each of *All My Children*'s four directors has a personal style: the actors must adapt to their strengths and weaknesses, while at the same time remaining true to their own character. "Francesca James [who won an Emmy for her performance as Kitty on *All My Children*] rehearses more for the actors. She finds the shots after we get down to the studio," Michael Knight/Tad tells us. "But Jack, he has everything all written down, he is the Alfred Hitchcock of daytime."

RUN-THROUGH

All My Children's studio is as large as a city block. Ten sets have been erected on either side of a central aisle, down which travel five cameras and three booms. There are two stage managers—one for each half of the studio. Working from the floor, the director views each shot from a monitor mounted on a movable lectern. He communicates with the control room and the crew via a microphone on the lectern. "If I had to come running out of the control room every time I needed to adjust a shot on an hour show, I'd be running the Boston Marathon every day."

Now the extras arrive and are told to find seats at the motel or Benny's Place. The studio is a mass of noise and movement: the lighting man calls his assistants on a walkie-talkie; his people move ten-foot ladders and adjust spots, while the set designer tells his people to move pots and cushions and rearrange flowers. The movie theater set has not been nailed into final position, because a portion of it interferes with the wagon carrying a special effects contraption —an ingenious arrangement of mirrors, water trough, and an electric fan, which creates the look of splashing surf at the See Spray Motel.

"Fax time!" booms a voice over the PA system. *Fax* means "facilities": all the machinery is turned on. It's costing several thousands of dollars a minute, so, please, let's get on with the show.

A show this length has several hundred shots. Each camera operator clips the list of his or her shot numbers to the camera, like a shopping list. With this run-through, they will learn what each numbered shot is supposed to look like. The crew must learn as quickly as the performers. We hear Camera 2 say to the director, "Jack, I can do it if I get really low and shoot up." He lowers the camera and sits on the floor, "How's that? Isn't that a better angle, Jack?"

Coffey says, "You're right." Then he calls, "Where's Camera 3? Larry, come back here. You went to the wrong motel."

The actors can get no sense of the scenes' dynamic. They stop for lights, for boom shadow, for a squeaking door; stop and start until the technical aspects have been smoothed. Yet the next run-through will be dress rehearsal. Feeling the constant need for more rehearsal, this cast asked management to schedule a line rehearsal with the A.D. after every scene run-through. They argued that it would make for a better show. Management agreed.

By noon most of the show has been blocked. The schedule says it's lunchtime.

Actors are free to leave, knowing that when they come back they must be ready for dress rehearsal. Somewhere in this period they will have to get into costumes, makeup, and hair. Extras too.

Munching on her sandwich in the deserted theater set, one of them tells us, "This is like being paid for learning! Have you ever seen anything like this? This is my first time on a soap. I think I would have flipped out if I had to say anything!"

The actress playing with David Canary is having problems. Producer and director have vetoed her first outfit. She has to try on another gown. She also has to get her long hair into another style, because it photographs heavily. She can't seem to get into a position in the spotlight focused on the doorway, where she must make an important gesture. It's her first time on the show and her strong characterization is melting slowly.

Coffey, aware of her growing anxiety, reassures her. "The actor's discipline is not just showing up on time and learning the lines. It's having to accept without question all direction that I call for, because I need it for my pictures, and incorporate that into the character. And these people are terrific."

Coffey uses this lunch break for the weekly meeting with his fellow directors. "We have to tell each other how we are handling things. We have to have unity and cooperation on all our shows."

DRESS REHEARSAL

Closer to two o'clock, the dress rehearsal begins. The set is closed to all outsiders. The extras have been assigned places and activities: An actor who must cross to the bar at the See Spray becomes more inebriated as the scene progresses. An actress reapplies makeup, over and over, loving her reflection.

In the control room, producer Jacqueline Babbin loves Pamela Blair/Maida's clever bit of letting the camera see her cheat at solitaire. She wants to know, "Why is Dottie carrying that bag? That's much too expensive. Dottie has no money. It should be plastic." While the scene continues, the wardrobe assistant runs to get a replacement. Within seconds, he is in the control room with a transparent vinyl carryall. Ms. Babbin approves.

The producer calls such comments as: "That scene is meandering; there's a possible cut here." Coffey says, "Give me a note to fix a line at the top."

"And let's fix Mark's tie."

The A.D. records all their comments:

"We need more voice from Steve."

"Tell him to be supercharming when she leaves."

"That's the wrong music on that cue."

"When the motel door opens, I want to hear some sea gulls, please."

"He should have more of a crush on her and not handle it so well."

These notes will be passed on to actors and staff at the break.

"Everyone into the movie set, please!" Coffey has five minutes to give actors' notes. He has decided that they will stop the tape between scenes. There is too much to do to maintain a quiet set. The actors applaud. "Oh, good, then we don't have to bring my bathing suit down to the studio. I'll have time to change in my dressing room, right?" asks Dottie. "Right," says Coffey. She blows him a kiss.

He walks back to the control room, smiling as if to himself. "You know, another director told me, you give the same direction in different words until you see the actor's eyes click. With these actors, they click right away."

TAPING TIME

"Places, people, everyone in the prologue, places, please. This is the show."

A hush falls over the studio. The countdown begins in the control room. A chalk slate, giving the show name, episode number, and air date, is held up to Camera 1. When the A.D. counts down to five, the stage manager on the floor picks up the count, "Four, three, two, one," and "Cue them!" Dottie and Tad start to shout. The camera catches them in midargument and the scene goes. *Cut* to Greg and Robin in his dark room, and that scene goes. *Cut* to Erica's room and . . . What's the matter?

"Jack, we can't open the door."

"Stop the tape, everybody. What's the matter with the door?"

A voice yells into the boom, "We fixed it! It's OK."

"Have her try the door," Coffey tells them. Susan/Erica calls, "I've done it, Jack. I think it's OK now."

"All right, everybody. We're going from the top. This is take 2."

Tad calls, "Dottie's gone to change into her bathing suit. Do you want us to do this scene again?"

In the control room Coffey mutters, "I *did*. Hold on a minute."

The tape is replayed on his monitor. He and Jacqueline Babbin agree to go with take 1 of that scene. Coffey announces over the talk-back, "We will begin with Greg and Robin in the darkroom. That's OK, Tad."

The A.D. now talks to the technical crew, "Ready in the darkroom. Let's get the slate in there."

Countdown. Cue. This time the door opens. Erica rushes up the stairs and the show goes as scheduled. The taping of part 1 ends at 6 P.M.

Coffey still must rehearse and tape the movie theater sequence and David Canary's dual-role scene. He sighs, "Doing an hour a day. I have six days off to recover, but some of these people will come back tomorrow. We almost don't make it, every day."

A veteran movie director asked the director of one of Hollywood's daytime soaps, "How much do you shoot each day?"

"How much do you see?" the soap director answered.

"Well, that show of yours is an hour," the veteran said.

"That's how much I shoot."

"But that's not possible," said the film director.

"I know, but we do it just the same."

THIRTY MINUTES OF PRIME TIME

Judith Light, two-time Emmy Award winner for her performances as Karen Wolek on *One Life to Live*, has gone from the pressure of a one-hour-a-day show to the relative ease of a half-hour weekly show, *Who's the Boss?* She describes that routine for us:

We get a new script on Sunday. On Monday morning at eleven there is a "table read." That is over at noon, after which we discuss costumes for the show, and directions.

The following day I have a costume fitting, at 9:00 A.M., then there is a blocking rehearsal at 10:00. We do the entire show. Late in the afternoon, 3:00 to 5:00, we do a run-through for the network, writers, producers, and pertinent personnel. Afterward there are notes.

The next day, Wednesday, we rework the sections that need it. We have another run-through between 4:30 and 5:00.

On Thursday we report at 10:00 A.M. and spend the entire day on camera blocking, till 3:30, 4:00, or 5:00. There is a run-through, followed by notes. Usually this is a late day.

Friday is makeup and hair at 11:00 A.M. At noon we have a run-through till 2:45. We have forty-five minutes for touch-ups, then we perform for a live audience at 3:30 and another live audience at 6:00. We are usually finished by 8:00 P.M.

We are constantly cutting, changing jokes, reshifting something. There is an amount of flexibility, and you have to do it immediately.

There is no time to have an ego. There are people with titles, who are important because of those titles, but when we sit in production meetings, titles don't exist. Everybody has input. The director is from the theater. The writers and producers want creative participation; they want to discuss problems. We work like an ensemble.

We do this for three weeks, then have a hiatus on the fourth week. Our season ends at the end of February. We are off March, April, May, and June. We begin again in July. This year we are doing twenty-four episodes.

COMMERCIALS AND MOVIES

To actors accustomed to soaps and the multicamera technique, filming commercials is like sleepwalking. How can it take a whole day to do a minute? they ask.

On one-camera film shoots, the camera sees and magnifies everything. Every detail must be perfect. Technical perfection becomes an attainable goal. The product is the star.

Actors called for eight or nine o'clock know that they may not be called to the set until after lunchtime. Yet, they must be ready. There is a great deal of waiting.

The number of people and the noise will equal that of a soap set. Everyone moves with careful speed: spraying down the shine on the refrigerator handle, masking the light behind the window. The director decides to put the table on blocks. The lights must be repositioned.

The director has broken the script down into short shots. Each of these moments will be filmed again and again from different angles and at different distances. For each change the lights will need to be refocused. These changes may, in turn, reveal other details that will require attention. If the cake frosting melts under the hot lights we will need another take. If the camera wobbles on the dolly back, we will need another take. The cookie crumbles; the paper tears; the lettuce wilts. The actor sneezes or squints or sweats visibly.

The shot is perfect! But a light blows. Take it again.

Technical problems. Human error.

On location, the sun disappears; a passing plane ruins the sound track; someone forgets the bug spray.

Saying the lines is the easy part. Synchronizing words, picture, and product can take a whole day. And it does.

In a movie, everything is the same, minus the product shots. Tasia Valenza, Dottie on *All My Children*:

In soap operas you have to learn fast. I liked that. Film is more technical. You do one line ten times. In soaps you can become more of an actor.

AND ON STAGE

We are assuming that our readers have some familiarity with theatrical production—the relatively long rehearsal period and the hoped for long run of performances. In this medium the challenge is to keep the performance fresh, to bring the illusion of the first time to every day.

As Lester Lewis recalls:

There are some actors, you don't see them in the first weeks of the run, forget it. They're bored. That disturbs me. There is a classic story about Alfred Lunt. He always grew in performance. The tour of O Mistress Mine *was closing. The matinee before the final performance Mr. Lunt told Dick Van Patten, who was playing his son, to come to his dressing room before the show. Lunt said, "I think if you say this line at this particular point, we can get another laugh." Van Patten did, and got it. This was after two years of performing! That's what actors should never forget!*

Chapter 12
They Want You to Sign a Contract

You are going to sign a personal contract. You are going to create a definable character on stage, on a soap, or in a movie! It is a great feeling.

You will be paid a salary every week, for as long as the project, or your story line, lasts.

Your agent will do the negotiating for you. If you have managed to win your role without an agent, this may be a smart time to get an agent or theatrical attorney to represent you. Many performers think this is giving away 10 percent of their salary. Try to see it as an investment: the agent will try to get as much for you as you are worth—actors are not as knowledgeable as they can be about the subtle business aspects of their jobs. Moreover, the agent may start seeking additional work for you, work that does not conflict with your new job. Think about it.

Be sure you understand the terms of your contract. Are you precluded from doing commercials or any other jobs?

Once you're working steadily, it invariably follows that other people will want to hire you. If you are presented with a better career opportunity, what are your options?

On soaps, actors generally need to give six weeks' notice for four weeks out, after their first six months on the show. These things are negotiated before you sign.

As Sam Goldwyn used to say, "A word-of-mouth agreement isn't worth the paper it's written on."

One thing to understand deep in your soul is that once you join any company—film, TV, or stage—you are part of a business family. Respect it.

Avoid the childish temptation to test their love for you by behaving sloppily—forgetting to learn your lines, losing your script, forgetting to set the alarm, showing up late, or not showing up at all. You are considered too grown-up for that sort of kid stuff.

Remember how hard you have worked for this reward. Love it. Love yourself. And have fun with it.

Chapter 13
Coping with Success

Let us assume that you are *working* and have become *highly successful* and very *visible*.

Your television and feature film exposure have enabled you to move into a bigger house or to buy a condominium, to expand your wardrobe. Your celebrity gets you invited to only the "in-crowd" soirées and guarantees you the best tables at posh restaurants. In California you drive a Mercedes to the lot; the parking space has your name on it. Perhaps, someday a chauffeur will be driving you around in your own Rolls.

You have had to hire a business manager to take charge of your finances, a publicist, and a secretary who handles the deluge of fan mail and related correspondence. A personal manager has become indispensable for decision making about career moves.

You have also invested in fashion consultants, hair stylists, masseuses, housekeepers, and most important, a bodyguard. You've got what you have always dreamed about.

But what is missing? Where's the support system you relied upon as you were climbing the ladder? Those trustworthy friends and family members? What happened to the agent who got you your first big breaks?

What sacrifices you have made!

And for what? To lose your privacy? To be chased by paparazzi? To be the darling of a bunch of parasites? To succumb to excessive drinking and dope taking? What do you see when you look in the mirror? Who is that drawn, anorexic-looking, burnt-out image? The dream has become a nightmare!

What could you have done to avert this self-destruction?

The short scenario we have just detailed is not an exaggeration.

You frequently read about a celebrity's cocaine habit, drunk-driving arrest, barroom brawl, overdose, and the predictable visits to clinics, detoxification centers, and courtrooms.

After all the hard work, the dues paying, and rejections, it is essential that you maintain your sense of self.

Judith Light offers excellent advice:

No career is more important than the way you are as a human being. That philosophy has enabled me to go through just about everything. Nobody stays a star. A long-range goal or a series of goals is important for a long-term career. You have to have a foundation, be a person of integrity.

Find the right support system—people you trust. Agent, manager, teacher, psychologist, friends, spouse. It is important to put everything in the proper perspective.

I was very lucky to have wise agents who told me to work well with my money. I hired a business manager. I still allowed myself to live well. There is this old myth about the "struggling actor who lives in a cold-water garret and starves for his art!" When you can move yourself up from the poverty level, move up. If you know where you are coming from, all things are possible. Focus on mental health. There has to be some greater energy source that you can tap into.

When I came out to California, I didn't know how to drive a car. I had to learn, and I was terrified. But I made the adjustment. You work very hard. You have to get up very early. You can't be out all hours of the night partying. You have to be at your best on the set, in rehearsal, and in performance. These are the requirements of your career, and you must be prepared to meet them . . . because you love it and you want to be there.

Coping with the pressures of staying on top must be difficult for those who have been catapulted to stardom without training and experience—they haven't paid their dues. Actors who have extensive stage credits and who have studied for years with such teachers as Uta Hagen, Stella Adler, or Sanford Meisner are ready to accept the accolades and applause of an adoring public and press and are not fazed by them.

But the very young—whether exceptionally beautiful, handsome, or offbeat types—who are lucky enough to be selected from an open call or relocated to New York or Los Angeles to assume contract roles in soap operas or features, have the most difficulty keeping their perspective. They are ripe for the temptations of drugs and alcohol and partying all night long and believing their publicity.

They lack a solid support system. They have no family, teacher, mentor, close friend, or sweetheart to exert a positive moral influence or give them a reality base.

Actors become commodities associated with dollar signs—that loathsome word *bankability*. They must remember that their *art* lies within themselves. They have the option to continue to grow in their craft or to stagnate and become lazy.

Respected and successful industry professionals have shared with us the following valuable insights.

According to Kathleen Noone:

> *Some young actors who become matinee idols are coddled instead of being reprimanded. They don't know what it's like to get out there and be in a play that's a flop, to make an absolute idiot of themselves. At sixteen or seventeen, when have they ever had to risk anything?*

Fifi Oscard, veteran talent agent:

> *I think the young actor of today has more importance than he should have. I'm impressed with dues paying, and I think young people becoming stars vitiates the education process and the respect process.*

Gillian Spencer, Daisy on *All My Children*:

> *If you're picked up in a limo for everything, you fly first class . . . it's not your money. At seventeen or eighteen it would be difficult for me to forget that this doesn't have anything to do with me. At my age I know very well it doesn't have anything to do with me. But at eighteen, you're swept away. Unless there's something to ground them. I think staying in the theater world for someone in TV is important. There's something much more earthy about it. It doesn't have a façade.*

Here are some suggestions to help you realize your worth as a successful human being and artist:

First, keep in touch with your reality base. This is easy to do if you have a family. Kids don't treat you like a star, but just as a parent.

Second, live well, but not beyond your means. Don't try to create an image or a life-style for yourself that is exaggerated and dishonest. Don't play a role.

Third, invest in yourself. Keep going to classes, rehearsing plays, participating in creative projects such as writing and/or producing. Get a sense of controlling your life.

Love yourself so much that you keep your psychological and physical well-being. Do nothing to harm your body or alter your consciousness, otherwise it will not only show on camera but in life and will seriously jeopardize your personal life.

Keep your sense of humor.

Continue to enjoy the process.

Chapter 14
The Little Stars

It has been rumored that adult stars of the vaudeville circuits refused to appear on the same bill with children because they were constantly upstaged by them.

In movies during the 1930s and 1940s, an appealing moppet like Shirley Temple or Freddie Bartholomew or a wide-eyed, sweet-voiced Margaret O'Brien could steal the focus from any adult in the picture. Can anyone forget Margaret O'Brien's Tootie in *Meet Me in St. Louis*?

W. C. Fields always denigrated Baby Leroy, and while his sarcasm was hilariously funny, there was true fury behind it.

Feelings about stage children were further colored by the behavior of their parents. The pushy stage mother, epitomized by Mama Rose, has been immortalized on stage and screen in *Gypsy*, the saga of Mama Rose and Gypsy Rose Lee. Gypsy's sister, June Havoc, wrote about Rose in her autobiographies—*Early Havoc* and *More Havoc*. June told us that when she was three years old Mama dragged her to a prestigious Hollywood party and forced her to perform for the guests, even though she was deathly ill.

Stage musicals such as *Oliver*, *The Music Man*, *Annie*, and *The King and I* have employed scores of children ready to get out there and give their all, singing, dancing, and acting. Danielle Brisebois was six years old when she was cast as the littlest orphan in *Annie*. She had already appeared in a major motion picture and had been studying singing, dancing, and speech.

Today's gifted children have more opportunities than ever before to work in commercials, soap operas, films, and theater. Commercials probably use children more than any other medium. Movies are noticeably employing more young people than adults. By definition, TV's family shows require several children in every family. Soap operas feature roles for babies, preschoolers, grade-school children, and of course, teens age fifteen to nineteen.

Danny Pintauro, costar of the ABC comedy series *Who's the Boss?* was a regular on *As the World Turns* when he won a major role in the movie *Cujo*. His stunning portrayal of an asthmatic child in that film brought him to the attention of ABC's talent and development division. He was a handsome eight-year-old, with an appealing look and an engaging personality that, combined with his instincts for concentration and characterization, helped launch his career.

Justin Henry was a first-grader at a school in Westchester County, New York, when he was discovered in a nationwide talent search. He possessed such incredible ability to take direction that Dustin Hoffman selected him over many youngsters with better training and more experience to play his son in *Kramer vs. Kramer*. The child's performance—and it was his first—received critical acclaim.

We hope that this chapter will enlighten both parent and child about the right ways to seek stardom or simply good, honest work opportunities for a child. The most important rule of thumb is, *The child must want to do it!* We think it is appalling when a parent forces a young person into a life of commercial auditions and tap, singing, and acting classes when the child would prefer to be playing softball with the neighbors' children or baking cookies. It is dangerous to attempt to live vicariously through children. Let the choice be theirs.

Letters pour in to casting directors and agents from anguished parents seeking breaks for their beautiful babies, talented dancers, or child prodigies. Bogus talent scouts lurk around grade schools, ready to charge unwitting parents a fee to get their Drew Barrymore or Ricky Schroeder on television or into the movies. These charlatans take advantage of the parent who envisions the monetary rewards of having a successful child in show business. Greed should not be the motivation for pushing a child into the limelight.

The Business offers a life of intense competition, not necessarily made better by the insensitivity of directors and producers. In commercials, children are frequently treated like adults. They may lose touch with their schoolmates, who sometimes ostracize them out of jealousy. Much too soon they can begin to feel like part of the adult world. It is not uncommon at auditions to hear children comparing their residuals. If they become miniadults or if they behave like little automatons who cry but without real motivation, it is time to end the career and get them back to the real world.

Young people are extremely impressionable and, like adults, sensitive to rejection. They can become hard as well. They need encouragement and a solid support system at home. Parents who disagree about the wisdom of a show business career for their child often become so hostile over the subject that the marriage is jeopardized. We hope such cases are rare.

OPPORTUNITIES FOR YOUNGSTERS

New York, Chicago, and Los Angeles offer the greatest number of job opportunities for young performers. There is continuous production. They have the best photographers, as well as the largest reservoir of teachers and coaches who specialize in working with young people. And there are talent agents who handle children exclusively—in New York alone there are approximately forty-five talent agencies and forty managers for kids. The agents are listed in *Ross Reports* and in the trade papers.

How does a family living far from the production centers help the child or support the talent?

You can begin by inquiring about children's theaters, community theaters, and university theaters in your area. In many cities, plays that need children, such as productions of *A Christmas Carol*, are annual events. There may be a regional outdoor drama produced every summer that utilizes children. There may be a summer camp nearby catering to children interested in the performing arts.

Find out if local talent agencies send out children for commercials, local features, or modeling jobs.

These are all ways of gaining experience at a more leisurely pace than you will find in high-powered production centers. As far as pictures are concerned, snapshots will do for very young babies and until a child is about four years old. Children change so quickly that it's foolish to invest in professional photos before the child is at least five.

SPEAKING AND READING ABILITY

While children who grow up in the metropolitan New York area may have the added advantage of plentiful theater and television jobs, they are often disqualified from major roles *because* they sound like kids who live in New York—they talk with a New York accent, which means their intonation and pronunciation are peculiar to Brooklyn, the Bronx, Queens, New Jersey, Long Island, or Yonkers. Any regionalism is limiting, be it southern, midwestern (the Chicago *a*), New England, or Texan. Children whose speech shows signs of becoming so accented should go to authorized speech teachers who specialize in mid-Atlantic or standard speech. The earlier these children start their lessons, the easier it will be to develop good speech habits and a good ear, so that they will be able to assume whatever dialect a role demands.

It is shocking nowadays to discover that a great many high school graduates cannot read properly. Reading skill is vital to every audition and should be developed as early as possible.

All children should be encouraged to read aloud. Parents should set aside the time to hear poetry, a story, or an essay, perhaps even one that the child has written.

Very often, a parent will coach a young child with commercial copy or with a scripted scene. The child ends up sounding just like an adult and may, out of terror, forget the words he is supposed to say because he is unable to read phonetically or divide the words. Such a child may become very frustrated and tense.

Proper training and study habits will enable the young actor to have a better chance at winning the part without the parents' constant support.

CHILDREN'S CLOTHING

Some mothers have been known to dress their daughters to look like dolls in a toy store window rather than real people. The child should be permitted to wear something comfortable and should have a choice in the outfit. The casting director, the director, and the producer may be completely won over by the individuality and personality expressed by the clothing. Boys tend to wear certain caps or T-shirts or football jerseys, and that is appropriate.

If the casting director wants a specific wardrobe for the audition, the parent will be told in advance.

TALENT SEARCH

The open call is perhaps the fastest way for a casting director and producer to see a great number of children. Possibly you remember hearing about the international searches for *the* perfect little girl to play *Annie* in the movie; *the* Dorothy in the recent *Oz* movie. In 1984, NBC, with Hughes-Moss Casting, held such a search in New York, for a child who would personify a new character—Punky Brewster.

Here is Andrea Wolper's heartfelt eyewitness account of that event, courtesy of *Back Stage* publications:

It is a cold and rainy Saturday morning in late January. Mothers, fathers, and assorted seven- to twelve-year-old girls are shivering in the line outside the Minskoff Building, waiting for a shot at stardom. Some of the girls are seasoned professionals, clutching 8″ × 10″ glossies and résumés boasting enviable credits. For others, this is a new experience, as likely as not the first and last time they'll ever see the inside of a rehearsal studio.

Why with all the pro talent available hold an open audition? Publicity maybe. The fact that "star quality" and charisma are not acquired traits nor do they necessarily belong to the most talented or well-trained performers. They didn't want a kid so slick that she delivered her lines like a Borscht Belt comic. They want to find a little girl so appealing that all America would want to eat her up with a spoon.

So talented or not, experienced or not, if you're the right age and are assertive without being obnoxious, smart without being precocious, and have a sense of comedy and fun, you might find yourself a—SUPERSTAR. The show's creators intend to build the story around the girl they ultimately find.

At this preliminary audition, they come in every shape and size. There are eight-year-olds who look twelve, six-year-olds whose parents told them to say they're seven, girls dressed in frills, girls dressed in blue jeans. Ten or twelve at a time they are brought into the studio, and after a few friendly words in-

tended to ease the tension, each is asked to tell her name, age, and where she lives.

One group of girls is asked if they want to be stars. The smallest of the bunch shoots her hand into the air and says most emphatically, "Yes!" Why? "Because you get lots of money." Would she like to be a star if such was not the case. "No!"

In another group, a smaller girl with a sweetly funny face starts in on her vital statistics. As she speaks her name, her lower lip begins to quiver. On her age, the voice breaks. By the time she gets to where she lives, she is into full-fledged tears and is looking desperately for some place to hide. It's heartbreaking and adorable at the same time and raises an important question. How many of these kids are here because they want to be? And more important, how many of the actively working, auditioning, lesson-taking kids are doing those things because they really want to?"

Behind every stage child there is a parent, frequently an ambitious parent. And more often than not it is the child's mother.

Most agents do not want to work with children whose mothers are intolerable. They become *persona non grata* on a set or backstage. Commercial directors and producers will tell casting directors never to use certain children again because of their parents.

BEGINNING A CAREER EARLY

Experience has always proved to be the best teacher. We asked Danielle Brisebois and her mother/manager, Mary, to tell us what it was like at the beginning of Danielle's career, and we now reprint excerpts of their reflections. We will start with what it was like for the mother:

At the age of three, pictures were taken of Danielle at a department store. The photographer was impressed with Danielle's bright eyes and energy. He suggested that we should put her with a commercial agent and gave us the name of an agent. Not knowing what to expect, I took her to the agent and she was immediately signed.

I was then informed about what is involved. First you have to invest in pictures and then be willing to be on call at any time to get to an audition. From that time on my time was always planned.

It is quite a learning experience to go to your first audition. Danielle's first one was for a shampoo. It was what in the business is called a "cattle call." It seemed like there were wall-to-wall kids. That was my first realization of what a competitive business it is. Danielle started getting a lot of the calls she went on. So she became a hot item in the kid market. From there I was told to give her voice lessons and dance. That started another obligation. Along with auditions she took tap, voice, jazz almost every day. This led to going out on the weekends to do a lot of charity work, which also took up more time. Danielle then landed her first movie at five years old. She then appeared on soap operas. Her really big break came in the musical Annie. She landed the part of Molly in the original cast on Broadway. That show was also a real learning experience. The competition was very strong. Danielle gained a lot of popularity and fame from Annie, and she got good reviews—which I attribute to all the time that was put into preparing her so when the opportunity arrived she was ready.

Stage work is a very disciplined part of the business. A child must perform like an adult and therefore end up having the pressures of the stage at a young age. The child has to really be strong-willed and love what she is doing.

After Annie, I took her to Los Angeles to audition for the studios there. She landed two contracts within two weeks. She met Norman Lear, and he decided to use her in one of his shows. Archie's Place turned out to be a turning point in her career. Knowing how important public relations is, I hired a publicist, and she then started appearing in magazines and newspapers.

The move to Los Angeles caused us a great deal of sacrifice. We had to leave our home and move to a place where we knew no one. It was quite a transition.

After Archie's Place, Danielle returned to the stage and television shows such as Knots Landing. I feel this is a very changeable business. You constantly walk a tightrope. An important thing to remember is, Think ahead and don't ever believe that you are set because at any given moment it can turn around. You have to be a strong person and respect the business.

Now here's Danielle:

Being a child in this business is almost the same thing as being an adult in this business. The difference is that children don't get taken as seriously. They work harder and they get paid less.

Rarely will you find a successful or nonsuccessful person in this business who treats a child as an equal. I personally think that most adults who have put lots of money and training into their career find it hard to accept that a child is doing the same thing as they are. What they don't realize is that in most cases children have also put as much work and dedication into their career as well.

Sometimes, children have it harder. They're trying to be successful at many hard things all at the same time. They're growing up (which is hard enough on its own), going to school, taking lessons in singing, dancing, acting, and whatever else, going on auditions, dealing with competition, setting values for themselves, living in an adult world while their parents are still telling them what to do, are expected to take on the same responsibilities as an adult—working, making money, sometimes getting famous— and are expected to stay sweet and cute like a "normal" kid. There are a lot of demands and pressures put on the younger professional. I started in the business when I was three. The most prominent memory I have from back then is taking dancing and singing lessons. It's almost as if I grew up in a dance studio. I formed a special relationship with my teachers that I will always treasure in my heart. They taught me more than how to sing and dance. They taught me how to have confidence in myself, how to strive for perfection (if there is such a thing), taught me discipline and many other things. They were like second fathers to me. If it wasn't for the studio, I wouldn't have come so far in my career.

If it wasn't for my mother, I wouldn't have come so far either. She took me everywhere I had to go—auditions, lessons, etc. She gave me most of her time so I could be successful. Even though we lived in Brooklyn, we were hardly ever there. Being in this business is a full-time job and we found that out quickly. It was even getting hard to fit school in. I was going to public school at first, but eventually I started getting tutored by my next door neighbor who was a teacher. I would go to her early every morning and she would work with me for about three hours at a time. Because we'd only get together for about three hours at a time, I'd have to get tutored on the weekends too. Luckily, I was pretty bright, so school wasn't hard for me.

My career started picking up. I started getting more and more commercials. Classes were getting easier for me. The older you get, the more parts there are. I started knowing all the kids at the auditions and all their mothers. Usually, I was the only dark-haired kid there. But even though they like to use fair-complected kids better, I was still getting jobs. I guess it is because I worked hard at it.

I was also doing a lot of charity work. I would go with my singing teacher and sing songs and dance at old-age homes, hospitals, and places like that. It was good experience. I started working in dinner theaters. Then, when I was five I got a part in a feature film called The Premonition. That's when things started to happen. I did press for the film, which gave me a little credibility and more confidence. I got the chance to do a nightclub act (I was six). It was approximately forty-five minutes. It was filled with all sorts of numbers from a sweet Shirley Temple song to Mae West imitations. I was pretty excited about doing this act, and I was also pretty nervous. My mother rehearsed me so much for the act that I almost became afraid of it. But all went well. It was another credit on my résumé that another kid didn't have.

One day as I was leaving dance class, someone told me about an audition for a new musical called Annie. So I went down to the audition and forced my way into it. I got the part. My mom and I hoped we made the right decision. Taking this job would mean going to Connecticut for a month. Our hope was that the play would make it to Broadway.

We went to the Goodspeed Opera House. My role was Mary-Jane (which later became Molly), the littlest orphan. I was the first cast member to meet Sandy. When the run was over in Connecticut, the play got a new producer, reopened in Washington, D.C., went to Broadway, and the rest is history. I was in Annie about three years. I only missed one performance and that was due to a job on a movie. All of us kids were jealous of each other, even though we never let the others know it. We all were friends, but there was always that sense of competition between us. No one wanted any of the other kids to have more than them. Annie taught me a lot about discipline. It made me learn that if I want to be the best, I have to make myself the best. Every day I would go to school (with my tutor), take lessons, audition, and do the play every night.

Then one day I got too big for my part and had to leave the show. So I went out to Hollywood to find work. My mom got me appointments with some casting directors and producers. I was really well prepared for my meetings. At this time I met Norman Lear who remembered me from Annie, and he loved me. As I was leaving my meeting with him, Carroll O'Connor saw me in the hall and remembered me from Annie too. He and Mr. Lear came up with the idea for my character on All in the Family. It just so happened that Sally Struthers and Rob Reiner were leav-

> *ing the show and they needed someone to fill in the gap. This is where luck and timing were on my side. They called me and presented me with the character of Stephanie. I did the show for five years, and I've been working hard since.*
>
> *I've kept up with my lessons and my dedication to the craft of show business. I don't think I'll ever stop. I love what I do, and I'd be willing to give up anything for it.*

Christian Slater, whose experience includes film, commercials, soap opera, and Broadway, started at the age of nine. He accompanied his mother, casting director Mary Jo Slater-Wilson, to a local talk show and ended up singing "Zippity Doo Dah." The famed choreographer/director Michael Kidd happened to be watching the show, tracked him down, and ended up hiring Christian to play Winthrop in a revival of *The Music Man*, starring Dick Van Dyke. He spent nine months on a national tour, prior to opening on Broadway.

Christian remembers:

> *I was terrible. They almost fired me. I had no discipline, no technique. I didn't know what I was doing. I couldn't do the same thing twice. I would wave at the audience as if it were a school show. Mom helped me. They kept me.*
>
> *When we came back to New York, I went to Professional Children's School and kept on auditioning.*

Mary Jo is not a typical stage mother:

> *I didn't want my child to go into the business. Commercials were something else. He was adorable and had this typical American face they were looking for and it was easy. But when I saw him in Reno where the show opened, there was this wonderful little person! You had to admit he had something special. And Christian loved it, he wanted it! He kept getting jobs. Now he is very good.*

Christian's goal is to alternate plays with films. Plays allow him opportunities to grow as an actor. Films allow for versatility and different challenges.

What's most important is that the joy of performing as a child must carry over into adolescence and, one hopes, adulthood.

GROWING UP

When kids reach puberty, their bodies are changing and they become so aware of themselves that their *performance* can become inhibited. Young girls frequently wear too much makeup and elaborate hair styles and too sophisticated clothing that may mask their genuine appeal. This is sometimes engineered by a pushy parent who thinks the thirteen-year-old will have more job opportunities if she looks eighteen. The teen years are so important that to deprive anyone of them is unforgivable.

Unfortunately, the teens who get cast on soaps and features are sometimes expected to behave as if they have the emotional experience and sexual confidence of their older siblings. If they lack the support system of balanced parents or a strong spiritual foundation, they may experience traumas that will take years to resolve.

There are some teens whom we will call the "old souls." They come into the world with a history. Adults marvel at their poise, maturity, sensuality, concentration, focus, intellectual acumen, and artistic instincts. They are the ones who clearly know what they want to do and how to go about it.

Judith Light, two-time Emmy Award winner for her portrayal of Karen Wolek in *One Life to Live* and star of the ABC comedy series *Who's the Boss?*:

When I was little, about three years old, I started to memorize poetry. I enjoyed performing for people. I had a revelation that I would be doing this and I would be successful. It hit me in the gut, rather than in my head.

Tasia Valenza, Dottie Thornton in *All My Children*:

My mother read in Back Stage *that Louis Malle was looking for the right teenage girl for a role in his next film. She took my pictures to Mr. Malle. He brought me in for a meeting and I was hired. Louis Malle said I had an "old soul."*

Some of our illustrious performers of stage and screen, the established reputable working actors, tell when they decided to pursue their acting career.

Kathleen Noone, Ellen Dalton Chandler in *All My Children*:

At the age of thirteen, I was terribly shy. I would cower, afraid to say hello to anybody. When I got into high school, there was a music teacher there who urged me to audition for the all-stage chorus, which I got into. Then he wanted me to audition for the school musical, which I did and got the part. It was through this one teacher's encouragement and belief in my ability. Right after the musical comedy in high school I decided, This is what I want to do! I want to be a part of something where the people love to have fun and where it is a joy to work.

Tony Call, Herb Callison in *One Life to Live*, much nominated Emmy Award contender:

I wanted to be a stage actor. I was born in that tradition. At a young age I did plays, wrote plays. We did slow-motion football between acts. I was in the fifth-grade play. When I was eleven, I did every school play, three or four a year.

Robin Strasser, Emmy Award winner for her portrayal of Dorian Lord Callison in *One Life to Live*:

I turned to acting as an escape from being myself. I looked to my toys and my little space as a fantasy retreat. Early photos indicate my makeshift sets and props for my performances. Between four and five I was taken to see Peter Pan. That cinched it. It was the only thing I wanted to do with the rest of my life.

Jim Dale, Tony Award winner for leading actor in the musical *Barnum*:

When I was nine, my father took me to a live performance of For Me and My Girl. We sat in the second balcony. It cost one pound apiece and the people were very tiny. I watched those little people and I said to my father, "That's what I want to do." He said, "Well, then I think you should learn to move." And I started taking lessons—all kinds of lessons in dance, ballet, tap.

Gillian Spencer, Daisy Cortlandt in *All My Children*:

My family was in the theater, so it was a natural. I grew up in that atmosphere. I saw a book of Helen Hayes's life and saw pictures of her acting and I thought, "Oh, you could put everything in your head that you fantasized out, outside of yourself," and that is when I became interested in acting. I wrote plays in my basement and put them on in my basement and that is all I wanted to do.

As you see, kids come into the business by different routes. Sometimes a mother will read about a talent search or a beauty pageant that features a talent competition in the local paper. Judges at these events might be casting directors, agents, or managers who specialize in young talent. Competing for awards is excellent preparation for a career in the business. Parent and child will be able to tell whether or not the desire is real. School plays, choir and instrumental recitals, and dance festivals afford opportunities to perform in front of an audience and acquire a sense of discipline.

In high school, participation in the drama club or oratorical contests or speech events such as debate, original oratory, humorous or dramatic or oral interpretation, and extemporaneous speaking are invaluable. They develop good speech, projection, poise, timing, and appearance, as well as acting and writing skills.

THE NATIONAL FOUNDATION FOR ADVANCEMENT IN THE ARTS (NFAA)

You should know about an innovative program concerned with the future of America's new generation of artists, especially if you are a young artist or the parent of a gifted teen. NFAA is a nonprofit philanthropic and educational institution that assists young artists at various stages of their development. Its Arts Recognition and Talent Search (ARTS) program has had the greatest impact on young artists across the country. Its helping hand reaches out to every state and major city in the United States and embraces teenage hopefuls of every artistic discipline.

Approximately five thousand high school seniors participate in ARTS annually. They have an opportunity to share in scholarship aid worth $3 million and cash awards of $400,000. Each year about five hundred national ARTS awardees are named in dance, music, theater, visual arts, and writing. ARTS is the exclusive vehicle through which the White House Commission on Presidential Scholars annually selects twenty Presidential Scholars in the ARTS.

Awardees are also recruited extensively by major universities and professional schools such as the Juilliard School, Yale, Harvard, New York University, and the University of Michigan.

ARTS has its own affirmative action program, designed to ensure widespread participation by all who are eligible, regardless of race, creed, color, geographical location, economic disadvantage, physical disability, language, or sex. Through information networks and telephone consultations, minority and disabled youth are assisted in participating in the program.

Since 1980, awardees have launched their careers as working artists. Through NFAA sponsorship, young performers have had a play produced at Wolf Trap Performing Arts Park and have performed in workshops and special activities at the American Dance Festival, Jacob's Pillow, the Eugene O'Neill Theatre Center, and the American Conservatory Theatre.

If you want to be considered for an ARTS award, you should know that the formal ARTS prospectus is distributed nationally to every public and private high school and various arts and education associations. Eligible applicants are high school seniors or other seventeen- to eighteen-year-old youths who are U.S. citizens or permanent residents. When they register in ARTS, they receive a detailed application packet. These packets are evaluated by prescreening panels of experts. Portfolios (there were nearly 1,500 in 1985) are then reviewed by five national panel of ARTS adjudicators who select a maximum of thirty applicants in each art form to be brought to Miami at NFAA expense for live performances and related activities. In this final phase, applicants in dance, music, and theater present prepared auditions and participate in observed master classes and exercises to evaluate their talents. Each applicant is evaluated as an individual according to applicable standards of excellence at that age in the given art form.

More than one hundred major universities and arts institutions subscribe to the NFAA Scholarship List Service. These subscribers receive the names of ARTS registrants and awardees. The foundation supports young people in the arts in their formative years of growth by informing them about the special scholarship opportunities that are offered, thereby helping them achieve their educational and artistic goals.

Registration for ARTS begins each spring with an early registration deadline of mid-May (for high school juniors) and a late registration deadline of early October (for high school seniors).

For further information, specific eligibility requirements, and registration materials, write to: ARTS, 300 Northeast Second Avenue, Miami, Florida 33132.

A NETWORK OF PERFORMING ARTS SCHOOLS

The popularity of the movie and television series *Fame* has brought New York's LaGuardia High School of the Performing Arts national recognition. However, the recently organized network of performing arts high schools indicates that there may be at least one and possibly more accredited secondary schools of the arts in practically every state in the Union.

Most of the schools require an audition and a certain academic excellence as entrance criteria. Others are not as stringent or sophisticated. It is exciting to know that the individual states have responded to the need for specialized training centers for artistically motivated teenagers.

A selected list of performing arts high schools is included in the Appendix. If there is no school listed for your neighborhood, inquire of the local school authorities. We hope the network will continue to expand.

You should also investigate opportunities at community theaters dedicated to young people.

THE WALDEN THEATRE

We think you should know about a very special organization in Louisville, Kentucky. The Walden Theatre was founded in 1976 by producing director Nancy Niles Sexton. The theater trains young people from grades four through twelve in acting and writing. Its

Theatre in the Making program, instituted as a showcase for young talent within the company, offers productions of new works by young playwrights and classics adapted and directed by the students. The Folk Heritage program produces dramatic plays based upon Kentucky's rich historical heritage. The professional theater training program offers afternoon, evening, and Saturday classes in movement, voice, improvisation, vocal music, playwriting, and auditioning. Graduating seniors of the Walden Theatre receive special attention in college selection.

Performing is part of an actor's training: Walden Theatre offers four productions during the regular season, October through May; a summer academy performs in July. Advanced students have the opportunity to perform in the annual Humana Festival of New Plays at the prestigious Actors' Theatre of Louisville. They also audition for roles in major motion pictures and television.

The theater sponsors seminars with actors, playwrights, and musicians. Classes have been taught by Nicholas Pennell of the Stratford Ontario Shakespeare Festival, voice specialist Robert Dunn, playwright John Pielmeier (*Agnes of God*), and actress Patricia Neal, as well as other outstanding professionals.

Walden Theatre is supported in part by grants from the Kentucky Arts Council and the Council and the Community Arts Council of the Greater Louisville Fund for the Arts, as well as various other corporations and individuals.

Nancy Niles Sexton has worked with young performers for more than twenty years and is recognized as one of the outstanding drama teachers in the country. She has lectured and conducted workshops for the Stratford Ontario Shakespearean Festival Foundation, the Arts Councils of Kentucky, Indiana, and Illinois, as well as resident theater training projects at Boston University School of the Theatre and the California Institute of the Arts. She produced the first Shakespeare festival by and for young people in the state of Kentucky and directed the AFTRA award-winning production of *The Taming of the Shrew*. She has also won several writing awards.

It is hoped that the Walden Theatre, as a caring unit designed to afford talented young people the opportunity to gain a solid foundation in the performing arts, will inspire similar programs in cities throughout the country.

Samples of original audition pieces written by the Walden Theatre's promising young actor-writers appear in chapter 15.

INCREASING OPPORTUNITIES

Outside Los Angeles and New York there are agents or casting offices in cities throughout the country who are informed of the television and theater jobs locally available. Some of them have video equipment and are frequently contacted by East Coast or West Coast casting directors to screen-test local talent and then send those tapes to them for consideration.

Movies for television, miniseries, and feature films shot on location will employ young actors from those areas to give authenticity to the project. The little boy and girl who played Sally Field's children in *Places in the Heart* were discovered in Texas.

Carmen Thomas (Hilary on *All My Children*) had just graduated from Northside High School for the Performing Arts in Atlanta when her agent put her on videotape at the request of the ABC casting department.

Deborah Morehart (Robin McCall on *All My Children*) enrolled in a Dallas soap opera workshop conducted by the show's casting director, Joan D'Incecco. Her class scene was videotaped and shown to the ABC-Daytime programming executives as well as to producer Jacqueline Babbin. The young actress was flown to New York, tested, and won the part.

A ten-year-old boy from Portland, Maine, was seen in a college production of *All My Sons* at the northeastern regional competition of the American College Theatre Festival. His stage presence, concentration, and timing were impressive to a network casting executive, and the boy got the chance to audition for a major children's series.

In all these cases, the common denominator is that the young people were all taking classes, attending professional schools, and actively performing in their communities. They were prepared for the audition.

In New York, a marvelous curriculum of courses is offered by the Weist-Barron School's Teen Division. Director Rita Litton, whose acting career began at UCLA and San Francisco's American Conservatory Theatre, has appeared in more than a hundred roles off Broadway, in regional, stock, and dinner theaters across the country. She has extensive television credits and has taught improvisation classes and advanced commercial workshops and has consistently been recommended by industry professionals. She has staffed the teen division with working actors and qualified teachers who understand the demands of the business and who respect young actors. They help the students realize their uniqueness and creative potential. Courses are offered in speech, commercial technique, and how to audition for film, soap, musical comedy, and theater. She prescreens the applicants to weed out those she feels are not completely dedicated to pursuing acting careers. Students from fifteen states and Europe, recommended by more than thirty agents and talent managers, have attended the teen workshops.

The classes are small so the actors can receive individual attention. A class in beginning commercial technique explored sense memory through exercises using mimed products, problems and solutions in commercial messages, understanding the character relationships and using real not forced energy, and benefited from video playbacks. There was an equal sharing of focus. One homework assignment featured three different interpretations of a one-liner slogan and the motivations. The students were very adaptable and positive, and their teachers treated them as people and young professionals.

SAFEGUARDS

If you are in doubt about a teacher's qualifications, if you find that certain schools are interested only in financial profits, or if they make false promises, report them to the local attorney general's office, the department of consumer affairs, or any local union office. There are a lot of get-rich-quick entrepreneurs who prey on naive parents and may be wanted in six states. Beware of them.

There are state laws to protect working children. The Children's Committee of Screen Actors Guild has assembled an information packet that states "the rules about obtaining work permits in the entertainment industry for children from birth to 18 years of age are quite explicit and in many cases difficult." It continues:

The work permit application must be signed by a qualified employer before the Labor Board will accept it. The application must also have the signature of a doctor who has examined the child within the six weeks prior to applying for the permit. The application must also be signed by the principal or teacher at the school your child attends.

Many times, in addition to this, the labor board will require you to produce the child's latest report card or progress report. The first time a child applies for a permit, he or she must appear in person at the labor board office. There is no charge for this permit, but it must be kept up to date because the child cannot work without it. Remember, if your child's grades slip below a C average, the work permit will not be renewed.

The packet contains important safety rules where stunts are involved or where there is any potential health hazard. There is general information about preparation before you get to the interview and when you arrive; a checklist for the workday, including getting homework from the child's school for the teacher on the set and having three hours of schoolwork for your child to do; arranging for an authorized guardian if you can't accompany your child; the dos and don'ts on the set; and rules about unemployment and education. There are sections entitled Studio Teacher/Labor Law Representative Parent Evaluation Form; Teacher's Hints for Parents; Agents' Hints; Theatrical Contract Summary; Commercial Code Definitions; Commercial Contract Summary; and a State by State Summary of Laws, Rules and Regulations Applicable to the Employment of Minors as Actors in the Film Industry.

This guide was compiled in March 1983. Some laws may have changed, but the basic rules remain the same. For a copy of the packet, write to: Screen Actors Guild, 7750 Sunset Boulevard, Los Angeles, CA 90046.

It is extremely important that the pursuit of a career does not upstage education. They should *grow* hand in hand. Studies in science, languages, social sciences, history, geography, and English literature expand the mind, open the doors to the imagination, provide comparisons, and increase comprehension of the peoples and religions of the world. This awareness will produce better actors and more enlightened, articulate, and well-developed adults. The professional standards of the future are formed during these years.

There are thousands of successful, working children and teens, but one young person's dedication to his craft is a striking example of what it takes to make it and to keep growing.

Robert MacNaughton, at eighteen, was interviewed by Gary Ballard of *Drama-Logue*. He had been a professional for six years. He had performed in numerous stage productions including *The Diviners* at the Circle Repertory Theatre in New York and in *Henry V* with Kevin Kline for the New York Shakespeare Festival. Among his screen credits was the portrayal of the older brother in the Spielberg classic, *E.T.* He has the distinction of becoming the youngest member of the Circle Repertory Theatre's resident company.

Robert's grandmother declared that he knew he wanted to be an entertainer at the tender age of two and a half when he fashioned a microphone out of a spoon and did a Tom Jones imitation. His ideas about film, television, and the stage are very focused and epitomize what the aspiration of every dedicated young professional should be:

I find the speed of TV frustrating because you can have a good director, a good script, but not the time to explore. Even in film you can rehearse it a few times. Sometimes in TV, I'll say, "Can we reshoot that because I'm not satisfied with what I did?" They'll answer, "Sorry, we can't. It was okay." In TV I find myself wondering what happened with the last scene instead of thinking ahead and getting ready for the next one. . . .

I've seen E.T. seven or eight times, but I don't think I'll watch it again. I'm too critical of my performance. I keep seeing things I'd do differently.

I want to do stage all my life. I got a little cocky after I'd done some TV and movies, but when I went back to stage and realized how hard it is, I knew that is where I'm constantly learning.
(Drama-Logue, August 29–September 4, 1985)

Parents whose children have become popular in any or all phases of the entertainment industry know the hard road it took to get there: the hours spent driving the child to classes, the waits, the auditions that seemed interminable, baby-sitter fees, meals out, clothing expenses, class costs, photographs and résumés, the sacrifice of a personal life just so these efforts could be made. The rewards are obvious: a trust fund for college, working with celebrities from the stage and screen, first-class treatment, travel to a variety of locations, help with family finances, and most gratifying, the pride in talent being recognized.

Part 3
Script Analysis

In this and the next few chapters, we offer you the chance to work on new material—the same kind of copy you will be called upon to read or perform at an audition for a play, a repertory company, a commercial, a soap opera, or a film.

These pieces of copy are, in a sense, waiting for you to bring them to life. They are not snippets from standard, classic plays or contemporary hit shows; no one's previous performance has been stamped on any of this material. They are all as new as your next thought. So you are free to make any choices you can think of to illuminate the text.

Chapter 15
The Theater Audition

MONOLOGUES, DUOLOGUES, AND DIALOGUES

In her acclaimed book *Respect for Acting*, the brilliant actress and teacher Uta Hagen defined the *monologue* as "an actor talking to himself out loud, or to absent characters, or to objects surrounding him at a given time in a given place for a specific reason at a moment of crisis." Even though the words must be heard in the last row of the balcony, the monologue "will always be words that represent the character's thoughts or a part of his thoughts."

Only when you are talking aloud when *alone* is it a monologue. Anything else is a *dialogue*.

When someone can talk back to you with a look, a snort, a yawn, by turning away, by smiling, by giving you a concentrated look of attention (as in Strindberg's play *The Stronger*, which consists of one actress's long speech, punctuated by the reactions of the person she is talking to, who speaks no words) that is actually a dialogue.

The term *duologue* is used to define those times when an actor is called upon to talk to the *audience*. The audience becomes the actor's partner.

In accord with Ms. Hagen's definitions, this chapter will focus on one *mono*logue, three *duo*logues, and four *dia*logues.

Any of these selections can serve as audition material for agents or casting directors or as class exercises.

The four short pieces which follow are extracted from two full evenings of theater, *Glimpses* and *Rites*, created by the young playwrights at the Walden Theatre. The full texts can be obtained from the publisher, and they may be performed upon payment of a royalty. For texts and/or permission to present these works, write to: The Dramatic Publishing Company, P.O. Box 109, Woodstock, Illinois 60098.

A MONOLOGUE SELECTION

An original member of the Walden Theatre Company, Charles Sexton was seventeen when he wrote *Hut, Hut* as part of the Young Playwrights Program. At eighteen, he coauthored *Point/Counterpoint*, a one-act play published by the Dramatic Publishing Company. He has recently received a degree in theater from Southern Methodist University, performed at the Dallas Shakespeare Festival, and served as a summer intern/teacher for the Children's & Teen Theatre at the Dallas Theatre Center.

HUT, HUT by Charles Sexton

CHARLIE *(running in).* Hut, hut, hut . . . *(He takes a football stance.)* Down, set, hut, hut, hut. *(He mimes the action.)* Charlie takes the ball from Center . . . Drops . . . He's going to pass, ladies and gentlemen! No, folks, he's going to run with it! *(He mimes more action and moves to C on the sidewalk.)* Oh, my gosh . . . he plows over the whole defensive line for the T.D.! *(He mimes "spiking" the ball.)* The fans go absolutely bananas! Oh, yes! Thank you, thank you. They mob him and carry him on their shoulders. *(He mimes the action . . . then slowly removes his football helmet and takes a solemn pose.)* The mayor presents him with the key to the city. *(He mimes receiving the key.)* Oh, thank you, mister mayor . . . and thank you, beautiful people . . . but now . . . *(He dons the helmet again.)* He must play defense. The fans return to their seats. A hush falls over the stadium as we kick off. *(He mimes the action.)* Touchback! First play at scrimmage . . . Charlie at linebacker . . . every eye riveted on the "rumbling wrecking machine" . . . the opposing quarterback calls the cadence. Down . . . set . . . Charlie is poised, ladies and gentlemen . . . hut, hut. The play. A thirty-yard drive up the middle! Charlie plunges the hole and *slams into the fullback popping the ball loose like a kidney stone, picks it up and rumbles for the T.D.! Oh, ladies and gentlemen! The induction committee for the Pro Football Hall of Fame has just announced that the Louisville kid, Charlie, will be inducted today. What a day for Charlie! Thank you. Thank you.*

Analysis of Hut, Hut

Character: Charlie, teen

Charlie's dream is to be inducted into the Pro Football Hall of Fame. He is not addressing the audience or another person. He is in his own world, a world he has created of football heroes, pivotal passes, crowd worship, keys to the city, the strategy that leads to the winning touchdown, and his acceptance speech. We watch all the moves; we hear his dream, but for Charlie, we don't exist. This is his secret world, like that of James Thurber's Walter Mitty.

The actor who uses this monologue should *connect* with the sport. Only if you fully understand the game will the language and the actions be believable. There is a specific rhythm and timing to the "Hut, hut, hut" and "Down, set, hut, hut, hut." The attack at the start is bursting with energy and that must be present to carry you through to the final thirty-yard drive up the middle to the touchdown! There should be a breath following that line before the speech to the imaginary crowd. You could use your own name and town in this audition piece to make it your own. Use it as the humorous selection.

If you were to write your own monologue, this is a wonderful prototype for a range of sports events: a swimming competition, a tennis match, a baseball game, or any athletic feat that you enjoy or do well.

THREE DUOLOGUES

Remember that the term *duologue* is used to define those times when an actor is called upon to talk to the audience.

DUOLOGUE #1

After joining the Walden Theatre in the seventh grade, Ned Oldham wrote *The Box* when he was thirteen. His work was selected by Jon Jory, producing director of Actors' Theatre of Louisville for presentation at the Humana Festival of New American Plays as part of Walden Theatre's *New Generation.*

THE BOX by Ned Oldham

(The ACTOR enters in the darkness and begins speaking in the darkness.)
ACTOR. My dad has a box. It's little. About like this. *(Quick lights up in small pool, revealing ACTOR sitting on a stool.)* There's something in it, it's heavy, real heavy for being so small. I can't open it. It's locked and Dad's lost the key. He said that the thing that's in it doesn't have a name. He has the only one like it. The box stays in my dad's *closet.* It leaves little marks in the closet from the metal studs all over it. He'll never show me what's in it. I know he won't. He says he will, though. He says nothing important is in it. He won't show me, though. He says someday when he dies that I can have the box but I don't want it. I just want to see what's inside, I think! Yes, that's all. I only want to see and I want him to show me. I don't want to have to see it by myself. I wonder why he won't show me? Nothing can be that good or bad, I don't think! It's not being able to know what it is that makes me want to know. It's not my curiosity that makes it so bad. It's that my dad won't tell me. I wouldn't be satisfied if I found out what was in it. I need him to show me. *It's his box.* *(beat)* I'll get my own box and put something in it, then I'll lose the key.

Analysis of The Box

Character: Teen, male or female

This is a naturally written and realistic account about a mysterious box in the closet. You should be able to relate to this person's curiosity. We've all experienced a desire to know why a door was locked, a drawer was never opened, or something was placed specifically beyond our reach.

Put yourself in that frame of mind. See the box. It has metal studs that "leave little marks in the closet." How small is it? Feel the heaviness of it. Find the closet. What else is in it? What does it smell like? Moth balls? Tobacco? After-shave? Musk? Use your own dad. Think about his telling you he lost the key, that he has the only one like it, and that when he dies, you can have that box.

The actor is verbalizing his thoughts and suspicion and wonderment about this box. He just doesn't understand why his dad won't show him or tell him what is in the box. He doesn't want to discover it for himself. He wants his dad to show him. He wants his dad to relate to him and to trust him. In talking about it, in getting it off his chest, he makes a discovery! He'll get his own box and put something in it . . . then lose the key.

This final point cannot be anticipated. It must come as a solution to the box, as if he had just discovered it.

When you start this duologue, you must break it down into moments or thought groups. You must sound natural and extremely sincere and the speaking rhythm has to be conversational!

As a practice exercise, describe an *object* that you know in your own home: an object you admire, perhaps a vase, a perfume bottle, a sports trophy, a clock, a painting, a chandelier, an ornate book, a hat, a cigar box, and so forth. Describe every detail of it. Explain why it means so much to you. Then add a dash of mystery to the object. Give it a shady past. Perhaps it is an heirloom. Use your imagination and share your feelings, create a problem and find a resolution. Use *The Box* as a model and be inventive. The key to understanding *The Box* is simplicity. It's not out to impress with fancy language or an elevated tone. It follows a logical thought process. Avoid complication and you'll discover truth!

DUOLOGUE #2

Caroline White was fifteen when she wrote *Happy Birthday*. She is currently a liberal arts/English major at Princeton University. She is a member of the staff of the student literary magazine. Her work has been published in *Rites* by the Dramatic Publishing Company.

HAPPY BIRTHDAY by Caroline White

The curtain is up. The stage is dark. Light comes up by way of a match lit in the darkness of a full-stage blackout. We see the face of a young girl in the light. She lights birthday candles. As the area spot slowly rises, we hear:

GIRL
(singing)
Happy Birthday to Claire . . .
Happy Birthday to Claire . . .
Happy Birthday to Claire . . .
Happy Birthday to me . . .
(Lights up full in spot. The girl holds one birthday candle in her hand and she blows it out at the end of her song. Beside her are a litter of pictures, some birthday candles and a scrapbook. She sits on the floor.)

GIRL
Sixteen . . . sixteen candles . . . I'm the only person my age in the world who's never been on a date.
(She drops the candle and lights another and begins to sing again.)
Happy Birthday to me . . . *(spoken)* well . . . not on a real date . . .
(She blows out second candle.)
I mean, like, I go to parties and movies with my friends, but no guy has ever called me up and asked me out . . .
(She shuffles through her pictures. She finds a newspaper clipping of a high school athlete from the sports page. She practically faints at the sight of the picture as she begins gushing about him.)
Oh, God, he's so gorgeous . . .
(She shows the picture to the audience.)
His name's Ben, and he's got blond hair and bright blue eyes that make me melt every time I see him . . . *(She gazes at the picture.)*
And one time I was standing in back of him in the lunch line . . .
(She raises the picture slowly to her nose and inhales deeply.)
and I could smell his after-shave, even above the lasagna . . . It smelled . . . just like he should smell.
(She places the clipping in her scrapbook.)
Anyway, Ben called me one Thursday night a few months ago. I was so excited! My stomach . . . my stomach did four flips. He asked me for the math homework . . . 'cause he had slept through class . . . and . . . I knew it was just a way of starting the conversation. Well . . . it wasn't. He just said, "Thanks a lot. 'Bye."
(She embraces a Pizza Hut menu from her scrapbook.)
Well . . . I have gone on a sort of date. It was set up . . . by my friend . . . My friend Jan. She got this boy she knows to come pick me up and take me to a movie and then to Pizza Hut. He was okay-looking . . . medium-tall . . . brown hair . . . brown eyes . . . Nothing

special, but okay-looking. We didn't talk on the way to the movie or all through it. What can you say to someone you don't know? He didn't smell of anything, like . . . well . . . after-shave . . . No . . . a . . . bright blue eyes . . . When we got to Pizza Hut we had a deep dish pizza with pepperoni and mushrooms and sausage . . . and even anchovies . . . disgusting . . . But he wanted them . . . so we had them. And onions . . . on the first date . . . onions . . . God! We ordered, or rather he ordered . . . and then . . . well, silence. God! What to say! Well, *something* had to be said . . . so . . . I asked him what classes he was taking, and he said . . .

(She takes a piece of paper from her collection and reads from it.)

English, French, precalculus, physics . . .

(She flings the paper aside.)

Or something incredible like that. And I said, "Oh." He didn't ask me anything. He just answered my questions . . . like he didn't even care about me. What a DUD! I was bored to death! Why? Tell me why Jan would set me up with that STUD! er, I mean dud, dud . . . She must think I'm really desperate or something! I don't want her feeling sorry for me! It's not like I'm a social outcast or anything!

(She hums a few bars of "Happy Birthday" while rummaging through her scrapbook.)

I go out with my friends for God's sake . . . *(She stops short.)* But not with guys. I mean on dates . . . I . . . a . . . guess . . . well, maybe . . . maybe they just don't like me . . . I'm not . . . desirable . . . I guess I'll just go through high school . . . without a . . . date.

(She lights another birthday candle.)

Maybe college, too . . . I just wait every day for THAT phone call . . . Everyone else gets them.

(The lights go down slowly.)

Why not me?

(She blows out the candle as we BLACKOUT.)

Analysis of Happy Birthday

Character: Female, sixteen

The problem Claire experiences in this piece is universal. What "sweet sixteen" doesn't think about dates, popularity, the blond, blue-eyed jock who smells of sexy after-shave? At this age, the greatest fear is the thought of sitting home waiting for the phone to ring. Claire is obsessed with Ben. Anyone else, like her blind date, is just "okay-looking." She realizes Ben has used her crush on him to get her math homework. That leaves her vulnerable to her friend Jan's matchmaking. She describes the date in great detail: the pizza with the anchovies ("disgusting") and onions ("on the first date . . . God!"); the horrible silence. She was forced to keep the conversation going when it was apparent he had no interest in her. The result was boredom and her questioning why her friend would set her up with such a dud. She doesn't want pity, but she feels undesirable and unliked and considers her situation to be hopeless.

This is an excellent example of character revelation. You can substitute your own name and experience and your scrapbook memorabilia . . . to remind you of dates and dinners or Pizza Huts, blind dates, phone calls, the first kiss, junior prom, and so forth. Create a real place, mood, situation.

This duologue has several major transitions in thought and feeling. The first one occurs after she says "but no guy has ever called me up and asked me out." Ben's picture causes a change. She shares her feelings with the audience. Use sense memory for the smells of after-shave and lasagna. Picture the cafeteria lunch line. The mood change is cued by placing the clipping in the scrapbook. "Anyway, Ben called me one Thursday." Another change on "Well . . . it wasn't." Then there is the change cued by the Pizza Hut Menu. "Well . . . I have gone on a sort of date." This detailed description of the date should be animated and believable! You are sharing the moments with us. Next change: "Why? Tell me why Jan would set me up with that STUD! er, I mean dud, dud." Here she shows her sense of humor. Humor is the element that will keep Claire from complete despair. If she can get through high school, she'll probably blossom in college. She is bright and witty. Someone will connect with her personality down the road.

As an actress, try not to give in to self-pity. There is a drop in energy in the last section. The character goes from "I go out with my friends for God's sake . . . But not with guys" to "Why not me?" There is a sense of low-key frustration. Rehearse this part in the mirror. Believe it!

DUOLOGUE #3

Ruth Jacobson was fifteen when she wrote *Angie's Song* for Walden Theatre's Young Playwrights Project. She began her training at the Walden Theatre in the sixth grade. Her work is published in *Rites*. She majored in theater at Southern Methodist University and continues to write plays. Her latest, *Roberta/George*, will be showcased during Walden Theatre's Young Playwrights '86.

ANGIE'S SONG by Ruth Jacobson

GIRL. I guess I've always been of "dubious reputation" as my minister puts it. I never thought much about the rights or wrongs of it all when I was panting in the backseat of someone's car. It wasn't that I especially enjoyed it. If you want to know the truth, it was more like mild distaste. I never heard any bells. I don't know why I did it. I just didn't mind it. I got lots of friends that way, I guess.

I always was really careful—I was on the "pill" since eighth grade. I never missed it. But then—I don't know what happened. My dad started giving me a bunch of garbage about my life. He always does that, but it was really starting to bother me. It wasn't much—he'd slap me around a little and then tell me to go away . . . and I would. I'd go right to Steve's or Phil's or Mike's and just go to it.

Well, around that time I kind of stopped taking the "pill." I kept forgetting, and finally I ran out and didn't refill my prescription. I thought I could last a little while without it. Well, I sure didn't. When I found out I was pregnant I didn't cry. I don't know how I felt—kind of relieved. I didn't feel any of that "miracle of life" bull that you're supposed to. I just felt kind of relieved, like I'd finally done something right. I don't know. That's kinda dumb, I guess.

Well, my dad wanted me to get an abortion. I couldn't. I said I wouldn't and he got mad again. I racked him, and I mean HARD, and I ran out of the house blubbering like a jerk. Later that night I called from a pay phone and Mom kept askin' me to come home. I had to. I didn't have a job or anything.

Everything went fine. Then I was getting really big, about six months along. My dad got mad. The toothpaste was missing. He got so mad he pushed me down the stairs—by accident. I screamed. It hurt so much—like someone taking a knife and scraping out your insides. I just kept screaming and screaming. I think I was bleeding. My mom called an ambulance, and I think I kept screaming until they clapped that mask over my face and whisked me away . . .

I had a fracture in my elbow. Angie wasn't so lucky. She was so far along, they could see her face and everything. I didn't see it but I know she was very pretty. I know she was smart, too. When we were alone I would talk with her. She would bump around and I would talk to her and everything . . . she was a good kid, I know . . .

Now I just kinda walk around. Above it all. Nobody bothers me. Nobody touches me. I still talk with my Angie. I don't know what I'll do. I don't know if I care. I don't know. *(Lights slowly out . . .)*

Analysis of Angie's Song

Character: Female, fifteen to seventeen

This confession could be shared with an audience or one person. The girl could be talking to an old friend. It is important not to play it to elicit sympathy. She has accepted what has happened to her until that final acknowledgment where she says, "Now I just kinda walk around." We realize she hasn't let the baby die. It is here we realize how alone she is.

She is very direct about her promiscuity. The pill started in eighth grade. Her dad has been berating her about her life, and his abuse would send her to the "backseats." Her ignorance about the pill helped get her into trouble. We must understand her when she says, "I'd finally done something right." She stood up to her father on the abortion issue. She ran away, but she had to return because she had no place to go. There is a great deal of pain, emotional as well as physical, in her life. Yet when she describes her father's violence and beating, she is not judgmental. This was the way it happened. Her suffering was intense; the screams were real. Yet it was her mother who called the ambulance. Where was her father?

She will never be the same after the death of Angie. The poignancy of her story and the depth of her feelings are truly realized if the actress chooses not to bring attention to it by commenting on emotional choices or becoming too self-indulgent. Let it happen, let it unfold. Don't play results.

Imagine what it would be like to live in a loveless home. Imagine not having a childhood. Do you have a close friend or relative who has had a similar experience? As a sense memory exercise, put a cushion under your dress. Observe in the mirror how pregnancy would alter your shape; practice sitting, rising, lying down. Take the cushion away abruptly. Project the loneliness by simply being quiet and reflective. Think about an ambulance, an emergency room, anesthesia, bright lights, strangers in white, the cold of an operating room. Visit a hospital; sit in a waiting room. Get a sense of place.

Write a duologue describing in detail an accident you witnessed, a fight you observed in your neighborhood, a schoolroom brawl, a verbal tirade you overheard, a scolding you received from your parents—any conflict you can relate to. Make us see it and hear it with you. You will increase your understanding of how to give truth and meaning to *Angie's Song*.

FOUR DIALOGUES

Each of the following selections is excerpted from a complete play. Each character is talking to someone who might yawn, smile, cry, turn away, giggle, start to interrupt, or even leave the room.

In the audition you have to focus on an object or an empty chair for an imagined physical presence.

You must concentrate on whom you are trying to reach.

Alice Spivak, one of New York's finest acting teachers and coaches, suggests three ways to achieve this concentration:

1. Make believe you are rehearsing the speech to tell the person on your next encounter.
2. Imagine that the person you are talking to is in an adjoining room or behind a screen.
3. Put yourself at a mirror where the person you are addressing is behind you and you are talking to the mirror image.

In your mind the other person must be fully pictured and specific.

William Hathaway, the author of the material in this section, received an MFA from Catholic University in Washington, D.C., in 1981. He has won the Joseph P. Kesselring Playwriting Award twice for his plays *Bless Me, Father* and *That One Talent*. His plays have been performed in New York and in Washington, D.C. We are deeply grateful to him for allowing us to use his work in your behalf.

Any inquiries about the plays should be addressed to the author: William Hathaway, 1128 Garden Street, Hoboken, NJ 07030.

DIALOGUE #1

Father O'Brien in *BLESS ME, FATHER* by William Hathaway

FATHER O'BRIEN: If you haven't been around the stockyards, you haven't been to Chicago. Meat stinks, Father. Worse than any of your automobile factories. Of course growin' up next door to the meat plants, you don't really think about it. It's a smell and that's it. Besides those yards gave my brother and me something to do. Every Saturday morning we'd walk over to where they unloaded the cows. And we'd do what kids do when they see cows.

(O'Brien lows.)

Mooooooooo. Mooooooooo. But this one Saturday on our way to greet the cattle, I said something that my brother didn't like and he squared off and punched me in the mouth. Son of a bitch. Of course, Thomas being older and bigger, I wisely turned around and roared home—bleeding, crying and accusing. Mother immediately took charge. She slapped me a good one to stop my crying and then she ordered Thomas inside and gave him a good whack. Then she got a cold, clean, wet cloth and stood directly over him while he cleaned my lip. And she made him apologize. Which he did. And she made me forgive him. Which I did. Then she sent us into her room. That usually meant the brush, followed by two rosaries, on our knees and out loud. But not that day. She sat on the edge of her bed and pulled me up and to her left and put Thomas on her right. Well, my mother wasn't much for words. Dad influenced that. God love him. She simply said, "Thomas, do you want to be the doctor or the priest?" He didn't even blink. "Doctor," he said. Son of a bitch. Then she turned to me and said, "James, you'll be the priest. Now go on, both of you, get out."

(O'Brien pours himself another drink.)

And, no, I'm not saying it's in the stars. When I took my vows, it was my decision. But I am saying, Father Mosley, that he called on me and you, long before we made any decision to call on him. So believe me, man, you're already spoken for. If you really love this girl, you tell her to go away.

Analysis of Father O'Brien

Character: Father O'Brien, character actor, fifty to sixty

The pastor is an alcoholic. Although he is drunk during this dialogue, his thoughts are still coherent.

The play *Bless Me, Father* deals with a young, revolutionary priest, Father Mosley, who has fallen in love with a young woman. He is struggling with the decision whether or not to remain a priest. Father O'Brien, his pastor, has just found out about the affair. In this speech, he confronts Father Mosley.

It is important that the actor practice degrees of inebriation. Start with extreme lack of control and work backward, slowly, to trying not to let anyone know you are out of control. Work on this exercise physically and vocally.

An alcoholic will never admit that he has a problem. He is a moderate drinker, not a lush.

Father O'Brien is a victim of frustration, bitterness, personal failure, and self-pity. Although he loved his family, his childhood was difficult with a domineering father, a strong mother, and an older brother with a temper. He tells the story of his brother's attack and his mother's decision to give him the vocation in order to make a point with the love-struck priest. He implores him to put his personal feelings aside, to remember he was called by God to serve Him, and to give up the young woman.

O'Brien is a human being underneath the priestly robes. He is from a poor neighborhood of Chicago. He would say "son of a bitch," and when under the influence, more than once. We have here a flesh-and-blood, imperfect man, capable of harsh language and submitting to alcohol. He is colorful.

This dialogue is a good exercise for storytelling, sense memory, and variety.

DIALOGUE #2

Henry in *THAT ONE TALENT* by William Hathaway

HENRY

You're only here because I let you feel sorry for me. I wanted you to feel sorry for me. "Poor Henry, he can't go beyond imitation. He's nature's dupe." I went to the library. I looked up *dupe*. It means the same as fool. And that's what I've been. But not nature's dupe. I let myself be your dupe. Just a big, dumb dupe.

(He takes a finger painting from the wall.)

Will you look at this? Look what I've let you do to me. Finger painting. In Sister Charles Borromeo's art class this wouldn't be on

the bulletin board. It would be in the wastepaper basket. And that
was second grade.
   (*Henry crumples the painting and tosses it on the floor.*)
You know, I know that you know more than I know. But what gets
me is the way you have of letting me know that you know . . . more.
Hey. I didn't put in a request to be born in the Upper Peninsula.
How would you like it if you'd been born in Iron City, Michigan,
and say I'd been born in Parlee-poopoo, France, and I was the one
with all the learning about history and poetry and art and how one
day someone does this and the next day someone does that and it
leads to wherever we are now and tomorrow. But do you think I'd've
made a dupe out of you?
   (*Henry makes his way over to the still-life composition of green
   balloons.*)
And these balloons prove I know exactly what I'm talking about.
You know I like balloons so you brought a bunch along. But not
just because I like them, but because you can use them to help me
get to my soul. So you can say, "Henry, you're a sucker for balloons.
But why? Look closely at them, and as you come to realize why you
like them, I want you to paint. But don't paint the balloons you see,
paint the balloons that you don't see." What'd you call it this morning? "The balloon of my mind"? Yeh. "Paint the balloon of your
mind and find the true meaning behind the balloons or beyond the
balloons or better yet, inside the balloons." Ann, my dear, you might
not understand what I'm about to say, since I'm about to state a
fact. I know what's inside a balloon. It's the same thing that you're
so full of. Sad but true. Air, air, only air.

Analysis of Henry in That One Talent

Character: Henry McPeak, twenty-five to thirty

   The play *That One Talent* is a comedy. The time is 1954. Henry
McPeak is a realistic painter who has been taking art lessons from
Ann Theofilopolous, an abstract painter, because he loves her and
it's the only way she would agree to see him.
   Desperate to find out if she cares for him, he plots with another
woman to see if they can get a rise out of her. Completely misreading
her smile to mean that she doesn't care for him, he lets off all that
has been building since the lessons began.
   This is a "moment of truth" dialogue as well as a confrontation.
The feelings are on the table. What are you, who have provoked
me to this "moment," going to do about it?

Henry not only claims he allowed himself to be duped by her approach to painting, but he now feels impelled to tell her what he thinks of it and that makes him aware of her personal feelings. She, like the balloons, is full of air.

His straightforwardness and openness are what ultimately win her over.

Find his sense of humor, and don't be afraid to expose his vulnerability.

DIALOGUE #3

Mo from *A CROOKED FLOWER* by William Hathaway

MO

Mom, after I told you and Daddy what you could do with your expectations of me, I came down here and I thought I had it made. I was where it was at, right at the bottom. This is where I'd make the difference. I got a job tending bar, and for a while I'd paint furiously during the day and work and play just as furiously at night. But it seems I forgot about sleep and pretty soon it caught up with me. I stopped painting. Just sleep, work, party and sleep . . . Then I met Scott. Talk about a rush. Can't be anything better than the first few weeks of being in love. Can't be. He was beautiful. Brown eyes to hypnotize and the smoothest skin, so black it was blue. But color aside, he was my spittin' image. From money, best schools, sky's the limit potential, all that crap. Princeton, 1963. And three years later he had a room above a liquor store and was writing poetry about junkies and whores and magazines like the *New Yorker* were lapping it up. He was perfect. A match made in heaven, as you'd say, Mom. He got me to cool out my night life and got so damn excited about my art, it scared me. I'd anguish over every painting wondering whether or not he'd give it his seal of approval. He was the one who put me in touch with the gallery in New York that still gurgles over anything I churn out. Mom, what he was doing with his poetry I wanted to do with my art. Reach out and shake up all of you that we'd left behind. "Hey, we're down here and we're making it!" I saw the future perfectly. My painting and his poetry and from out of the ashes of Detroit, beauty and truth.

(Mo laughs softly.)

It was September. Almost two years? Hot and humid and I couldn't work. So I walked over to Scott's. Up the stairs that had more steps missing than steps. I had to kick open the door. He never locked it. Just the heat made it stick. He was there. Sitting on the floor. He never sat on the furniture. I don't know if he heard me come in or not, it didn't seem to matter. He was only interested in finding a vein. I watched. He'd put the needle in, pull it out, put it in, pull it out. When he finally hit one, he let out a sigh of a relief and looked up at me and shrugged. I turned around and closed the door, jumped over the missing steps, and walked fast through the streets. And back here, I threw up. Just threw up. It turns out everybody on the street knew, except me. Talk about your little girl in pigtails. Mom, I thought he had a handle on this place, but all this time it had him. And if it could get him, it could certainly get me.

Analysis of Mo in A Crooked Flower

Character: Maureen (Mo) Boisvert, female, twenty to twenty-five

Mo resides in a crime and drug-infested area of Detroit. The year is 1969 and she's been living there for three years. Coming from a well-protected environment, her ignorance about certain people and situations slowly comes to light. Her first affair was one of her first lessons. In this dialogue, she tells her mother about it.

This young woman has had an awakening. All of her idealism has been shattered by a drugged-out lover's insensitivity. Yet she has learned from it and related the joy and the pain in exacting, vivid detail. Imagine talking to your own mother about an affair that turned sour. Scott must be alive in your mind as the photograph he may have given you. Perhaps as an artist you painted him. This is a woman who paints pictures with words.

Paint the building where you lived, the room, the liquor store, hear the street sounds, imagine the smells, the horror at finding your lover "shooting up," seeing the "sky's the limit potential" burned out.

Think about the nausea and the gradual realization, the moment of truth, and the sense of triumph that you were strong enough to "close the door."

This is not a character plagued by remorse or full of despair. She is strong, rebellious, crusading, vulnerable, and filled with pride. Find her humor.

DIALOGUE #4

Kate Love in *A CROOKED FLOWER* by William Hathaway

(Kate is helping decorate the Christmas tree. One ornament catches her eye.)

KATE

Richie made an ornament somethin' like this. Oh yeh, it reminds me of our first Christmas together. It seems like just yesterday now. Yeh, about a week before that Christmas, we had this real bad ice storm, and I was hurryin' around the apartment gettin' ready for work. Because I knew those buses'd be slow and I'd be late. I had to ride two buses when I worked at that ol' Big Boy over at Six Mile and Woodrow Wilson. Anyway, Richie come a huffin' and a puffin' in from school and he run right inta the bafroom and yells, "Mama!" He was only five years ol'. "Mama, am I a good boy?" "Child," I says, "the worl' didn't know good until you was born." "I know, Mama, and I tol' Miss Fisher you tell me that. But, Mama, could you get hold of this man called Sanda Claws and tell him what you tell me. Because this man he got a red suit and a white beard, Mama, and he a white man. And he been goin' to all the boys and girls since they was babies. He even go to Ralf's house and Ralf's bad, real bad. Even Miss Fisher says he bad . . . Mama, this man Sanda Claws, he only come when we sleepin' and he ridin' around in the sky on sompin' like horses, but they ain't horses 'cause they got ears that look like dead trees. And then he parks the horses on the roof and then he come down the chimney or through the fire escape, whatever the best way. And, Mama, he got a bag full of toys, candy, gum and everythin'. But ya got to bring a tree inside, a Christmas tree, real soon. You got to find this white man and tell him I be real good and tell him where I live."

(Kate hangs the ornament.)

I don't know why, but I always need to be pushed to get things done. But, baby, let me tell ya, that man Sanda Claws made up for the five years he missed our apartment. Yeh, oh yeh, we had ourself one hell of a Christmas. And that boy, he loved it.

(Kate fights back the tears.)

At nights I wake up sometime and I expect him to come up the fire escape and through the window and try ta sneak inta his bed after stayin' out past when he should. Oh Lord, how I keep forgettin' he's dead.

Analysis of Kate Love in A Crooked Flower

Character: Female, black, thirty to forty

Kate Love lives in a poor section of Detroit. Her sixteen-year-old son, Richie, recently suffered a violent death during a robbery in their apartment. It's Christmas, a time that conjures up memories of an earlier Christmas with her boy.

Get a sense of place. Environment is crucial in this dialogue.

This piece could also be a duologue.

This type of speech is a flashback. It should be delivered by an actress who is capable of the regional dialect.

The character's life has been filled with tragedy. The Christmas ornament she is about to place on the tree motivates her to talk about her son. He made an ornament like this one. What kind of ornament is it? The angel for the top of the tree? A star? A reindeer? A "Sanda Claws"? It was probably simple, but priceless. What were the days like (have a picture of him, perhaps a kindergarten photo) when Richie was at home or out playing? Who were his friends? What did Ralf look like? What food did he enjoy? Did he love to dance or tell jokes or sing or play games?

What does working at Big Boy pay? What kind of job did you have? Cook? Waitress? Cashier? What were the hours?

Can you remember the night of the robbery? Were the murderers apprehended? Did his pals come to the funeral? Did any of his teachers attend?

Have you ever experienced an ice storm? Imagine subzero temperatures and treacherous, slick roads and trees weighed down by heavy sheets of ice. There would be power outages and blackouts.

It is vital to your portrayal of the grief-stricken mother to relive the incidents with energy and to bring humor to the story about Sanda Claws.

Then there is a major emotional shift in gears. When Kate starts the line, "I don't know why . . ." there should be an urge to cry and an attempt to fight the tears.

Forcing any natural feeling will result in a lack of believability.

There is probably a physical reaction like a sudden chill that she might experience when she tells about her nightmare.

All these choices are yours.

Chapter 16
The Soap Opera Audition

In this chapter we are fortunate to have three examples of authentic audition material. If you have watched *One Life to Live* and *All My Children*, you will have seen the actors who won the auditions—performers who looked over these pages, as you are doing, and connected with the material so forcefully that the producers, directors, writers, and network executives agreed they were the ones who must be chosen for the role.

GENERAL DIRECTIONS

Read each scene over several times. Sense the rhythm, structure, character relationships, and mood changes.

Read both parts. Imagine your partner's reactions, temperament, energy, and physicality.

Look for emotional buttons in the script. Mark them. Clues exist in the parenthetical directions, which are always in capital letters, and in stated intentions.

Examine the central conflict in each scene.

Who is the antagonist?

Who is the hero?

Who is the "third person"? The third person is a presence, not physically in the scene. Someone who is talked about or who has influenced the character's behavior and philosophy, such as a teacher, parent, spouse, or mentor. This third person can be living or dead, historical or fictional.

What is the secret each character is keeping from the other?
What has happened before the scene starts?
What will happen at the end of the scene?
Use your imagination.
Find obstacles to the scene's resolution.

AUDITION SCENE #1

We are grateful to Peggy O'Shea, head writer of ABC's *One Life to Live*, for allowing us to use this scene, with the understanding that it may not be republished or broadcast.

Nikos and Cassie in *One Life to Live*

Cassie is on a one-way phone call with Dorian when there is the sound of a doorbell.

CASSIE

I gotta hang up and collect my daily dozen . . . of course Nikos again! Talk to you later, Mom. (She HANGS UP and hurries to open the door.)

NIKOS

I thought instead of a card this time . . . (TRAILING OFF)

CASSIE

Nikos!

NIKOS

You're even better than I remembered.

CASSIE

I've missed you. (BURYING HIS HANDS IN HER HAIR, LIFTING HER FACE TO HIS. SHE WRENCHES FROM HIS EMBRACE, BACKING AWAY. HER EYES SMOLDERING.) Not again Nikos!

NIKOS

You won't let me touch you? Tell you that I've left my family and my country to be with you again?

CASSIE

You're two years too late, Nikos. You've no right to come here and try and shake up my life again.

NIKOS

We belong together and you know it, Cassie.

CASSIE

Don't you belong to that rich Greek woman your father *made* you marry?

NIKOS

We're separated.

CASSIE

I see.

NIKOS

I don't like that "tone."

CASSIE

Well I didn't like your "Dear Cassie" letter.

NIKOS

Not from my thoughts—not from my heart. I never forgot you, Cassie, and I'll prove it to you.

CASSIE

I don't believe how arrogant you are.

NIKOS

Don't be this way. I remember you as soft and tender, I've torn up my life to be with you again.

CASSIE

Without bothering to ask if I wanted you back in my life.

NIKOS

I should have made love to you.

CASSIE

Why? Would that have "branded" me?

NIKOS

Yes.

CASSIE

I don't think so.

NIKOS

I know so.

CASSIE

Well, it didn't happen. Aren't we lucky?

NIKOS

Have you made love to another man?

CASSIE

You've no right to ask me that.

NIKOS

I still love you and I claim the right.

CASSIE

(BEAT, THEN) I'm in love with someone else.

NIKOS

Answer my question.

CASSIE

(AN EXPLOSION) Damn you, Nikos. You can't march back into my life and— (START DEMANDING, ETC.)

NIKOS

(GRABBING HER AND WHIRLING HER TO FACE HIM) Did you make love to him?

CASSIE

No! (A FRIGHTENED MOMENT, THEN NIKOS RELAXES, SMILES, RELEASES HIS GRIP ON HER, BUT BENDS TO KISS HER VERY SOFTLY.)

NIKOS

And you never shall. Because you're mine. (AND SO SAYING, HE GIVES HER A JAUNTY WAVE AND EXITS, LEAVING A SOMEWHAT SHAKEN AND FEARFUL CASSIE STARING AFTER HIM.)

Analysis of Nikos and Cassie—One Life to Live

Cassie is on the phone at the start of the scene. To whom is she talking? The stage directions tell you that she is talking to Dorian. If you watch the show, you know that Dorian is her mother. She says good-bye Mom in her first speech. If you do not know who that character is, you must ask at the audition. It will color how you talk to her on the telephone. You must establish a relationship with the unseen person immediately.

What does the phrase "daily dozen" refer to? In the vernacular it refers to flowers, obviously roses. Who has been sending Cassie flowers every day? She says *Nikos* (pronounced Knee Kose).

The doorbell rings. The actress would walk to the door, open it, and find him standing there. How does she say his name? This is essential to the rest of the scene and the establishment of the relationship. She reacts to his touch by backing away. What does she mean by "not again!" This denial must be related to the past history of these two lovers—a summer fling in Greece that led to intense letter writing, feverish sentiments, vows of everlasting love that ultimately turned sour.

Cassie recoils from his advance. This causes Nikos to act offended and question her withdrawal. She justifies her action by reminding him of the past. He persists.

Ah, new information: Nikos is married, to a Greek woman, supposedly an arrangement made by his father.

Nikos assures Cassie he's separated. She says "I see." Here is an emotional clue; he gives it when he refers to her "tone." She retaliates by mentioning the Dear Cassie letter. The actress should imagine what that letter contained, how it was written. Hastily? Sympathetically? Curtly? Painfully? Illegibly? Elaborately? Or was it a telegram? Make a decision. When did she get the letter? At Christmas? On a birthday? During exams? Recount the circumstances, and how you felt. It's almost universal that teenagers have received or written Dear John/Dear Cassie letters. Let that feeling be evident in the tone of that line.

He is defensive; she calls him arrogant.

He swears he is different and so is she. She sets up obstacles to his declaration of love. "You didn't bother to ask me if I wanted you back." She reacts to his macho suggestion that he should have made love to her by using the word "branded"—a put-down to Nikos, who is acting as if she's some sort of prize heifer.

Her tone is cool and unreceptive.

And then we get to the main obstacle to Nikos' plan—she is in love with another. Cassie is on her way to an explosion. Structurally, the scene must build to her line, "Damn you, Nikos!"

The writer has given the actress suggestions for the completion of the line: "You can't march back into my life and—(*start demanding, etc.*)." Nikos can react and try to hurt her, forcing her to stop speaking with his line, "Did you make love to him?"

The climactic moment has come. It is Nikos' scene. He gets the last line, a threat that is implied, which leaves Cassie shaken at the intensity with which he has delivered the line. He is not the same Nikos. She is not the same Cassie. She has found true love.

She knows he is manipulative, arrogant, and self-serving, as opposed to her real love who is just the opposite.

flesh out the character, add dimension and texture, and make him a full-blown human being, not a stock, melodramatic, cardboard Casanova.

There must be a complete character analysis with every audition scene you do. There must be specific choices and character connections. It will become automatic after a while.

AUDITION SCENE #2

The following scenes from ABC's *All My Children* have been reprinted with the permission of head-writer Wisner Washam. They may not be reprinted or broadcast.

This is the character description each actress received with the audition scene. We have romanized the key words that give immediate clues to the appearance, emotional background, status, and environment of the character.

Robin McCall on All My Children

Seventeen and streetwise, *Robin has survived* horrendous upbringing *by means of her* wits *and with the help of her* older brother. *Robin and* Wade McCall, twenty, *were orphaned early in life in Chicago and, thanks to the court's concern, were kept together . . . but in a series of progressively worse* foster homes. *Three or four years ago they could no longer tolerate the system and ran away together to be on their own. Subsequently, they lived by means of* thievery *and small-time* con games, *eventually drifting to New York City. Their* hand-to-mouth existence *continued until Wade was arrested and sentenced to prison six months ago and Robin was forced to live on her own in the unfriendly city. Robin prides herself on being* cleverer *than most of the street kids who wind up on drugs or worse. She's never had to turn a trick to survive and she doesn't intend to.*

But Robin made a tactical blunder when she stole from Greg Nelson. He pursued her and, while trying to make her escape, she broke her ankle and had to be hospitalized.

Robin's spent most of her young life masking her feelings from others and from herself. Trusting no one but her brother, she's effectively written off the rest of the world. She does, however, possess a vulnerable streak *which she fears may be her undoing.*

She's been in the hospital for a day and this is the first time she's seen Greg since the accident.

SCENE   ROBIN AND GREG
             (GREG ENTERS AND THEY LOCK EYES.)

ROBIN: If you're here to apologize, forget it!

GREG: Apologize! *You stole my camera.*

ROBIN: It's your fault I'm here.

GREG: All I did was chase you. I didn't tell you to run in front of a cab.

ROBIN: I could've been killed on account of you.

GREG: If you're trying to make me feel guilty, forget it.

ROBIN: You a cop?

GREG: No.

ROBIN: Just some show-off, right? Getting your kicks playing Magnum P. I.

GREG: I caught you, didn't I?

ROBIN: Yeah. But you're not getting over on me. I'm suing you for every penny you got!

GREG: You're really amazing.

ROBIN: You look like the kinda guy who's got insurance. What's the big deal?

GREG: Don't you feel anything about stealing my camera?

ROBIN: I picked the wrong guy.

GREG: You're not sorry? Even after all this?

ROBIN: Sorry's for suckers. I'll do better next time.

GREG: There's not gonna be any next time. I'm pressing charges against you.

ROBIN: It's your word against mine.

GREG: That's where you're wrong. One of the waitresses saw you snag the camera and is willing to testify you stole it.

ROBIN: Nice try, *Ritchie Rich.* You're bluffing.

GREG: Try me.

ROBIN: You're gonna go through all the hassle of going to court . . . losing time from your job just so you can see me in the *slammer?*

GREG: Kids like you have to be taught a lesson.

ROBIN: Prison doesn't stop people from stealing. It just teaches them to be more careful. Besides, I'll get a *nickel bit max* and be back out in six months. No sweat.

GREG: Just out of curiosity, what would it take to get you to go straight?

ROBIN: Just out of curiosity, what would it take to get you to tell the cops you chased the wrong girl? (PAUSE, FEIGNING SEDUCTIVENESS) You're not all that bad-looking.

GREG: You just don't understand, do you?

ROBIN: (ANGRY) Sure I understand! I understand you're some *rich bastard* who can afford to be all high and mighty! That camera equipment of yours would feed me and my brother for a month. Why don't you try being poor sometime?

GREG: You can make all the excuses you want . . .

ROBIN: Get out! Get out or I'll call the nurse.

GREG: I'll see you in court.

ROBIN: (ON HIS EXIT) *I'll see you in Hell!* (HER CONFIDENCE SHATTERS AND WE SEE HER REAL FEAR BENEATH . . .) Oh, Wade, why did you have to get busted?

Analysis of Robin McCall on All My Children

Robin is a complex character who is defensive, scared, alone, hurt, bitter, vulnerable, seductive, and sensual, and from the script we know by her phrasing that she probably has had little or no schooling. She is compulsive and without a support system.

During the course of the scene we learn what has happened:

1. She stole Greg's camera.
2. He gave chase.
3. She ran in front of a cab.
4. She was taken to the hospital.

The actress must be specific about the injury. Did she hurt her leg, suffer bruises or a broken bone, merely get stunned, or incur a slight concussion? There must be a specific choice. If you've ever been in a hospital because of an accident or illness, try to remember how you felt, where it hurt, the strangeness of the place, how alone you felt, what it smelled like.

From the description of this character we know that she would never apologize to Greg. He, then, is justifiably angered by her behavior. She starts to needle him, call him names like show-off and, derisively, Magnum P.I.

The build is very clear in this scene. She threatens to sue. He says he'll press charges; tells her he has a witness. She says he is bluffing. She's been on the streets and is skeptical of strangers. She thinks, too, that even if she is identified and put in the slammer, she'll get a light sentence and be released.

From that emotional moment, her compulsive nature compels her to feign "coming on" to Greg. It doesn't wash. She then resorts to yelling at him, asking him how he'd like to be "poor sometime." Then there is her explosive, "Get out!" Her final line, after his exit, is to herself. It can be said in a number of ways, but the actress must communicate the vulnerability and pain she is feeling because of the absence of her only support system, her brother.

Robin knows she is in trouble. Her confidence and her cover have melted. "Oh, Wade, why did you have to get busted?" is an important line and moment for this character. Her mask is off. We have to see the frightened, lonely little girl she really is. There is a tendency among inexperienced actresses to throw away that moment.

Give yourself enough time and make it count. It's the moment that might get you the screen test, and very possibly the job.

Let's find out something of Greg Nelson's background.

He was married to the young, innocent, beautiful Jenny Gardner. A jealous lover tried to kill Greg, but got Jenny instead. Greg has not been the same since the funeral. He tried to date a girl who bore a strong resemblance to his wife, but in the end he knew he was dating her for the wrong reasons. Luckily he has good friends —Angie and Jessie—but no steady romantic entanglement.

So Greg is fair game for the likes of Robin McCall. She is beautiful, cunning, and helpless. He is angry with her, but fascinated. He has never met anyone like her.

It has been established that Greg is a photojournalist. That's why he always travels with a camera. It was this camera that Robin thought she could pawn for her next meal.

Greg is no match for Robin in this scene. Her life has been so different from his that his sermonizing falls on deaf ears. She tells him "Sorry's for suckers" and "Prison doesn't stop people from stealing." She gets to him, finally, with her phony come-on. And he gets to her with his rejection. She tops his "I'll see you in court!" with "I'll see you in hell!"

Where does Greg go when he leaves the hospital room? To phone the police? To call a lawyer? To think about what has happened? To find out more about Robin McCall? To heal his bruised ego with the help of old friends?

Is Robin going to try to escape by running out of the hospital? Is she going to plan revenge on Greg? Will she act contrite on the next encounter with Greg or his attorney? Is she going to give herself up and ask for leniency?

Try to decide what this character might do after this confrontation with Greg.

Also, try to visualize her hair, makeup, and clothing choices. Explore her fantasies. Does she want to be rich and famous? How does she hope to do it? Does she have any heroes or role models? Imagine what kind of life experiences this kid has had on the road. She may have been attacked in prison or in a foster home, or gone hungry for days. Give her reasons for her defensiveness. Give her a life other than the character description.

Write your own miniautobiography!

MINI-BIOGRAPHY

A young actress from California chose to write a character profile of Robin McCall—her wishes, likes, and dislikes. It helped her audition and we hope it will help you with your future preparation. Here is an excerpt from Lezlie Deane's life of R. McCall:

New York City is different from Chicago. It's faster and tougher. There's a lot of people to hit on in the city, but they're a lot smarter. They're on to you . . .

We first started with panhandling. You know, just asking people for money. We'd make up stories like . . . "My boyfriend just abandoned me and I don't have any money to take a cab home. I'm really scared, could I have a couple of bucks to make it home?" This plan worked okay, but it got old after a while. I also remember if we wanted to go somewhere, we would hail a cab, take the ride, and when the cab stopped we'd jump out and run for our lives! Sound fun?

There was one good friend we had on the streets. His name was Carl. He was cool because he would feed us everyday. See, he had one of those hotdog stands you see on just about every corner. He would also let us work sometime.

Me and my brother rely so much on each other. We always vowed we'd be together through thick and thin! We took care and looked out for one another. Wade was taken away from me about six months ago just for stealing a car. As he was hot-wiring it, the cops caught him. I really don't know what the big deal was. I mean, he was just doing it for kicks. Dig this, when the cops asked him who I was, he said he didn't know. He did that just to keep me out of trouble. Now that's cool. My brother saved my neck because he loves me!

Since Wade's been gone, I admit, it's sorta been tough on me. But I'm not gonna give up. I will survive! I have for six months. Carl has been watching out for me, but no one will take the place of my brother. I stuck to panhandling and pickpocketing.

My luck caught up to me recently. I zeroed in on this preppy-looking guy who had this awesome-looking camera equipment, so I figured if I pegged him, he would just freak out and not know what to do. So I followed my plan. I grabbed the equipment and ran. Dig this, as I was running I tripped, fell, and broke my damn ankle. Can you believe that? Well, this jerk caught me and now I'm in the hospital. How am I gonna get out of this mess? I mean, this guy could really get me in trouble. He's probably some rich guy who can do anything. You know what I mean? I'm not gonna let him beat me at my own game. If only Wade was here, we would get out of this mess . . .no problem.

So now you know about me. Are you happy? Are you gonna hang me by my toenails? You better not because I got a broken ankle!

AUDITION SCENE #3

This scene has no character description because the character had already been established on the show. A new actress was being sought for an existing role. The scene used for the audition was lifted from an aired show. To the actresses auditioning for the part, this meant that they had to work themselves up to the emotional intensity that exists at the start of the scene with very little preparation.

Liza Colby in *All My Children*

SCENE LIZA AND TAD
(The Martin living room)

TAD: What the hell are you talking about?

LIZA: Oh, don't give me that innocent act. You're having an affair with my mother!

TAD: Liza, you don't know what you're saying.

LIZA: Save your breath, you slime! When I think of all the times I came home and found you and my mother "getting better acquainted"—isn't that what you said? And me, thinking you were there to see *me*! What a laugh you must have had!

TAD: I *was* there to see you. Your mother doesn't even like me.

LIZA: You know something: You're right. I don't think she does like you. But that hasn't stopped her from climbing into bed with you, has it?

TAD: Liza, your imagination has gotten the best of you.

LIZA: Was it my imagination that my mother phoned you at the Hearth? Oh, but wait, that was because she was helping you pick out a present for me, wasn't it? What present? And I suppose I just imagined that remark your mother made at the yacht party—that it was good to see you with someone your own age. Well, no wonder!

TAD: You've got it all wrong.

LIZA: Oh no, I haven't. Obviously, a lot of people know about your sordid affair. Your mother for one . . . and Bob . . . who else, Tad? Who else knows what a sick piece of garbage you are?

TAD: Okay, Liza. You've had your say but you've got no proof of any of this. Go on, rant and rave all you like . . .

LIZA: I *have* proof!

TAD: (SLIGHTLY SHAKEN) You couldn't possibly.

LIZA: I've got good news for you, Tad. Remember the gold chain you had—the one you "bought for yourself."

TAD: (MOMENTARILY FLUSTERED) What about it?

LIZA: I found it! Would you like to know where I found it? At my house . . . where you left it after making love to my mother!

TAD: Liza, no . . .

LIZA: Shut up! I don't want to hear another word out of your mouth. You and my mother are the most despicable people in the whole world. I hate you . . . do you hear me? I hate you both! (WITH HATRED IN HER EYES SHE TURNS AND RUNS TO THE DOOR WHERE TAD CATCHES UP WITH HER AND HIS FACADE CRUMBLES.)

TAD: Liza, wait. (SHE PULLS HERSELF FREE FROM HIS GRASP.) What are you going to do?

LIZA: You'll just have to wait and see, won't you? (SHE SLAMS OUT.)

*Analysis of Liza Colby—*All My Children

Here is a thumbnail sketch of the characters:

Liza: Beautiful ingenue, passionate, manipulative, spoiled, self-involved, troublemaker, governed by emotion. Capable of deceit, lying to get what she wants and self-destructive.

Tad: Handsome, conceited, manipulative, juvenile. Self-involved and yet capable of vulnerability and even sincerity and integrity. Unfortunately, more opportunities occur to play the cad.

What has gone on before this scene starts? You must ask yourself this question. Liza has found evidence that Tad and her mother have been having an affair while she and Tad have been having an affair. She has come to his house to denounce him. Structurally we are starting in the middle of the scene and presenting a climactic scene that has taken possibly months of scripts to reach. There will be times when you will get an audition scene with very little background information and you will have to be very careful that you don't start too high at the beginning or you won't have anywhere to go with it emotionally.

There is a definite structure and momentum to this scene. Once Liza unleashes her fury and hatred for Tad, there is no stopping her. This is her moment of triumph!

Try not to get carried away with the melodrama of it; don't sacrifice Liza's reality. You must imagine yourself in the situation, even though it couldn't possibly happen to you. Imagine the boy you love, who you have thought was solely devoted to you, giving the special gift you presented to him on his birthday to another woman. Remember all the times he was too busy to come over or wasn't feeling very well or the times he didn't answer the phone. Imagine how angry that would make you feel and how humiliated. Now try to sense what it would be like if you discovered your mother in bed with your boyfriend. Okay, this only happens on soap operas or in movies but you have to place it in your reality to understand Liza's feelings. Your own mother had been deceiving you! Think specifically of that time at the yacht party when your boyfriend's mother implied it was nice seeing him with someone his own age! Picture that place, time of day, what you wore, what she wore, what kind of time you were having before she dropped this little bombshell. Imagine friends who kept you in the dark about the situation. You must somehow infuse your own emotional life into Liza's. The scene is also about the wonderful times you shared before you knew you were being deceived by Tad and your mother. You have to look at the whole relationship not just the end of it.

The actor playing Tad must visualize both women. He can't win in the situation, and he has to convey a drowning man who's trying to come up for air. The gold chain motivates the sinking feeling. Desperation is evident when he asks her what she is going to do. Liza must be triumphant when she replies that he will "just have to wait and see."

Where does Liza go when she leaves him?

- She could have a confrontation with her mother.
- She could drive out of town to calm down.
- She could seek the help of a girlfriend.
- She could get drunk and have a fling with someone she doesn't care about, to get even.
- She could take an overdose of sleeping pills.

What does Tad do?

- He could call Liza's mother and enlist her aid.
- Does Liza's mother know how deeply involved her daughter is with Tad?
- He could start to pack a suitcase to leave town—the coward's way out.
- He could go after Liza to try to make her understand what really happened.
- He could call an old girlfriend to forget.
- He could decide to tell the truth for once.
- He could leave it to fate.

Whatever you decide, think through that moment after.

Let's go through the scene moment by moment. Tad has the first line: "What the hell are you talking about?" It is obvious Liza has just said something inflammatory. Tad has been juggling affairs with a mother who brings him everything he wants and her daughter who pleases him sexually. He is not *in love* with either one of them. He has been caught with circumstantial evidence—the "gold chain." The actor playing Tad has to sound sincerely incredulous at Liza's accusation.

Liza gives the actor the emotional clue when she says, "Oh, don't give me that innocent act."

Tad holds his own.

Liza retaliates bitterly. She could cry. The choice is not to let him see her resolve weakened.

Tad counters. He was there to see Liza, not Liza's mother. After all, Liza's mother doesn't even like him.

Liza knows her mother and Tad have shared the same bed.

Tad accuses her of an overactive imagination.

Liza recounts incidents to justify herself.

Tad, beginning to squirm, says, "You've got it all wrong."

Liza lists people who knew about the affair.

Notice all along what she chooses to call him: "slime" and "sick piece of garbage."

Tad is certain she has no proof to convict him.

Liza moves in for the "kill."

She dangles the chain. (Actresses who would audition for this scene might bring this prop.) Tad panics. Liza utters her hatred for both Tad and her mother and exits dramatically.

Tad is left with the close-up revealing his desperation at being caught.

Chapter 17
The Film Audition

We are indebted to Joyce Eliason for this excerpt from her teleplay *Right to Kill*, an ABC Movie-of-the-Week, Frank Konigsberg and Larry Sanitsky, Executive Producers for Telepictures Productions, Inc. Ms. Eliason was particularly eager for newcomers to have the opportunity to work with authentic, current material. It is published with the understanding that it may not be reprinted or broadcast.

ACT THREE

FADE IN:

86   EXT. JAHNKE DRIVEWAY—SUNDAY MORNING   86
Doors are open on the Scout. Deborah sits at the steering wheel while Richard disconnects the odometer. Deborah seems on the edge of hysteria. Her eyes red and swollen from crying.

DEBORAH (V.O.)
(nervously)
He'll notice something . . . He will . . .

RICHARD
He's not gonna know . . .

DEBORAH
Why does he hate me so much? I mean what did I do?

RICHARD
It was me. I had a great time last night. . . . He couldn't stand it. He took it out on you. . . .

87   INT. SCOUT—SAME   87
Richard pulls door shut.

                        RICHARD
        C'mon now . . . Turn the key.

Deborah is shaking . . . all thumbs.

                        DEBORAH
        He's gonna catch us?

                        RICHARD
        They went to the mall. They'll be there for hours. You al-
        ways say you don't know how to drive. This is your chance.

Richard reaches over and turns on the key. The car jerks as
Deborah releases the clutch.

                        RICHARD
        Keep your foot on the clutch . . . Like I told you . . . Let
        it out slowly . . .

The Scout jumps, jerks forward. Deborah puts her arms up in
the air.

                        DEBORAH
        What do I do? What do I do?

                        RICHARD
        Steer it!

She cranks the wheel. The car jerking forward again.

                        RICHARD
        Let the clutch out!

More JERKS. Suddenly they both break out into laughter.

                        RICHARD
        You're doing it!

88   EXT. SCOUT—SAME   88
In jerks and starts, Deborah gets Scout onto the road. We watch
as it proceeds erratically down the bend.

                        RICHARD (V.O.)
        That's the way, Deborah! That's the way!

More LAUGHTER.

        CUT TO:

89   EXT. PRAIRIE—LATER   89
The Scout is parked at the side of the road. Richard and Deborah clamber up a rolling hill through the prairie grass. They
are both in better spirits after the rather exciting ride.

RICHARD
(reciting)
There was a young man named Flower.
Whose nose was as long as a tower.
　　He hated the charge,
　　　That his beak was so large . . .
He could smoke a cigar in the shower.
(calls back to Deborah)
It's your turn.

DEBORAH
I don't know any . . .

She gets to the top of the hill, hands up, twirling around.
Feeling free. Her face is shining, glowing as she looks out across
the prairie. The road running straight into the distant horizon.

DEBORAH
Richard . . . Look . . .

90   ANOTHER ANGLE   90
As Richard flops down in the grass beside her. Both of them
looking out across the vastness of the prairie.

RICHARD
We could follow this road and never come back.

DEBORAH
(sinking down, rolling over)
We could go to California.

RICHARD
(happy, looking up at the sky; full of dreams)
Maybe I'd be a photographer.

DEBORAH
I want to be a writer. A poet.

RICHARD
(playfully)
There was a young woman named Claire.
Whose chest was covered with hair.

DEBORAH
(laughing, playfully hitting him)
Ritchie . . .

RICHARD
(stretching his arms)
I wonder what Dad would do? If we just ran away.

DEBORAH
He'd get the IRS out to look for us.

RICHARD
(breaking into laughter)
Are you kidding? He'd get the National Guard. The Secret
Service. The FBI. He'd get the Canadian Mounted Police!

They are both laughing, caught in a moment. In the clear white
Wyoming morning light.

RICHARD
(laughter fades)
He'd take it out on Mom.

DEBORAH
(spirits sinking)
We can't leave her, can we? Ever.

RICHARD
(getting up)
It was a stupid idea. He'd find us anyway. We better go
back. It's getting late.

Analysis of Right to Kill

Characters: Deborah Jahnke, sixteen; Richard Jahnke, seventeen

Notice that in a movie script each scene consists of a sequence
of numbered shots. The shots indicate the camera setup for that
moment in the story. The first part of the audition scene consists
of shots 86—outside the Scout, 87—inside the Scout, almost on the
driver's seat with them, and 88—from a distance, as the Scout makes
it down the road. In the second part of the scene, shot 89 gives us
a wide, exterior shot of the open country, with the Scout parked on
the road and Deborah and Richard clambering up the hill; shot 90
is a closer look at the two of them. The director will probably shoot
the scene from several angles—concentrating on Deborah, concentrating on Richard. Later, in the editing process, the shots will be
alternated to give the effect of looking first at one actor, then the
other. The entire sequence is filmed outdoors, on location.

Read all of the camera directions (which go across the page) as well as the lines of dialogue (which are always centered on the page). They will help you visualize how the writer wants to tell the story.

Deborah and Richard are the prisoners of their sadistic, schizophrenic father and are trapped. Deborah is getting a driving lesson from her brother, because her father refuses to let her drive. They have to do this when the parents are away from home.

For this scene, you would have to know what has gone on before to cause Deborah to be on the verge of hysteria, her "eyes red and swollen."

Richard's function is to calm her down and assure her that their father is angry with him, not her.

There is a great deal of action in the scene. For the audition, you could mime the jerkiness of the car, the releasing of the clutch, the cranking of the wheel, and the turning on of the key.

It is easy to empathize with the first driving lesson. Most of us have experienced the frustration. We have also felt the exhilaration of taking the risk to learn and the laughter at our mistakes.

Cut to prairie. The kids are climbing a hill. Richard recites a limerick. The mood is carefree and happy. Looking at the vast expanse of land before them, they can articulate their dream of escape from their prison. Their playfulness is infectious.

They are extremely fond of one another. They are best friends. They are totally dependent on one another. Suddenly they realize escaping would hurt their mother because he would take it out on her! The mood of happiness changes to one of bitter resignation.

Their relationship is clearly developed even without a knowledge of the entire script. The fear of the father is still present despite the lighthearted spirits of the brother and sister.

Imagine life in a small town, strict parental discipline, not being allowed to go on dates, having abnormal demands placed on you, never knowing any peace, parents who argue constantly, a father who beats his wife for no reason, never being allowed to dress in the latest fashion, living in a constant state of fear, walking on eggs.

When you have created the environment, the other characters, and your relationship to them, you are ready to write a short autobiography of your life, your likes, your dislikes, your goals, dreams, and interests, what you think of yourself, your brother, your sister, and your parents.

The film script can be an adaptation of a play, novel, biography, or original story. It depicts a cross section of families, ethnic groups, occupations, set in a variety of locales. Because of the time frame, there may not be a lot of attention given to fleshing out the life of each major character. Part of your homework is to prepare an in-depth character profile from childhood to the present.

The outcome of *Right to Kill* involves Richard's plot to kill his father. He can't take any more abuse nor can he watch his sister and mother suffer because of it. He takes a gun from his dad's collection and ambushes him when he returns home one night.

It is essential to character motivation and development that you understand the psychology of each person, originating from the earliest traumas of a battered childhood. Check out case studies and newspaper accounts. The more you research, the more finely tuned your instincts will be.

Chapter 18
The Commercial Audition

The filmed or taped commercial is normally a sales message, from ten to sixty seconds, about a product or service.

There are several types of commercials: a spokesperson delivering the sales pitch directly to the audience; a dramatization, involving husband/wife or sister/brother or mother/child or a group of people who might gather at a ski resort, cocktail party, bank, anniversary, seasonal celebration, and so forth; an off-camera announcer may deliver the message as we watch the action. Some commercials are funny; some are low-key or "soft sell," some use a forceful "hard sell."

The actor's approach to commercial copy will utilize training in sense memory, improvisation, mime, characterization, voice production, concentration, and timing.

There is a facility that comes with constant auditioning which affects the reading so that it may sound too glib or rote. We hope that understanding the overall purpose of each commercial message presented in these samples through exploring the dynamic, language, punctuation, or emphasis, copy points, structure, and rhythm will provide you with guidelines for all future auditions and will help keep you from becoming too slick.

A recommended exercise is to write your own commercial about a product you enjoy using. Practice telling a friend about the product; attempt to persuade the person to buy it. All of us do commercials every day—whenever we tell a friend about a book we enjoyed, the cologne we just purchased, the camera we simply have to buy. Notice your energy and concentration at those moments. Bring that enthusiasm into the audition with you.

To feel natural with any piece of copy, you may want to put it into your own words. Just remember, at the audition, you may keep it natural, but read the *copywriter's* words.

Always read over the copy at least five times. Make this your general rule for all auditions.

COMMERCIAL #1

Wind Drift After-Shave and Cologne* (thirty seconds)

You're tired.
You've had a rough week in a grimy city.
But now you're at the shore.
The sea is pounding and the air is fresh.
You fill your lungs and
breathe deeply of clean, fresh air with
a tang of salt and the sound of waves.
You're not tired anymore.

WIND DRIFT does that to you
because WIND DRIFT is about the sea.
WIND DRIFT After-Shave and Cologne.

Analysis of Wind Drift Commercial

● Voice over—action on camera

● Motivation: To help a tired friend feel revitalized by using the correct and most refreshing after-shave and cologne.

● Objective: Compare the soothing influence of the shore to the product using sense memory.

You are using yourself to reach that friend. Personalize the copy. Talk to someone you know. Be specific. It will be far more effective than trying to sound like the stereotypical announcer.

Visualize the grimy city and the shore, the color of the sea. Hear the sound of the waves, taste the salt that is connected to the waves. Sense the filling of the lungs with clean, fresh air. Hear the pounding of the sea on the beach.

---

*Reprinted with the permission of Mem Company, Inc., Northvale, NJ 07647.

In your mind you can see that tired, sweaty, pale, bedraggled nine-to-fiver. Think about August in New York or Scottsdale or Dallas or when you have been uncomfortable from the heat. Bus fumes pollute the air. Soot is everywhere and litter and the smell is unpleasant. When you have this picture clearly drawn from your own experience you'll be prepared to tackle the first line.

There will be a certain tone used. The second line elaborates on the "tired" state. Underscore the words "rough" and "grimy." They describe the unpleasantness you are trying to express. Then there is a major transition on "But now . . .?" which takes you and your tired friend to the shore. There should be an implied feeling of Ahhhhhhhh! You are praising the sea and its clean, fresh environment. "Tired" no longer exists. The metaphor is complete for the product pitch. Wind Drift takes you to the seashore. It makes you feel just as clean and fresh as the sea air. By appealing to your senses, the qualities of the after-shave and cologne are enhanced. The sponsor doesn't have to tell you to buy the product. The message speaks for itself. This is a "soft-sell" commercial, a mood piece.

COMMERCIAL #2

Easy-Off® Oven Cleaner* (thirty seconds)

ANNCR (EXCITED BUT CONFIDENTIAL): America, here's a wonderful new way to clean your oven:
EASY-OFF® Oven Cleaner. We cut the fumes, kept the power. Let's discover the difference.
WOMAN: It'll take EASY-OFF® to get grease this bad.
ANNCR: How's this smell?
WOMAN (SNIFFS): Nice 'n fresh. Bet it won't work like EASY-OFF®!
ANNCR (VO), STILL CONFIDENTIAL: The EASY-OFF® power cleaners cut through grease *fast*.
ANNCR (LIVE): Okay, wipe.
WOMAN: Sparkling clean!
EASY-OFF® Oven Cleaner! Smells great, works great.
ANNCR (VO): Get *improved* EASY-OFF®. We cut the fumes, kept the power.

---

*Easy-Off® is the registered trademark of American Home Products Corporation.

Analysis of EASY-OFF® Oven Cleaner Commercial

- Announcer/housewife
- Product demonstration commercial

This is the type of message that is shared with America—America's oven-cleaners. You will note the stage directions in the announcer's copy—"Excited but confidential." This tone is the one used by the sports announcer at the eighteenth hole as he describes the final putts that will determine the new winner of the PGA trophy.

The announcer must be dynamic and intent on informing us that this oven cleaner is improved because it has cut its fumes but kept its power. He establishes contact with a housewife who doesn't know about the new improved brand. Obviously there is a cover label hiding the EASY-OFF® label.

As a woman auditioning for this commercial, you have to imagine a grease-caked oven. She knows about EASY-OFF®, as is evident in her first line. Common sense dictates EASY-OFF® is emphasized in this line.

The announcer sprays some oven cleaner and asks the woman what she thinks of the odor. Now she must sniff. (Note: Clients and producers are very critical of sensory reactions. Actors have lost commercials because their coffee tasting wasn't convincing.) We know he has fooled her. She thinks the smell is nice and fresh, so it can't work like EASY-OFF®, which has industrial strength and a strong aroma.

The announcer still uses a one-on-one confidential method to address America. He reiterates that EASY-OFF® has the power (underscored) to cut through grease fast (underscored). Fast is the operative word. He instructs her to wipe her oven. She reacts with surprise and elation. Now he removes the cover label and reveals the hero of the day—EASY-OFF®. She is convinced. It smells great; works great.

The *voice over tag* is said over a product shot with a reprise of the opening claim—"We cut the fumes, kept the power."

This is not an easy commercial because its dynamic is intense and at a higher pitch than the "real" people commercial. It challenges the announcer to use low-voice excitement to address the nation with important news about oven cleaners. He is figuratively winking at us and playfully leading on the housewife with a Brand X he knows is the preferred cleaner. He is doing this so she will discover that the product does work minus the fumes. The word "improved" must get a headline emphasis. It is a major selling point.

The actress playing the consumer should know about cleaning an oven. She would probably be in the age range twenty-five to thirty-five. At the audition you won't have a dirty oven to relate to, so you'll have to imagine the grease-filled appliance. See the sparkling clean variety as well. That contrast in tone is important in the interpretation. The reactions must sound real, not forced. To anticipate the outcome is a common trap. You must play each moment—from doubt to skepticism to the thrill of discovery and joy.

COMMERCIAL # 3

Jergens Direct-Aid* (thirty seconds)

VIDEO	AUDIO
SFX Alarm Clock	SHE: Good morning.
2 hands touch	HE: G'morning. Hey—your *hands*.
	SHE: Mmmm?
His hand caresses hers.	HE: They're so *soft*.
She reaches out of frame. Bring in product.	SHE: I've discovered Jergens Direct-Aid.
	HE: You put it on before bed?
She takes out a tiny dab, rubs it on finger.	SHE: Uh, huh. And wake up to softer hands.
	HE: Hmm . . . smoother, too.
	SHE: Jergens starts working instantly to soothe and soften. S'non-greasy.
	HE: Can you use it during the day?
	SHE: Sure. Honey . . . ?
	HE: Mmmm?
	SHE: How about *you* making breakfast?

*Reprinted with the permission of the Andrew Jergens Company, Cincinnati, OH 45214.

Analysis of Jergens Direct-Aid Commercial

- Voice over/relationship
- Hand demonstration
- "Talking hands"

Imagine the place—bedroom, the bed, end tables, type of alarm clock, time of morning. Imagine how product feels to the woman and how her hands feel to her husband. Visualization will help the interpretation of the copy.

In the beginning, the voice should sound a little sleepy. We see hands groping for the clock. The contact prompts the dialogue. He says, "Hey—your hands." She has a throwaway reaction, "Mmm?" He then says, "They're so soft." A major selling point. No mention yet of the product. This is her discovery. She describes the method. Before bed she applies the lotion and then she wakes up to softer hands. He concurs that the hands are indeed smoother. She enlightens him, "Jergens starts working instantly to soothe and soften" (important selling words), as well as "S'non-greasy." Another transition—"Honey," she purrs, "How about you making breakfast?" We must sense that she has him in the palm of her hands . . .

This dialogue is written in a very conversational rhythm. The product message is important, but it is not sledgehammered home. Read both parts so you can get a sense of how to listen and react. Notice the contractions used in the dialogue: "G'morning" and "S'non-greasy." Relaxed people don't punch every word in a dialogue, especially in bed. Therefore the writer intended that there be an ease in the couple's conversation. Practice saying "soft," "soften," "smooth," "smoother," and "soothe." The video direction has his hand caressing hers. The voices can sound just as caressing relating to the product. That is your objective.

When auditioning with a partner, see if you can find out in advance who that person will be; get together and rehearse. You won't have much time so make each moment meaningful!

COMMERCIAL #4

White Cloud Tissue* (sixty seconds)

SFX:	BREAKFAST SOUNDS
MAN:	Ann . . .
WOMAN:	Yes, dear.
MAN:	Why is bathroom tissue on our breakfast table?
WOMAN:	You noticed!
MAN (VO):	I noticed.
WOMAN:	Harold, I am such a terrific shopper . . . listen . . . I found White Cloud. *One* touch, and I *knew* it was for us . . . C'mon, I want *you* to touch it . . . just once!
MAN:	Can I have my coffee?
WOMAN:	After one touch. C'mon.
MAN:	Aw, what can one touch prove?
WOMAN:	You'll see. Feel ours.
MAN:	Feels soft.
WOMAN:	Now White Cloud—one touch, mind you.
MAN:	Feels different! Softer!!
WOMAN:	The softest.
MAN:	Smooth—like velvet. Feels *velvety*, like . . . your robe.
MAN:	Y'know Ann, you *are* a terrific shopper.
WOMAN:	And you're a terrific husband. Here's your coffee, Harold.
MAN:	One touch did prove it!
WOMAN:	One touch.
ANNCR:	White Cloud. One touch tells you it's softest. One touch tells someone you care.

Analysis of White Cloud Tissue Commercial

- Slice-of-life dramatization
- Husband and wife

---

*Reprinted with the permission of the Procter & Gamble Company, Cincinnati, OH 45201.

- Place: Kitchen
- SFX (sound effects): Breakfast sounds

In this sixty-second commercial, Ann and Harold discuss bathroom tissue. The White Cloud is on the breakfast table. "Touch," "Soft," "Velvet," "Caring" are key words in this copy. Ann convinces her husband of the special qualities of the product. As with EASY-OFF®, this is a comparison test. Our tissue versus theirs. Let's check the difference. Harold is more interested in his morning coffee than in complying with her "touch" test. He gives in.

Both characters have interesting personalities. She is outgoing and vivacious from the start. He is more tongue-in-cheek and skeptical. His major transition occurs naturally after he feels the White Cloud. He becomes sensually involved to the point of touching her velvet robe. Then the praise pours forth and he is a convert to White Cloud. Coffee is his reward.

The theme is restated by the voice-over announcer: "One touch tells you it's softest."

Do an improvisation using different products that would not normally be on the kitchen table at mealtime—shaving cream, perfume, hand lotion, bath powder. Have one person explain why one shaving cream is better than another.

In this commercial the wife is wearing a velvet robe. What is the man wearing? How long have they been married? He works for a living. What does he do? Does she work outside the home or is she a full-time housekeeper and mother? They are a happily married couple and appear to be very comfortable with each other. Be specific about their relationship.

The sixteen selections presented in this part of the book demonstrate the range of material you will encounter. They represent the kinds of scenes being done on stage, on television, and in film today. The material has also been chosen to illustrate the various formats employed in The Business—there are many ways to set down dramatic material on the printed page. Each medium has its own conventions. A scene from a play will not look like an excerpt from a television show. Commercial copy does not resemble a page from a film script.

Yet, for all their differences in appearance, these selections—and any others that you will work on—make the same demands upon the actor: careful investigation of the circumstances, exploration of the possibilities, consideration of the character's objectives, realization of the moments before the scene begins and after it ends, and, most important, they require a soaring imagination.

In all cases, what we hope to see is truth, illuminated by your singular talent.

Epilogue

We have come to the end of our guided journey.

What happens now is up to you.

You must ask yourself if it is absolutely necessary to journey to New York or Los Angeles.

Have you explored every possibility in your own neighborhood? Are you the outstanding talent in your group? Have you measured yourself against the best of what you see and hear?

Is it necessary to be in Los Angeles or New York to accomplish what you want to do? We have told you about excellent, respected theater companies flourishing outside the major production centers. Many of today's young playwrights prefer to have their works performed in these regional theaters. Actors like John Malkovich, Gary Sinise, Robert Prosky, and Ann Pitoniak come quickly to mind— examples of performers who were "discovered" in productions that originated thousands of miles from Broadway or Sunset Boulevard.

Jane Alderman tells us:

> *I think it's smart for a newcomer from Milwaukee, Minneapolis, Sioux City, Detroit, to come to Chicago. You don't have to go in leaps and bounds. You do leaps and leaps and then you bound. There is some fabulous talent in smaller markets. The* crème de la crème *are coming to Chicago, where they can raise families and get roots. Theatrical activity in Chicago has almost quadrupled. The entire city is an ensemble, like the British system, and they're very supportive.*

If the theater is what lures you, how strong is your foundation? Are you expecting your boundless enthusiasm to carry you too far?

Examine your motives and determination. Can you envision a life in The Business without being a star? Because that is what we are talking about. A life of work.

Mervyn Nelson's words are very moving:

If someone is going to be a star in spite of the masochistic nature of the business, I've never seen in all my years, talent go unrecognized provided the talent is dedicated because talent itself is an addiction. You don't need anything else but talent. That's your addiction. One day Roy Scheider came to me when I was teaching him and said, "I don't fit anywhere. I'm not a leading man, I'm not really a character. There is no cliché for me to be." I told him that has nothing to do with it. "You have talent. Hold on. Hold on."

I have never known really wonderful talent to be ignored. Somehow they have found their way, if they held on.

If the talent and the desire are so strong within you, perhaps the next question is which city: Los Angeles or New York? These are two differing cultures.

We rely on Mervyn Nelson again:

When I work out on the Coast, I find a lot of people belong in New York. Because I believe people are not born in New York, they're born for it. And I think people out there are lost because they went out there. Then I sit with people in New York, as I did with Tony Hamilton and others and say, "Go West!" People who can be put into a niche. Hollywood is a place of niches. You must be able to be given a title by them. If you can do that, if you have that kind of charisma, New York is wrong for you. If you are an actor/actress with a lot of stretch and don't seem to fit into a particular category, you shouldn't go to the Coast, but to New York. If Hollywood finds you in New York, then they'll take you, no matter what.

I think people come to New York too soon because the competition in the most important cultural city in the world is such you can't come here too soon. You're going to be a waiter the rest of your life. The competition is too strong. You must be able to compete with the best. What is considered off Broadway in Hollywood and lasts for a year would last in New York off-off-Broadway one night.

The working actor who continues to grow and keeps his soul intact to preserve his sanity is the one who will last.

Such actors are ready when the wonderful accident happens—the sudden, unpredictable marriage of preparation and opportunity that is the true meaning of luck.

Wherever you are working—Minneapolis, Cleveland, Seattle, Chicago, Louisville, New York, Los Angeles, or Denver—what is important is to be professional. And that is an ongoing process.

Everything in this book is geared to your professionalism—as well as to your ultimate and continuing success.

Appendix

WHERE TO GET IN TOUCH WITH THE UNIONS

Actors' Equity Association (AEA)

MAIN OFFICE (NEW YORK)
165 West Forty-sixth Street
New York, NY 10036

LOS ANGELES
6430 Sunset Boulevard
Hollywood, CA 90028

CHICAGO
360 North Michigan Avenue
Chicago, IL 60601

SAN FRANCISCO
182 Second Street
San Francisco, CA 94105

CANADA
64 Shuter Street
Toronto, Ontario, Canada
M5B2G7

American Federation of Television and Radio Artists (AFTRA)

MAIN OFFICE (NEW YORK)
1350 Avenue of the Americas
New York, NY 10019

LOS ANGELES
1717 North Highland Avenue
Los Angeles, CA 90028

CHICAGO
307 North Michigan Avenue
Chicago, IL 60601

LOCAL OFFICES:

ALBANY
341 Northern Boulevard
Albany, NY 12204

ATLANTA
3110 Maple Drive, N.E.
Atlanta, GA 30305

BINGHAMTON
50 Front Street
Binghamton, NY 13905

BOSTON
11 Beacon Street #1000
Boston, MA 02018

BUFFALO
635 Brisbane Building
Buffalo, NY 14203

CINCINNATI/COLUMBUS/DAYTON
1814–16 Carew Tower
Cincinnati, OH 45202

CLEVELAND
1367 East Sixth Street # 229
Cleveland, OH 44114

DALLAS/FORT WORTH
3220 Lemmon Avenue
Dallas, TX 75204

DENVER
6825 East Tennessee
Denver, CO 80224

DETROIT
24901 North Western Highway
Southfield, MI 48075

FRESNO
P.O. Box 11961
Fresno, CA 93776

HAWAII
P.O. Box 1350
Honolulu, HI 96807

HOUSTON
2620 Fountainview
Houston, TX 77057

INDIANAPOLIS
20 North Meridian Street
Indianapolis, IN 46204

KANSAS CITY/OMAHA
406 West Thirty-Fourth Street
Kansas City, MO 46111

LOUISVILLE
730 West Main Street
Louisville, KY 40202

MIAMI
1450 N.E. 123 Street
North Miami Beach, FL 33161

MINNEAPOLIS/ST. PAUL
(TWIN CITIES)
2500 Park Avenue South
Minneapolis, MN 55404

NASHVILLE
P.O. Box 121087
Acklen Station
Nashville, TN 37212

NEW ORLEANS
808 St. Ann Street
New Orleans, LA 70116

PEORIA
2907 Springfield Road
East Peoria, IL 61611

PHILADELPHIA
1405 Locust Street
Philadelphia, PA 19102

PHOENIX
3030 N. Central #919,
Phoenix, AZ 85012

PITTSBURGH
1000 The Bank Tower
Pittsburgh, PA 15222

PORTLAND
915 North East Davis Street
Portland, OR 97232

RACINE/KENOSHA
929 Fifty-second Street
Kenosha, WI 53140

ROCHESTER
1 Exchange Street
Rochester, NY 14614

SACRAMENTO/STOCKTON
1216 Arden Way
Sacramento, CA 95815

SAN DIEGO
3045 Rosecrans Street
San Diego, CA 92110

SAN FRANCISCO
100 Bush Street
San Francisco, CA 94104

SCHENECTADY
1400 Balltown Road
Albany, NY 12309

SEATTLE
158 Thomas Street
Seattle, WA 98104

SOUTH BEND
826 South Twenty-fifth Street
South Bend, IN 46615

STAMFORD
117 Prospect Street
Stamford, CT 06901

ST. LOUIS
818 Olive Street
St. Louis, MO 63101

WASHINGTON/BALTIMORE
35 Wisconsin Circle
Washington, DC 20015

Screen Actors Guild (SAG)

MAIN OFFICE (LOS ANGELES)
7750 Sunset Boulevard
Los Angeles, CA 90046

NEW YORK
1700 Broadway
New York, NY 10019

BRANCH OFFICES
In many instances, AFTRA and SAG locals are merged for all practical purposes. If the address of the SAG branch office is the same as that for the local AFTRA office, it's likely that the same executive staff administers the contracts for both unions. A visit to the office will give you the opportunity to learn about the activities of both unions in the area.

ATLANTA
3110 Maple Drive North East
Atlanta, GA 30305

BOSTON
11 Beacon Street
Boston, MA 02108

CHICAGO
307 North Michigan Avenue
Chicago, IL 60601

CLEVELAND
1367 East Sixth Street
Cleveland, OH 44114

DALLAS
3220 Lemmon Avenue
Dallas, TX 75204

DENVER
6825 East Tennessee Avenue
Denver, CO 80222

DETROIT
28690 Southfield Road
Lathrup Village, MI 48076

HOUSTON
2620 Fountainview
Houston, TX 77057

KANSAS CITY
406 West Thirty-fourth Street
Kansas City, MO 64111

MIAMI
146 Madeira Avenue
Coral Gables, FL 33134

MINNEAPOLIS/ST. PAUL
2500 Park Avenue
Minneapolis, MN 55402

NASHVILLE
P.O. Box 121087
Nashville, TN 37212

PHILADELPHIA
1405 Locust Street
Philadelphia, PA 19102

PHOENIX
3030 North Central
Phoenix, AZ 85012

ST. LOUIS
818 Olive Street
St. Louis, MO 63101

SEATTLE
158 Thomas Street
Seattle, WA 98109

SAN DIEGO
3045 Rosecrans
San Diego, CA 92110

WASHINGTON
35 Wisconsin Circle
Chevy Chase, MD 20015

SAN FRANCISCO
100 Bush Street
San Francisco, CA 94104

THEATERS OPERATING UNDER THE LORT CONTRACT

Theater and Address	Salary Category*	Artistic Director and/ or Business Manager
ALABAMA Alabama Shakespeare Festival P.O. Box 20350 Montgomery, AL 36120-0350	(**B**)	Martin L. Platt Jim Volz
ALASKA Alaska Repertory Theatre 705 W. Sixth Ave., Suite 201 Anchorage, AK 99501	(**B**)	Robert J. Farley Paul V. Brown
ARIZONA Arizona Theatre Company 120 W. Broadway Tucson, AZ 85701	(**C**)	Gary Gisselman
CALIFORNIA Berkeley Repertory Theatre 2025 Addison St. Berkeley, CA 94704	(**C**)	Mitzi Sales None
Berkeley Shakespeare Festival Box 969 Berkeley, CA 94701	(**D**)	Dakin Matthews John Maynard, Jr.
South Coast Repertory Theatre Box 2197 Costa Mesa, CA 92626	(**B**)	David Emmes Martin Benson

*Actors' salaries effective September 2, 1985: **A** = $401.00.
B = $364.00.
C = $352.00.
D = $321.00.

Theater and Address	Salary Category*	Artistic Director and/or Business Manager
L.A. Stage Company 1642 N. Las Palmas Avenue Hollywood, CA 90028	(B)	Susan Dietz Joshua Schiowitz
La Jolla Playhouse P.O. Box 12039 La Jolla, CA 92037	(B)	Des McAnuff Alan Levy
Long Beach Civic Light Opera P.O. Box 20280 Long Beach, CA 90801	(A)	Martin Wiviott None
L.A. Public Theatre 8105 West Third Street Los Angeles, CA 90048	(D)	Peg Yorkin Suzan Miller
Mark Taper Forum Los Angeles Music Center 135 North Grand Avenue Los Angeles, CA 90012	(A)	Gordon Davidson William P. Wingate
California Repertory P.O. Box 1891 Monterey, CA 93942	(A)	Ben Benoit None
Old Globe Theatre P.O. Box 2171 San Diego, CA 92112	(B)	Jack O'Brien Thomas Hall
American Conservatory Theatre 450 Geary St. San Francisco, CA 94102	(A)	William Ball James B. McKenzie
COLORADO American Theatre Company Box 9438 Aspen, CO 81612	(C)	Tom Ward None
Denver Center Theatre Company 1050 Thirteenth Street Denver, CO 80204	(B)	Donovan Marley Gully Stanford
CONNECTICUT Goodspeed at Chester c/o Goodspeed Opera House East Haddam, CT 06423	(D)	Michael Price None
Goodspeed Opera House East Haddam, CT 06423	(A)	Michael Price None
Hartford Stage Company 50 Church St. Hartford, CT 06103	(C)	Mark Lamos David Hawkinson

Theater and Address	Salary Category*	Artistic Director and/or Business Manager
Long Wharf Theatre 222 Sargent Dr. New Haven, CT 06511	(B)	Arvin Brown M. Edgar Rosenblum
Yale Repertory Theatre 222 York Street New Haven, CT 06520	(C)	Lloyd Richards Benjamin Mordecai
Hartman Theatre Company Stamford Center for the Arts 307 Atlantic Street Stamford, CT 06901	(B)	Margaret Booker Harris Goldman
American Shakespeare Theatre 1850 Elm St. Stratford, CT 06497	(A)	Richard Horner Associates Richard Horner and Lynn Stuart
Eugene O'Neill Memorial Theatre Center National Playwrights Conference 305 Great Neck Road Waterford, CT 06385	(C)	Lloyd Richards George C. White
DISTRICT OF COLUMBIA Arena Stage Sixth and Maine Avenue, S.W. Washington, DC 20024	(B)	Zelda Fichandler Thomas C. Fichandler
Folger Theatre Group 201 E. Capitol St. SE Washington, DC 20003	(D)	John Neville-Andrews Mary Ann Di Barbieri
The American National Theatre Kennedy Center for the Performing Arts Washington, DC 20566	(A)	Peter Sellars Diane Malecki
FLORIDA The Caldwell Playhouse P.O. Box 277 Boca Raton, FL 33432	(C)	Michael Hall None
The Hippodrome State Theatre 25 Southeast Second Pl. Gainesville, FL 32601	(D)	Paul Bennet None
Coconut Grove Playhouse P.O. Box 616 Miami, FL 33133	(B)	G. David Black Barry Steinman

Theater and Address	Salary Category*	Artistic Director and/or Business Manager
Asolo Theatre Festival P.O. Box Drawer E Sarasota, FL 33578	(C)	John Ulmer Richard G. Fallon
GEORGIA Alliance Theatre Company 1280 Peachtree St. N.E. Atlanta, GA 30309	(B)	Edith Love
ILLINOIS Goodman Theatre Company 200 S. Columbus Dr. Chicago, IL 60603	(B)	Gregory Mosher Roche Schulfer
The North Light Rep Theatre, Inc. 2300 Green Bay Rd. Evanston, IL 60201	(D)	Michael Maggio Susan Medak
INDIANA Indiana Repertory Theatre 140 W. Washington St. Indianapolis, IN 46204	(B)	Tom Haas Len Alexander
KENTUCKY Actors Theatre of Louisville 316-320 W. Main St. Louisville, KY 40202	(B)	Jon Jory Alexander Speer
MARYLAND Center Stage 700 North Calvert Street Baltimore, MD 21202	(B)	Stan Wojewodski Peter W. Culman
MASSACHUSETTS The Huntington Theatre Company Boston University Theatre 264 Huntington Avenue Boston, MA 02115	(B)	Peter Altman Michael Maso
American Repertory Theatre Company Loeb Drama Center 64 Brattle Street Cambridge, MA 02138	(B)	Robert Brustein Robert Orchard
Shakespeare and Company The Mount Lenox, MA 01240	(C)	Tina Packer Alan Yaffe

Theater and Address	Salary Category*	Artistic Director and/or Business Manager
Merrimack Regional Theatre P.O. Box 228 Lowell, MA 01853	(**D**)	Daniel Schay None
Stagewest Springfield Theatre Arts Association 1 Columbus Center Springfield, MA 01103	(**C**)	Timothy Lear Ken Denison
MICHIGAN Meadow Brook Theatre Oakland University Rochester, MI 48063	(**B**)	Terence Kilburn Frank F. Bollinger
MINNESOTA Cricket Theatre 528 Hennepin Avenue Minneapolis, MN 55403	(**C**)	Louis Salerni
The Guthrie Theatre 725 Vineland Pl. Minneapolis, MN 55403	(**A**)	Liviu Ciulei Donald Schoenbaum
Actors Theatre of St. Paul 2115 Summit Ave. Saint Paul, MN 55105	(**D**)	Michael Andrew Miner Jan Miner
MISSOURI Missouri Repertory Theatre 5100 Rockhill Road Kansas City, MO 64110	(**B**)	George Keathley Diana Coles
The Repertory Theatre of St. Louis 130 Edgar Rd. Saint Louis, MO 63119	(**B**)	Steven Woolf None
NEW HAMPSHIRE Theatre by the Sea P.O. Box 927 Portsmouth, NH 03801	(**C**)	Tom Celli None
NEW JERSEY New Jersey Shakespeare Festival Madison, NJ 07940	(**D**)	Paul Barry Ellen Barry
The Whole Theatre Company 544 Bloomfield Avenue Montclair, NJ 07042	(**D**)	Olympia Dukakis Laurence Feldman

Theater and Address	Salary Category*	Artistic Director and/or Business Manager
George Street Playhouse 9 Livingston Avenue New Brunswick, NJ 08901	(C)	Eric Krebs None
McCarter Theatre Company, Inc. 91 University Pl. Princeton, NJ 08540	(B)	Nagle Jackson Alison Harris
NEW MEXICO Santa Fe Festival Theatre P.O. Box DD Santa Fe, NM 87502	(C)	Thomas Kahn Gardner Richard J. Caples
NEW YORK Capital Repertory Company P.O. Box 399 Albany, NY 12201-0399	(D)	Peter Clough Barbara Smith
Studio Arena Theatre 710 Main St. Buffalo, NY 14202	(B)	David Frank Raymond Bonnard
Queens Theatre in the Park P.O. Box 1336 Flushing, NY 11352	(C)	Lori Bassin None
Acting Company Touring (B) 420 West Forty-second Street, 3rd Floor New York, NY 10036	(C)	Margot Harley Mary Beth Carroll
Circle in the Square 1633 Broadway New York, NY 10019	(A)	Theodore Mann Paul Libin
Negro Ensemble Company 165 W. Forty-sixth St. New York, NY 10036	(C)	Douglas Turner Ward Leon Denmark
New York Shakespeare Festival Delacorte and Mobile Theatres Public Theatre/425 Lafayette St. New York, NY 10003	(B)	Joseph Papp None
The Roundabout Theatre Company 100 East Seventeenth Street New York, NY 10003	(B)	Gene Feist Todd Haimes
Geva Theatre 168 Clinton Ave. So. Rochester, NY 14604	(D)	Howard Millman Timothy Norland

Theater and Address	Salary Category*	Artistic Director and/or Business Manager
Department of Theatre Arts SUNY at Stony Brook Stony Brook, NY 11794-5450	(D)	Robert Alpaugh
Syracuse Stage John D. Archbold Theatre 820 East Genesee Street Syracuse, NY 13210	(C)	Arthur Storch James A. Clark
NORTH CAROLINA Playmakers Repertory Company 206 Graham Memorial 052A Chapel Hill, NC 27514	(D)	David Hammond Julie Davis
Ace–Charlotte Repertory Theatre Spirit Square 110 E. 7th St. Charlotte, NC 28202	(B)	Mark Woods Howard Alexander
North Carolina Shakespeare Festival P.O. Box 6066 High Point, NC 27262	(D)	Malcolm Morrison Pedro Silva
OHIO Cincinnati Playhouse in the Park P.O. Box 6537 Cincinnati, OH 45206	(B)	Worth Gardner Katherine Mohylsky
Cleveland Playhouse Box 1989 Cleveland, OH 44106	(B)	William Rhys Janet Wade
Great Lakes Theatre Festival 1501 Euclid Avenue, Suite 250 Cleveland, OH 44115	(B)	Gerald Freedman Mary Bill
Kenyon Repertory Theatre and Festival, Inc. P.O. Box 313 Gambier, OH 43022	(B)	Ted Walch Thomas Dunn
OREGON Oregon Contemporary Theatre 511 S.W. Tenth Street, #1301 Portland, OR 97205	(D)	Craig Latrell Bruce Siddons
VIRGINIA Barter Theatre Box 867 Abingdon, VA 24210	(C)	Rex Partington None

Theater and Address	Salary Category*	Artistic Director and/or Business Manager
Virginia Stage Company 108-114 East Tazewell Street Norfolk, VA 23510	(C)	Charles Towers Dan Martin
Theatrevirginia Boulevard and Grove Aves. Richmond, VA 23221	(C)	Terry Burgler Edward W. Ruckler
WASHINGTON A Contemporary Theatre Box 19400 100 West Roy Street Seattle, WA 98119	(C)	Gregory A. Falls None
Intiman Theatre Company 801 Pike Street Seattle, WA 98101	(C)	Margaret Booker Simon Siegl
Seattle Repertory Theatre Bagley Wright Theatre 155 Mercer Street Seattle, WA 98109	(B)	Daniel Sullivan Peter Donnelly
Tacoma Actors Guild 1323 South Yakima Avenue Tacoma, WA 98405	(D)	Rick Tutor Ruth Kors
WISCONSIN Milwaukee Repertory Theatre Company 929 North Water Street Milwaukee, WI 53202	(C)	John Dillon Sara O'Connor

CURRENT STOCK LIST (1985)

Theater and Address	Type and Salary Category*	Manager
CALIFORNIA		
La Mirada Civic Theatre 14900 La Mirada Blvd. La Mirada, CA 90637	NR(S)	Herb Rogers
Sacramento Music Circus P.O. Box 2347 Sacramento, CA 95811 *Winter address:* 262 Twenty-sixth Street Suite #B Santa Monica, CA 90402	RM	Russell Lewis Howard Young
COLORADO		
Elitch Gardens Theatre 4620 W. Thirty-eight Avenue Denver, CO 80212	NR(S)	Whitfield Connor
CONNECTICUT		
Sharon Playhouse P.O. Box 296 Sharon, CT 06069	RZ	David Watson
Westport Country Playhouse 25 Powers Court P.O. Box 629 Westport, CT 06880	NR(S)	James B. McKenzie Jack Booch

---

NR(L) = Non-Resident Dramatic Stock (COST) & Indoor Musical Stock (Large).
NR(S) = Non-Resident Dramatic Stock (COST) & Indoor Musical Stock (Small).
OD = Outdoor Dramatic Stock.
OM = Outdoor Musical Stock.
RM = Resident Musical.
Resident Dramatic Stock (CORST):
RX = Resident X.
RY = Resident Y.
RZ = Resident Z.

Actors' salaries effective September 2, 1985:
X = $408.08.
Y = $375.03.
Z = $341.88.

Theater and Address	Type and Salary Category*	Manager
GEORGIA Theatre of the Stars, Inc. Atlantic Civic Center 395 Piedmont Avenue Atlanta, GA 30308 *All correspondence to:* P.O. Box 11748 Atlanta, GA 30355	NR(L)	Christopher B. Manos
ILLINOIS Drury Lane Theatre South 2500 W. Ninety-fifth Place Evergreen Park, IL 60642	NR(S)	Anthony di Santis
Shady Lane Playhouse Route 20 West Marengo, IL 60152	RZ	Ray Curnow
Little Theatre on the Square P.O. Box H Sullivan, IL 61951 (217) 728-2065	RY	Tom Marks
INDIANA Starlight Musicals, Inc. P.O. Box 40517 Indianapolis, IN 46220	OM	Robert L. Young
MAINE Brunswick Music Theatre P.O. Box 656 Bowdoin College Campus Brunswick, ME 04011	RY	Victoria Crandall
Ogunquit Playhouse Route 1 Ogunquit, ME 03907	NR(S)	John Lane
MARYLAND Olney Theatre Route 108 Olney, MD 20832	NR(S)	James D. Waring
MASSACHUSETTS North Shore Music Theatre P.O. Box 62, Route 128 Exit 19 Beverly, MA 01915	NR(S)	Jon Kimbell

Theater and Address	Type and Salary Category*	Manager
The Cape Playhouse P.O. Box A Dennis, MA 02638	NR(S)	William Crowell Angelo Del Rossi
Cape Cod Melody Tent W. End Main Street P.O. Box 1979 Hyannis, MA 02165	NR(S)	William Carmen
Berkshire Theatre Festival Berkshire Playhouse East Main Street Stockbridge, MA 01262	RY	Josephine R. Abady Joan Stein
Williamstown Theatre Festival Adams Memorial Theatre Main Street, Box 517 Williamstown, MA 01267	RY	Nikos Psacharapoulos Gary Levine
MICHIGAN Barn Theatre Route 1, M-96 Augusta, MI 49012	RY	Jack Ragotzy
Birmingham Theatre 211 West Woodward Birmingham, MI 48011	NR(S)	Tom Mallow James Janek
Star Theatre of Flint Whiting Auditorium 1241 E. Kearsley Street Flint, MI 48502	NR(L)	Frank Kenley
Cherry County Playhouse Park Place Motor Inn P.O. Box 661 Traverse City, MI 49684	NR(S)	Neil Rosen William Hooton
MINNESOTA Old Log Theatre P.O. Box 250 Excelsior, MN 55331	RY	Don Stolz
MISSOURI K.C. Starlight Association 4600 Starlight Drive Kansas City, MO 64105	OM	Rob Rolhf Randy Gale
St. Louis Municipal Opera Theatre Forest Park St. Louis, MO 63112	OM	E.R. Culver Ed Greenberg

Theater and Address	*Type and Salary Category**	Manager
Westport Playhouse 600 Westport Plaza St. Louis, MO 63141	NR(S)	Wesley Van Tassel
NEW HAMPSHIRE Hampton Playhouse Winnacunnett Road Hampton, NH 03842	RY	Alfred Christie John Vari
American Stage Festival P.O. Box 225 Milford, NH 03055	RZ	Larry Carpenter
Peterborough Players P.O. Box 1 Off Middle Hancock Road Peterborough, NH 03458	RZ	Charles Morey Ellen Dinerstein
The Barnstormers Tamworth, NH 03886	RZ	Francis G. Cleveland G. Warren Steele
NEW JERSEY Paper Mill Playhouse Brookside Drive Millburn, NJ 07041	NR(S)	Angelo Del Rossi
NEW YORK Corning Summer Theatre P.O. Box 51 Corning, NY 14830	NR(S)	Dorothy Chernuck
The John Drew Theatre 158 Main Street East Hampton, NY 11937	NR(S)	William McGrath Amy McGrath
Coliseum Theatre P.O. Box 41 Latham, NY 12110	NR(L)	Joseph N. Futia
Artpark P.O. Box 371 Lewiston, NY 14092	NR(L)	Joanne Allison
Woodstock Playhouse Association, Inc. P.O. Box 396 Woodstock, NY 12498	RZ	Harris A. Gordon
NORTH CAROLINA Flat Rock Playhouse P.O. Box 248 Flat Rock, NC 28731	RZ	Robin Farquhar John Everman

Theater and Address	Type and Salary Category*	Manager
OHIO		
Tecumseh/Shenandoah The Scioto Society, Inc. P.O. Box 73 Chillicothe, OH 45601	OD	W.L. Mundell
Trumpet In The Land Ohio Outdoor Historical Drama Association, Inc. P.O. Box 567 Dover, OH 44622	OD	Rachael Redinger
Theatre of the Stars Packard Music Hall Box 1271 Warren, OH 44482	NR(L)	Frank Kenley
Blue Jacket First Frontier, Inc. P.O. Box 312 Xenia, OH 45385	OD	Tally Sessions
PENNSYLVANIA		
Allenberry Playhouse Route 174, P.O. Box 7 Boiling Springs, PA 17007	RZ	John J. Heinze
Totem Pole Playhouse 9555 Golf Course Road Caledonia State Park Fayetteville, PA 17222	RY	Carl Schurr
Mountain Playhouse P.O. Box 54 Jennerstown, PA 15547	RZ	Earl D. Gipson Louise S. Maust
Civic Light Opera Heinz Hall 600 Penn Avenue Pittsburgh, PA 15222	RM	Charles Gray
TEXAS		
Dallas Summer Musicals P.O. Box 26188 Music Hall at Fair Park Dallas, TX 75226	NR(L)	Tom Hughes
Casa Manana Theatre 3101 West Lancaster Ft. Worth, TX 76107	RM	Bud Franks

Theater and Address	Type and Salary Category*	Manager
Lone Star P.O. Box 5253 Galveston, TX 77551	OD	James Stoker
VERMONT St. Michael's Playhouse 56 College Parkway Winooski, VT 05404	RZ	Don Rathgeb Margaret O'Brien
WISCONSIN Peninsula Players Highway 42 Fishcreek, WI 54212	RZ	James B. McKenzie
Milwaukee Melody Top Theatre 2501 W. Hampton Avenue Milwaukee, WI 53209 *Theatre: Summer only:* 7201 W. Good Hope Road Milwaukee, WI 53223 (414) 353-7700	RM	Guy S. Little, Jr.

DINNER THEATER LIST (ARRANGED ALPHABETICALLY BY STATE, AS OF 3/1/85)

Theater and Address	*Size**	*Producer*
CALIFORNIA		
The Grand Dinner Theatre Grand Hotel One Hotel Way Anaheim, CA 92802	399	Frank Wyka
Lawrence Welk Village Theatre 8975 Lawrence Welk Drive Escondido, CA 92026	300	Robert M. Dias
Harlequin Dinner Playhouse 3503 S. Harbor Boulevard Santa Ana, CA 92704	M 515	Al and Barbara Hampton
COLORADO		
Country Dinner Playhouse 6875 S. Clinton Englewood, CO 80110 *All correspondence to:* 6570 No. Alpine Drive Hidden Village Parker, CO 80134	470	Bill McHale
CONNECTICUT		
Darien Dinner Theatre 65 Tokeneke Road Darien, CT 06820	500	Dennis Cole Peter Paradossi
Coachlight Dinner Theatre 266 Main Street East Windsor, CT 06088 *All correspondence to:* Janis Belkin	599	Samuel Belkin
FLORIDA		
Royal Palm Dinner Theatre 303 Golfview Drive Royal Palm Plaza Boca Raton, FL 33432	228	Jan McArt
Alhambra Dinner Theatre 12000 Beach Boulevard Jacksonville, FL 32216	398	Tom Fallon

*Size of theater determined by seating capacity: Petite: 0–279; Small: 280–399; Medium: 400–599; Large: 600–1,000.

Theater and Address	Size*	Producer
Burt Reynolds Jupiter Theatre 1001 Indiantown Road Jupiter, FL 33458	450	Karen Poindexter
Mark I Dinner Theatre 304 East Lemon Street Lakeland, FL 33801	150	Mark Howard
Celebrity Dinner Theatre 46 N. Orange Avenue Orlando, FL 32801	399	Rick Allen Tom McKinney
Showboat Dinner Theatre 3405 Ulmerton Road P.O. Box 519 Pinellas Park, FL 33565 *All correspondence to:* Maurice Shinners	428	Maurice Shinners Dow M. Sherwood
Country Dinner Playhouse 7951 Gateway Mall 9th Street North St. Petersburg, FL 33702	390	Patricia Tong
Golden Apple Dinner Theatre 25 N. Pineapple Avenue Sarasota, FL 33577	279	Robert Turoff
ILLINOIS Marriott's Lincolnshire Theatre 101 Half Day Road Lincolnshire, IL 60015	872	Kary M. Walker
Drury Lane Dinner Theatre 100 Drury Lane Oakbrook Terrace, IL 60126	L 980	Tony DeSantis
Pheasant Run Cabaret Theatre Route 64 St. Charles, IL 60174	S 348	Gilda Moss
Candlelight Dinner Playhouse 5620 S. Harlem Avenue Summit, IL 60501	548	William Pullinsi Tony D'Angelo
INDIANA Beef 'n' Boards Dinner Theatre 9301 W. Michigan P.O. Box 68329 Indianapolis, IN 46268	510/399	Doug Stark Robert Zehr

Theater and Address	Size*	Producer
MINNESOTA		
Chanhassen Courtyard Dinner Theatre Chanhassen, MN 55317	1,172	Richard Bloomberg
Chanhassen Playhouse Dinner Theatre Chanhassen, MN 55317	130	Richard Bloomberg
Chanhassen Dinner Theatre Chanhassen, MN 55317	575	Richard Bloomberg
Fireside Dinner Theatre 51 West Seventy-eighth Street Chanhassen, MN 55317	249	Richard Bloomberg
MISSOURI		
Tiffany's Attic Dinner Theatre 5028 Main Street Kansas City, MO 64112	S 340	Dennis Hennessy
Waldo Astoria Dinner Playhouse 7428 Washington Kansas City, MO 64114 *All correspondence to:* Waldo Astoria Dinner Playhouse, Inc. 5028 Main Street Kansas City, MO 64112	S 399	Dennis Hennessy
NEBRASKA		
Firehouse Dinner Theatre 514 S. 11 Street Omaha, NE 68102	304	Richard Mueller
NEVADA		
Union Plaza Dinner Theatre #1 Main Street Union Plaza Hotel Las Vegas, NV 89101	550	Maynard Sloate
NEW MEXICO		
The Wool Warehouse Theatre Restaurant First Street Roma N.W. Albuquerque, NM 87102 *All correspondence to:* P.O. Box 26838 Albuquerque, NM 87125	S 425	George M. Luce

Theater and Address	Size*	Producer
NEW YORK		
An Evening Dinner Theatre	372	William Stutler
11 Clearbrook Road		Robert J. Funking
Elmsford, NY 10523		
Lake George Dinner Theatre	P	David Eastwood
P.O. Box 266	150	
Lake George, NY 12845		
OHIO		
Carousel Dinner Theatre	518	David Fulford
960 East Main Street		Scott Griffith
Ravenna, OH 44266		
All correspondence to:		
P.O. Box 427		
Ravenna, OH 44266		
TEXAS		
The Country Squire Dinner	S	Peter Fox
Theatre	399	
I-40 and Grand		
Amarillo, TX 79120		
All correspondence to:		
Country Squire Dinner		
Theatre, Inc.		
P.O. Box 30520		
Amarillo, TX 79120		
The Red Windmill Dinner Theatre	398	Geraldyne Newson
390 Town and Country		
Houston, TX 77024		
VIRGINIA		
West End Dinner Theatre	350	Melissa Bassford
4615 Duke Street		Otilla Bassford
P.O. Box 9200		
Alexandria, VA 22304		
Hayloft Dinner Theatre	356	Frank Matthews
10501 Balls Ford Road		
Manassas, VA 22110		

The Equity Membership Candidacy Program may be in effect at all of the theaters listed in these directories. Prospective membership candidates should inquire at a theater before accepting employment. In addition, the membership candidate program may be offered at certain Chicago Area Theatres (CAT), Hollywood Area Theatres (HAT), Bay Area Theatres (BAT), Letter of Agreement Theatres (LOA), and University Resident Theatre Association (U/RTA) companies.

MOTION PICTURE BUREAUS
AND FILM COMMISSIONS

ALABAMA
Alabama Film Commission
340 North Hull St.
Montgomery, AL 36130

ALASKA
Alaska Motion Picture
3601 "C" St., Suite 722
Anchorage, AK 99503

ARIZONA
Arizona Motion Picture
  Development Office
1700 West Washington Ave.
Suite 330
Phoenix, AZ 85007

Nogales
Nogales Film Commission
P.O. Box 2465
Nogales, AZ 85628

Phoenix
Phoenix Motion Picture/
  Commercial Coordinating Office
251 West Washington Ave.
Phoenix, AZ 85003

Tucson
Tucson Film Commission
P.O. Box 27210
Tucson, AZ 85726

ARKANSAS
Office of Motion Picture
  Development
1 Capitol Mall
Little Rock, AR 72201

CALIFORNIA
California Film Office
6922 Hollywood Blvd., Suite 600
Los Angeles, CA 90028

San Diego
Motion Picture & TV Bureau
Greater San Diego Chamber
  of Commerce
110 West "C" St., Suite 1600
San Diego, CA 92101

San Francisco
Office of the Mayor
Motion Picture Coordinator
City Hall, Room 200
San Francisco, CA 94102

San Jose
San Jose Film and Video
  Commission
One Paseo de San Antonio
San Jose, CA 95113

Santa Cruz
Santa Cruz Film Board
P.O. Box 1476
Santa Cruz, CA 95061

Sonoma
Sonoma County Film Commission
637 First St.
Santa Rosa, CA 95404

Stockton
Stockton Chamber of Commerce
445 West Weber Ave., Suite 220
Stockton, CA 95203

COLORADO
Motion Picture and TV Advisory
  Commission
1313 Sherman St., Suite 523
Denver, CO 80203

CONNECTICUT
Connecticut Film Commission
210 Washington St.
Hartford, CT 06106

Stamford
Mayor's Film Commission
429 Atlantic St.
P.O. Box 10152
Stamford, CT 06904

DELAWARE
Delaware Development Office
99 Kings Highway
P.O. Box 1401
Dover, DE 19901

DISTRICT OF COLUMBIA
Motion Picture and Television
  Development
District Bldg., Room 208
Washington, DC 20004

FLORIDA
Motion Picture and Television
  Office
Collins Bldg.
107 Gaines St., Suite 510G
Tallahassee, FL 32304

Jacksonville
Motion Picture and Television
  Liaison Office
City Hall, Room 107
220 East Bay St.
Jacksonville, FL 32202

Metro-Dade County
Metro-Dade County Office of Film
  & Television
140 W. Flagler St., #1104
Miami, FL 33130

GEORGIA
Georgia Film and Videotape Office
Department of Industry and Trade
230 Peachtree St., N.W.
Atlanta, GA 30303

HAWAII
Department of Planning &
  Economic Development
P.O. Box 2539
Honolulu, HI 96804

County of Hawaii
Department of Research &
  Development
34 Rainbow Dr.
Hilo, HI 96720

IDAHO
Idaho Film Bureau
Capitol Bldg., Room 108
Boise, ID 83720

ILLINOIS
Illinois Film Office
100 W. Randolph St., Suite 3-400
Chicago, IL 60601

Chicago
Chicago Office of Film and
  Entertainment Industries
City Hall, Room 810
121 North LaSalle St.
Chicago, IL 60602

INDIANA
Indiana Film Commission
Indiana Commerce Center
One North Capitol
Indianapolis, IN 46204-2248

IOWA
Iowa Development Commission
600 East Court, Suite A
Des Moines, IA 50309

KANSAS
Kansas Film Commission
503 Kansas Avenue, 6th Floor
Topeka, KS 66603

KENTUCKY
Kentucky Film Office
Berry Hill Mansion
Frankfort, KY 40601

LOUISIANA
Louisiana Film Commission
P.O. Box 44185
Baton Rouge, LA 70804

MAINE
Maine Film Commission
P.O. Box 8424
Portland, ME 04104

MARYLAND
Maryland Film Commission
45 Calvert St.
Annapolis, MD 21401

Baltimore
Office of the Mayor
Film Coordinator
100 North Holiday St.
Baltimore, MD 21202

MASSACHUSETTS
Massachusetts Film Bureau
100 Cambridge St., 13th Floor
Boston, MA 02202

MICHIGAN
Office of Film and Television
   Services
Michigan Dept. of Commerce
1200 Sixth St., 19th Floor
Detroit, MI 48226

MINNESOTA
Minnesota Motion Picture and
   Television Board
100 N. Sixth St., Suite 478A
Minneapolis, MN 55403

MISSISSIPPI
Mississippi Film Commission
P.O. Box 849
Jackson, MS 39205

Natchez
Natchez Film Commission
P.O. Box 794
Natchez, MS 39120

MISSOURI
Missouri Film Commission
P.O. Box 118
Jefferson City, MO 65102

MONTANA
Montana Film Commission
1424 Ninth Ave.
Helena, MT 59620

NEBRASKA
Nebraska Film Office
Department of Economic
   Development
P.O. Box 94666
Lincoln, NE 68509

Lincoln
Lincoln Film and Television Office
129 N. Tenth St., Room 111
Lincoln, NE 68508

Omaha
Film Assistance Office
9773 Lafayette Place
Omaha, NE 68114

Mayor's Film Advisory Committee
Mayor's Office—City of Omaha
Omaha, NE 68102

NEVADA
Nevada Motion Picture
   Development
2501 East Sahara Blvd., Suite 101
Las Vegas, NV 89104

Carson City
Carson City Tourism and
   Convention Authority
P.O. Box 1416
Carson City, NV 89702

Reno
Motion Picture and Television
   Bureau Greater Reno
P.O. Box 4102
Incline Village, NV 89450

NEW HAMPSHIRE
New Hampshire Film and
   Television Bureau
Box 856
Concord, NH 03301

NEW JERSEY
New Jersey Motion Picture and
Television Commission
Gateway One, Suite 510
Newark, NJ 07102

NEW MEXICO
New Mexico Film Commission
1050 Old Pecos Trail
Santa Fe, NM 87501

Albuquerque
Albuquerque Film and Television
Services
P.O. Box 1293
Albuquerque, NM 87103

NEW YORK
New York State Motion Picture
and Television Development
230 Park Ave., Room 1155
New York, NY 10009

Nassau County
Nassau Department of Commerce
and Industry
1550 Franklin Ave.
Mineola, NY 11501

New York
New York City Mayor's Office of
Film, Theater and Broadcasting
110 West Fifty-seventh St.
New York, NY 10019

Suffolk County
Suffolk County TV Commission
4175 Veterans Memorial Hwy.
Ronkonkoma, NY 11779

NORTH CAROLINA
North Carolina Film Office
430 North Salisbury St.
Raleigh, NC 27611

NORTH DAKOTA
North Dakota Economic
Development Commission
Capitol Grounds
Bismarck, ND 58505

OHIO
Ohio Film Bureau
P.O. Box 1001
Columbus, OH 43216

OKLAHOMA
Film Industry Task Force
500 Will Rogers Bldg.
Oklahoma City, OK 73105

OREGON
Dept. of Economic Development
Film & Video Recruitment
595 Cottage St., N.E.
Salem, OR 97310

PENNSYLVANIA
Pennsylvania Film Bureau
461 Forum Bldg.
Harrisburg, PA 17120

Philadelphia
Philadelphia Office of Motion
Picture and TV Production
1660 Municipal Services Bldg.
Philadelphia, PA 19102

PUERTO RICO
Institute of Film & Television
G.P.O. Box 2350
San Juan, PR 00936

RHODE ISLAND
Rhode Island Film Commission
150 Benefit St.
Providence, RI 02903

SOUTH CAROLINA
South Carolina Film Office
State Development Board
P.O. Box 927
Columbia, SC 29202

SOUTH DAKOTA
South Dakota Film Bureau
Dept. of State Development
P.O. Box 1000
Pierre, SD 57501

TENNESSEE
Tennessee Film, Tape and Music
Commission
James K. Polk Bldg., 16th Floor
Nashville, TN 37219

Memphis and Shelby County
Memphis & Shelby County Film,
Tape & Music Commission
160 N. Mid America Mall
Suite 640
Memphis, TN 38103

TEXAS
Texas Film Commission
P.O. Box 12428
201 E. Fourteenth St., Suite 512
Austin, TX 78711

Corpus Christi
Corpus Christi Convention Bureau
1201 North Shoreline
Corpus Christi, TX 78403

El Paso
El Paso Film Liaison Office
5 Civic Center Plaza
El Paso, TX 79999

Houston
Houston Convention and Visitors
Council
3300 Main St.
Houston, TX 77002

San Antonio
San Antonio Convention and
Visitors Bureau
P.O. Box 2277
San Antonio, TX 78298

UTAH
Utah Film Development
6150 State Office Bldg.
Salt Lake City, UT 84114

VERMONT
Vermont Film Bureau
134 State Street
Montpelier, VT 05602

VIRGINIA
Virginia Film Office
Department of Economic
Development
Washington Bldg.
Richmond, VA 23219

WASHINGTON
Motion Picture/Television Bureau
Dept. of Commerce and Economic
Development
312 First Ave., North
Seattle, WA 98109

WEST VIRGINIA
Governor's Office of Economic
Development
Capitol Complex Bldg. 6
Charleston, WV 25305

WISCONSIN
Wisconsin Film Office
Department of Tourism
P.O. Box 7970
Madison, WI 53707

Milwaukee
Department of City Development
P.O. Box 324
Milwaukee, WI 53201

WYOMING
Wyoming Film Office
Interstate 25 at College Dr.
Cheyenne, WY 82002

Jackson Hole
Jackson Hole Film Commission
P.O. Box E
Jackson, WY 83001

PARTIAL LIST OF PERFORMING ARTS HIGH SCHOOLS (NATIONWIDE)

When you write to these schools for further information, address inquiries to Principal or Director of Theater.

ALABAMA
Alabama School of Fine Arts
820 North Eighteenth St., Box A16
Birmingham, AL 35202

CALIFORNIA
Los Angeles High School for the Arts
5151 State University Drive
Los Angeles, CA 90032

O'Farrell School for Creative and Performing Arts
6130 Skyline Drive
San Diego, CA 92114

School of the Arts
J. Eugene McAteer High School
555 Portola Drive
San Francisco, CA 94131

Crossroads School for Arts and Sciences
1714 Twenty-first St.
Santa Monica, CA 90404

CONNECTICUT
Academy of Performing Arts
C.R.E.C.
212 King Phillips Drive
West Hartford, CT 06117

DISTRICT OF COLUMBIA
Duke Ellington School of the Arts
3500 R St. N.W.
Washington, DC 20007

FLORIDA
Dillard School of Performing Arts
2501 N.W. Eleventh St.
Fort Lauderdale, FL 33311

Performing and Visual Arts Center
PAVAC
Miami Dade Community College
11011 S.W. 104th St.
Miami, FL 33176

Sarasota Visual and Performing Arts Center
3201 North Orange Avenue
Sarasota, FL 33580

GEORGIA
Northside School of the Arts
Northside High School
2875 Northside Drive
Atlanta, GA 30305

ILLINOIS
Creative Children's Academy
800 North Fernandez
Arlington Heights, IL 60004

INDIANA
Emerson School for Visual and Performing Arts
716 E. Seventh Avenue
Gary, IN 45402

Indianapolis Public Schools
Curriculum Division
120 East Walnut Street
Indianapolis, IN 46204

KENTUCKY
Youth Performing Arts School
1517 South Second Street
Louisville, KY 40208

LOUISIANA
New Orleans Center for Creative Arts
6048 Perrier Street
New Orleans, LA 70118

Louisiana School for Math
Science and the Arts
715 College Avenue
Natchitoches, LA 71457-3915

MARYLAND
Baltimore School for the Arts
712 Cathedral Street
Baltimore, MD 21201

MASSACHUSETTS
Walnut Hill School
12 Highland Street
Natick, MA 01760

Young People's School for the
Performing Arts
Box 86
Seekonk, MA 02771

MICHIGAN
Interlochen Arts Academy
Interlochen, MI 49643

MINNESOTA
Minnesota Arts High School
8713 Wood Cliff Circle
Bloomington, MN 55420

Children's Theatre Company and
School
2400 Third Avenue South
Minneapolis, MN 55404

MISSOURI
Central Visual and Performing Arts
High School
3616 North Garrison
St. Louis, MO 63109

NEW JERSEY
Performing Arts at Somerset
Vocational and Technical High
School
P.O. Box 6350
North Bridge Street and Vogt
Drive
Bridgewater, NJ 08809

Performing Arts High School
Jersey City Board of Education
241 Erie St.
Jersey City, NJ 07302

Red Bank Regional High School
Performing Arts Program
101 Ridge Road
Little Silver, NJ 07739

NEW YORK
Buffalo Academy for Visual and
Performing Arts
333 Clinton Street
Buffalo, NY 14204

LaGuardia High School of Music
and Arts
108 Amsterdam Avenue
New York, NY 10023

OHIO
School for Creative and
Performing Arts
1310 Sycamore Street
Cincinnati, OH 45210

Cleveland School of the Arts
2064 Stearns Road
Cleveland, OH 44106

OREGON
Jefferson Performing Arts Center
5210 North Kerby Street
Portland, OR 97217

PENNSYLVANIA
Philadelphia High School for
the Performing Arts
Eleventh and Catherine Sts.
Philadelphia, PA 19147

Pittsburgh High School for
Performing and Creative Arts
Brushton Avenue and Baxter St.
Pittsburgh, PA 15208

RHODE ISLAND
Hope High School Arts Magnet
Program
324 Hope St.
Providence, RI 02904

SOUTH CAROLINA
Governor's School of the Arts
P.O. Box 2848
Greenville, SC 29602

TEXAS
Arts Magnet High School at
  Booker T. Washington
2501 Flora Street
Dallas, TX 75201

High School for the Performing
  and Visual Arts
4001 Stamford
Houston, TX 77006

VERMONT
Governor's Institute of the Arts
c/o Castleton State College
Castleton, VT 05735

WISCONSIN
Milwaukee High School of the Arts
2300 West Highland Avenue
Milwaukee, WI 53233

Roosevelt Middle School of the
  Arts
800 West Walnut Street
Milwaukee, WI 53205

Recommended Reading

Allen, John. *Summer Theatre Guide*. Theatre Guide Update, P.O. Box 2129, New York, NY 10185. Includes detailed information on non-Equity theaters, from an actor's viewpoint.

Anderson, Virgil. *Training the Speaking Voice*. New York: Oxford University Press, 1977. (If you can find a copy of Marion Rich's book under the same title, written in the 1940s, grab it.)

Gielgud, John. *Gielgud, An Actor and His Time*. New York: Clarkson N. Potter, Inc., Publishers, 1980.

Glenn, Peter. *The Madison Avenue Handbook*. New York: Peter Glenn Publications, 1985. Annual.

Goldman, William. *Adventures in the Screen Trade*. New York: Warner Books, 1983.

Hagen, Uta. *Respect for Acting*. New York: Macmillan Publishing Co., Inc., 1973.

Herman, Lewis, and Herman, Marguerite Shalett. *A Manual of American Dialects*. New York: Theatre Arts Books, 1947.

Herman, Lewis, and Herman, Marguerite Shalett. *A Manual of Foreign Dialects*. New York: Theatre Arts Books, 1943.

Houseman, John. *Run Through*. New York: Simon & Schuster, 1972.

Houseman, John. *Front and Center*. New York: Simon & Schuster, 1979.

Houseman, John. *Final Dress*. New York: Simon & Schuster, 1983.

Hunt, Gordon. *How to Audition*. New York: Harper and Row, 1979.

Lewis, M. K. and Rosemary. *Your Film Acting Career*. New York: Crown Publishers, Inc., 1983.

Lewis, Robert. *Advice to the Players*. New York: Stein and Day, 1980.

Lewis, Robert. *Method Or Madness*. New York: Samuel French, 1958.

Lewis, Robert. *Slings and Arrows*. New York: Stein and Day, 1984.

Olivier, Laurence. *Confessions of an Actor*. New York: Simon & Schuster, 1982.

Richardson, Ralph. *An Actor's Life*. New York: Limelight Editions, 1982.

Schickel, Richard. *Intimate Strangers*. New York: Doubleday and Co., 1985.

Schulman, Michael, and Mekler, Eve, eds. *The Actor's Scenebook*. New York: Bantam Books, 1984.

Seldes, Marion. *The Bright Lights*. New York: Houghton Mifflin, 1978.

Shanks, Robert. *The Cool Fire*. New York: Vintage Books, 1976.

Shawn, Wendy, and Henderson, Judy. *Everything You Always Wanted to Know About Los Angeles' and New York's Casting Directors . . . but Were Afraid to Ask!* Samuel French, 1985. For information contact Cast Busters, P.O. Box 67C75, Los Angeles, CA 90067.

Shurtleff, Michael. *Audition!* New York: Walker and Company, 1978.

Silver, Fred. *How to Audition for the Musical Theatre*. New York: New Market Press, 1985.

Singer, Sheri, and Alderman, Tom. *Is Your Child Right for TV Commercials?* New York: William Morrow and Co., 1983.

Weist, Dwight. *On Camera!* New York: Walker and Co., 1982.